RAJ KAPOOR

RAJ KAPOOR

THE MASTER AT WORK

RAHUL RAWAIL

as told to PRANIKA SHARMA

BLOOMSBURY

NEW DELHI • LONDON • OXFORD • NEW YORK • SYDNEY

BLOOMSBURY INDIA
Bloomsbury Publishing India Pvt. Ltd
Second Floor, LSC Building No. 4, DDA Complex, Pocket C – 6 & 7,
Vasant Kunj, New Delhi, 110070

BLOOMSBURY, BLOOMSBURY INDIA and the Diana logo
are trademarks of Bloomsbury Publishing Plc

First published in India 2021
This edition published 2021

ISBN: HB: 978-93-88630-16-0; eBook: 978-93-88630-18-4
2 4 6 8 10 9 7 5 3

Typeset in Adobe Caslon Pro by Manipal Technologies Limited
Printed and bound in India by Thomson Press India Ltd.

MIX
Paper from responsible sources
FSC www.fsc.org FSC® C010615

This book is dedicated to Chintu, my truest friend, my rock, my brother. You not just pushed me into putting together this book but also showered me with abuses whenever I would get lazy about the writing. Chintu, you were truly my champion since our childhood—from the classroom to movie sets to the culmination of this book. My regret is that you could not read it but I know that wherever you are, you are cheering me on. I miss you immensely and look forward to seeing you on the other side!

CONTENTS

FOREWORD

I consider myself very fortunate to be writing the foreword to this book that talks about my father, Raj Kapoor, and the relationship he shared with his films. It's something that has never been documented before, and if there is someone who could share my father's facets as a filmmaker, it is Rahul Rawail, his erstwhile assistant director.

You see, making films is not a science, it is intuitive; it is a creative art that comes from within. Sure, there is some science involved, but unless it comes from the heart, it does not make a good film. Mechanically, anyone can write a film, but there are very few people who have the right passion and zeal to bring these stories to life. This was the first lesson my father taught me.

I still remember the day he narrated the story of *Prem Rog*. He had told me that this would be a poignant love story but the story that he narrated was of a young widow and the relationship between her and the patriarch of her marital family, the elder brother of her father-in-law. This story did not have a role for the hero, so where was the love story?

I asked. He laughed and said, 'How can there be a love story without a hero? *Who toh aajayega, film toh banne do.*' As it happened, the hero did arrive and the film turned out to be a memorable love story. That's how he made his films. Everything was plotted out in his mind and this was his way of working.

Raj Kapoor had his own brand of filmmaking. His thoughts about the film he was making were translated by him into celluloid. He worked on any film with complete conviction and the credit for a hit film or a flop film was his completely, and he took all feedback very gracefully and never had regrets if his film flopped. 'I accept responsibility for a film's success or failure. A film fails because of errors of the director.'

His ideas were always ahead of his time and his films reflected that. *Mera Naam Joker* was one such example—it was a major flop when it released but, with time and people understanding what the film was about, it is now recognized as one of Raj Kapoor's most appreciated films and a major profit point in my organization.

My misfortune was that I only got to observe Raj Kapoor, the director, but never work with him. Rahul, on the other hand, was not only fortunate to have worked with him but also become his favourite assistant. He took his work very seriously and followed Raj Kapoor to a tee. He had imbibed a lot of my father's way of working in him and translated those in his own ways in his films. I am so glad that this book bares open the creativity, eccentricities, obsessions and techniques of Raj Kapoor, and will lead people to know that my father was a man who lived for cinema and worked relentlessly to bring his visions to life.

Randhir Kapoor
Mumbai, October 2021

AUTHOR'S NOTE

At the outset I pay homage to:

the matriarch of the Raj Kapoor family, Krishna Aunty; his daughter, Ritu Kapoor Nanda; and his youngest son, Rajeev (Chimpoo) Kapoor.

To the three of them along with my late friend, Chintu, to whom this book has been dedicated, and Randhir Kapoor (Daboo Sahab), Rima Kapoor Jain; were the pillars of strength who made me take this step to honour my Guru, Shri Raj Kapoor.

When the thought of writing this book was planted in my mind, I first spoke to the Kapoor family to inform them about the narrative style I would adopt. They were all really excited about the same and Krishna Aunty told me, 'You must write this book! You are the only living person who has worked with my husband and observed his work from such close quarters. You are aware of the aspects that contributed to his being an extraordinary filmmaker. If you don't write this book, then an entire lesson in creativity will be lost.'

Thus started my efforts into jogging my memory to recollect all that I could about the extraordinary genius, Raj Kapoor. I did not want this book to appeal only to people associated with cinema, but a narrative that would appeal to one and all – those who have watched his films and those who have not as well.

As I progressed, I remembered more and more of my time spent on the sets of his films. My wife, Rita, was extremely patient in the time spent over Zoom calls with Pranika, who has not only written my narration but has huge contribution in the style of writing.

Shantanu Roy Chaudhary, a well-respected editor in the publishing world, egged me on and gave me the strength when I was losing hope. Thank you, Shantanu. I hope I have lived up to your expectations.

My friend, Rahul Mitra, never wavered in his faith in the book, so much so that he went the extra mile to ensure the book reaches readers in all four corners of the world. Thank you for that, Rahul.

To the readers, which I hope are plenty: this is not just a book about a showman but my tribute to a filmmaker, the one man who taught me everything I have learnt. It hopes to put you in the front row seat to understand the mind of the greatest filmmaker India has ever known. This book encapsulates his eccentricities, his obsessions and his techniques of filmmaking in vivid detail, and I hope that it helps you see the filmmaker in a light that he has never been seen in before.

Raj Sahab, I hope that you are proud of what I have strived to attain by making people aware that you were not just a showman but a master at work.

PROLOGUE: THE DREAM

On a particularly chilly evening, I woke up with a jolt when I sensed some movement in my room. To my absolute astonishment and bewilderment, a striking image presented itself in my blurry vision. It took a moment for me to process the fact that Raj Uncle or Raj Sahab or 'Boss', as I addressed him at various points in my life, was sitting on a chair right in front of me!

I was taken aback to see him there but, at the same time, I couldn't contain my happiness. 'What a pleasant surprise to see you!' I exclaimed.

He seemed angry, 'Where is my drink?' I scrambled about and got him a large Black Label whisky, his favourite drink.

He gulped the drink and said, 'Get me another one!' As I poured him a second drink, he kept staring at me. I started getting nervous; he said suddenly, 'I know you have not made a film in some time. If you are not inclined to making films, why don't you, like most others today, start assembling films?'

I was completely confused and replied, 'I'm sorry, I did not understand the question.'

He flared up and exclaimed, 'You're stupid!' I was taken aback and did not know what to say because I still hadn't understood what he had meant to say.

'Do people nowadays know what it means to "make" a film?' He was furious! 'Nobody makes films anymore. Barring a few conscious and genuine filmmakers, 90 per cent of the so-called filmmakers are not "making" films but are only "assembling" films!'

He seemed to be getting angrier with every word he spoke, 'The state of the film industry is in despair. I lived in the golden period of cinema where people actually strived towards "making" a film. There was passion involved in the filmmaking process but now the passion is in assembling a product for numbers and figures; a disastrous situation which has led to the deterioration of cinema.'

He further voiced his disgust by saying, 'Filmmaking has ceased to be a creative process and is now a mechanical process. I believe today's writers should be called "typewriters". They sit at computers typing a script, or better yet, the computer dictates the script to them! Directors, while shooting, sit in front of a television screen and decide whether it's a good take or not. Is this how films are made? What happened to using your creativity, intelligence and the human feel? These were the most essential ingredients for making a film! People who call themselves filmmakers are only interested in the big bucks raked in from the Friday, Saturday and Sunday collections. It's just about the numbers. If you're only interested in Friday, Saturday and Sunday, where have Monday, Tuesday, Wednesday and Thursday gone? Have they disappeared from the calendar and do not exist anymore?'

He was mourning the demise of cinema; mourning the fact that the indelible legacy of creativity had disappeared; mourning the fact that cinema had lost that heartfelt passion. It now functioned on the basis of calculations and economics.

'Filmmaking is an art.' A melancholic expression masked his face as he said, 'I feel like I'm one of the lucky few who are not living in today's times. I agree that there should be some kind of economics but, for a true filmmaker, the heart has to reign supreme. I am happy in my space. I would hate to live in an era where films are not being made as a creative pursuit but where numbers are motivating filmmaking!'

His words struck my heart and I was taken to the time when filmmaking was more than just about the money. It took me back on a journey to the past when films were being made with utmost precision. It took me back to 8 December 1968, on the sets of *Mera Naam Joker*, the day I first saw the Immortal Master weave his magic.

STARTING OUT

I had recently got done with the stressful ICSE board exams when I got a call from my childhood buddy Chintu, Rishi Kapoor, 'Dad's shooting the circus chapter of *Mera Naam Joker* at Cross Maidan from today, let's spend the day there. There will be some sexy female Russian circus artists…' And that had me convinced! Free time, after the gruelling ICSE board exams, added with the prospect of meeting young Russian circus artists in skimpy outfits, was definitely more alluring than sitting at home.

The invitation was very exciting for a fifteen-year-old like myself. It wasn't the shooting aspect that fascinated me, I had been to a fair share of shootings given that I am the son of director H.S. Rawail. I simply went there to ogle at the exotic 'foreign' girls.

You see, Chintu and I had studied together at Walsingham House School until grade four, after which it became an all-girls school. In those four years, Chintu and I had developed a bond of friendship that lasted over the span of our lives. Dad and Raj Uncle were both filmmakers and hence very friendly with each other.

When we reached Cross Maidan and entered the big top, initially, the girls there definitely grabbed my attention, but when I saw Raj Uncle and the way he was working, I forgot my original purpose of going there. I was mesmerized by the aura created by Raj Uncle working. It was like watching him conduct a symphony without a music sheet.

There was this single man controlling a crowd of 5,000 junior artists, Russian and Indian circus artists, crew members and actors. He was orchestrating all of them to perform, to the best of their abilities, to bring his vision to life. The scene that was laid out in front of me was one of chaos and organization working hand in hand. It compelled me to simply stand in a corner and observe, and by this time I was so enamoured that even the thought of the girls had gone out of the window!

When I got back home, I couldn't get over what had fascinated me at the shooting. It kept replaying in my mind over and over again. How Raj Uncle paid attention to the smallest of details while shooting and how particular he was about even the smallest movements being perfect. I knew nothing about his film, but seeing the way he executed it with so many people under his command was enough to keep my mind running. I was so captivated that I couldn't help but share my experience with my mother. I told her, 'Mom, I went to watch Raj Uncle's film's shooting today and watching him at work is a different experience altogether! I'm going back to the circus tomorrow to watch him shooting.'

I went to the circus again the next day and sat alone in a corner. Raj Uncle saw me there and asked me if Chintu was with me. I replied that I had come alone that day and he simply nodded and got back to the shooting.

I was amazed to observe how well he managed to store an overload of information in his brain. His eyes and ears were everywhere. He would look at everything. He firmly believed if the director required his actor to speak the dialogue or execute a particular movement, it was the job of the director to enact the same so that the actor could replicate it.

I remember Raj Uncle wanted Dharam ji, Dharmendra, who was playing the owner of the circus and a trapeze artist, to stand on the safety net after a jump. Dharam ji was a little confused about how to stand on the net because the net was very wobbly and difficult to balance on. So, Raj Uncle climbed the steps to reach the safety net to show Dharam ji how it had to be done. Raj Uncle was a bit on the heavier side but there wasn't a single trace of fear or embarrassment on his face.

This represented his dedication towards the art. He would never compromise on the things he wanted to achieve while filming. He had visualized camera movements, background movements, the action of actors and the rhythm of dialogues, which were dictated by the content of the scene being executed, and he would ensure that they were achieved.

His clarity and intuitive sense of filmmaking compelled him to take charge of every action and emotion in every single scene. If his visualization of a scene demanded that an actor had to move with his left leg first, he would insist that the actor moves with his left leg first. As I spent more and more time observing him, I realized that there was a reason for everything he did and what the layperson thought of as simple details, were what contributed to his genius.

There was another scene, where Dara Singh ji had to enter from behind the lion's cage and stand at his position beside the cage. He had a bullwhip in his right hand. Dara ji had said he'd come from behind and take a position where the lion would be on his right. Raj Uncle differed. He said that entering from behind, Dara ji must take his position where the lion would be on his left and the bullwhip in his right hand. The visual impact with the bullwhip and the lion flanking Dara ji would enhance the dramatic impact.

I came back from the shoot and paused to think about what I was doing. Was I enjoying my stint with Raj Uncle and did I want this to be my career ahead? I was not sure. I thought plenty about everything: my studies, my career and my future. My parents wanted me to carry forward the legacy that was created by my father but I had a plan and it was a simple plan. I was to go to Canada and pursue a degree in nuclear physics; films were never a part of my plan.

My academic course was due to start in the next seven months and I had nothing better to do, so I talked to my mother about it, 'See, I have seven months free with nothing worthwhile to do. I was thinking if I should be productive and join Raj Uncle as an assistant director till the holidays end.'

She was more than happy to see me work rather than while my time away. My apprenticeship started with my father accompanying me to the shoot the next day and speaking to Raj Uncle about the prospect of me working with him for seven months during my holidays. Raj Uncle called me and said, 'You are most welcome to come and work with me. I have noticed that you've been here every day for the last 15 days keenly observing me work but remember, you are not going to be H.S. Rawail's son here, but a part of the unit like the others. Second, I haven't opened a school but am more than happy to teach and guide you provided that hunger for knowledge is exuded by you.'

He turned to my father with a stern expression and asked, 'What are you still doing here? This is Raj Kapoor's assistant director here, not your son.' The two of them started laughing while I stood there mulling over the fact that I was indeed Raj Kapoor's assistant director!

A few days into my apprenticeship and I started to realize that Raj Uncle not only had a brilliant mind but also an eccentric personality. He had his own quirks which I encountered soon enough. One day on the shoot while Radhu Karmakar, his director of photography (DOP) since *Awaara*, was lighting a shot, he summoned me, 'Babbu, I can't seem to get the lighting right for this shot. I need someone to climb up the big top and stand on the platform, where the trapeze artist stands.'

I was wondering who would be the right person to climb so high up, when Khan Sahab, Raj Uncle's sound engineer since *Aag*, came to me and said, 'Don't just stand here, climb the big top and give a position on the trapeze.'

I was terrified and numb with the thought of going through this ordeal but before I could say anything, a safety harness was being fitted onto me. Khan Sahab was serious. He wanted me to climb a shaky, 40 feet rope ladder all the way to the top. I started climbing the ladder with my heart in my mouth. When I reached the top, Khan Sahab asked me to hold on to the trapeze with both my hands. If I wasn't terrified enough before, I was after listening to those words. I wasn't trained in circus stunts. How could I hold on to the trapeze without risking my life?

Raj Uncle also spoke up, 'Babbu [my ridiculous pet name], grab hold of the trapeze and try swinging to the other end. The trapeze artist standing there will help you.'

I was so terrified that I underwent a brain freeze and just then, the entire crew burst out laughing. I had been pranked! I looked down at them with tears in my eyes unable to comprehend the joke I had become.

I climbed down on shaky legs, my heart still pounding and Raj Uncle, for the first time, called me to have lunch with him, 'I understand you were terrified and humiliated by what you went through. Don't consider this a prank but consider it to be a very important lesson. In any creative pursuit, experiencing and understanding the emotions – fear, humiliation, defeat, losing a loved one, break-up of a relationship – are all necessary as they strengthen your understanding of life and thus make you creatively richer.'

His words imprinted themselves in my memory and my days spent with him were unveiling different facets of life at every step. My hunger for knowledge kept growing by the day. The circus schedule came to an end and so did my apprenticeship under the most distinguished filmmaker and the world's most competent teacher, Raj Kapoor.

WHEN RAJ UNCLE BECAME RAJ SAHAB

I WAS PASSIONATE ABOUT PURSUING nuclear physics but my interests seemed to have now brought me at a crossroads where an alternative passion had also been ignited. The *nasha* of making films and the 'man' himself was really taking over. Raj Uncle had rightfully said, 'Once you enter this field of work and get passionate about the same, it is very difficult to give this up. It gives you an adrenaline rush when you heroically conquer all challenges hurled at you and this is what creates a sense of euphoria within you.' At that point, the idea of continuing to work as an assistant director appealed to me more than leaving it all to go to a different country to pursue a different career altogether. I was like a child who had graduated from dreaming of becoming a postman, slowly changing to a fireman, further changing to a policeman and to finally becoming a 'filmman'!

I had to speak to Raj Uncle and see if he would be willing to let me carry on working with him. This time around, my father wanted me to talk to him myself. Raj Uncle had an office at the studio but worked from the revered 'cottage', which was sacrosanct to him. I stood at the entrance, very confused whether I should enter or not and if I should knock before entering. I was contemplating at his doorstep when John, his cook, saw me there and asked me who I was and what I was doing there.

'*Sahab se milna hai. Bolna Babbu milna chahta hai*,' I answered.

I had always addressed him as Raj Uncle but with the realization that I wanted to be employed by him, the term

'Sahab' seemed more appropriate. As I nervously entered the cottage, he asked, 'Yes, Rahul, tell me.'

That was a monumental day for me. For the first time he addressed me as 'Rahul' and not 'Babbu'. I simply stood there with a puzzled expression on my face. He said, 'Don't look so confused at the fact that I called you Rahul instead of Babbu. I know why you are here and you are welcome to carry on as an assistant director.' His gift of reading faces and associating them with your thoughts was unparalleled.

Then Raj Sahab asked me about my future plans, 'So, will you also go to college from June?'

I replied, 'Yes Sir, I'll take admission at St. Xavier's College at Dhobi Talao.'

'What are your college timings?'

'From seven in the morning to one in the afternoon.'

'How will you commute to the studio?'

'In the morning, I will take a train from Bandra to VT to attend college. From college, I'll take a train to King Circle from VT, then take a bus from there to Sion and then a bus to the studio. I have found out what the routes are.'

'Good! I love your dedication and pray that this quality stays with you forever.'

I walked out of the cottage smiling and happy since Raj Sahab's support infused more confidence in my plans for the future. Following that conversation, I secured admission to St. Xavier's College and thus ensued my hectic schedule of attending lectures in the mornings and going to work in the afternoons. Even though it was hectic, I couldn't have asked for a better start as an official assistant director at RK Studios (henceforth referred to as RK).

A week or two after my confirmation as an assistant director with Raj Sahab, I got my first salary like the others. I had joined the crew in December, but it was May when I started getting paid. Payday in RK was as unusual as everything else that happened there. The seventh or tenth day of every month was when we got paid. I went to the account section to collect my pay. There used to be a huge line of employees, but we were privileged because we were assistant directors and we could just walk in.

When I entered the room, I was told that I would be getting a salary of ₹72 and I was thrilled to the core (there is a unique pleasure in being paid for your work). The accountant made me sign a voucher but I did not get the money in hand. The cash was passed on to the second table where the canteen owner sat. RK had a canteen and we used to go there once in a while to have a Coke or something. A Coke cost 4 *annas* and the canteen guy used to keep our account. The canteen chap on the second table would cut his dues and hand over the remaining cash to the man on the next table, the *paanwala*. I used to smoke in secret but I never used to buy my cigarettes from him because if Boss came to know, I would be as good as dead. Thankfully, I had no account with the *paanwala*, so he would pass the cash to Dambara ji, the head projectionist, who was running a clandestine bookmaking racket on the side. He would deduct his dues and whatever was left after the cuts was what one got in hand.

That day, since I smoked on the sly and was not into illegal gambling, I got the whole ₹72 as my first salary. I hadn't even realized then that the salary was actually ₹84 and medical insurance and Employee Provident Fund (EPF) contribution were deducted from that. However, such days didn't last long. I started eating at the canteen, buying my cigarettes from the *paanwala* and indulged in illegal betting with Dambara ji, all on credit. The result was that after three of them cut what I owed them, I would not get my salary on paydays but an IOU of what I owed them further because my salary didn't compensate it fully. Like most of the world, I had entered into a debt trap! I think I even owed the *paanwala* ₹30 or ₹40 when I left RK.

And thus, my journey at RK continued. It had been a year since I joined and in December that year, I had my prelims for the final exams. We were editing *Mera Naam Joker*. I went to Raj Sahab and told him, 'Sir, I may not be able to come for the next three weeks.'

His one-word reply was, 'Why?'

I said, 'I have got to study for my prelims.'

He was nonchalant about it and said, 'It's okay, you're intelligent enough. I know you'll manage your studies even if you continue coming to the studio.'

Now that Raj Sahab had told me not to worry about the exams, I continued working and didn't prepare for the prelims. I flunked! Needless to say, my parents were upset at my non-performance and even I felt stressed because of it. When I went to the studio later, I shared my distress with Raj Sahab. I told him, 'Sir, big problem, I didn't study and I have flunked my prelims.'

Looking at my worried face, he was very sympathetic about the situation and said, 'Don't worry about it, okay? Let me come with you. We'll go to St. Xavier's and meet the principal. I'll convince him that he should allow you to go on and give him the reason why you didn't pass.'

A wave of relief washed over me because I was confident that Raj Sahab would convince our principal. I was very happy that he was coming with me and I took an appointment with the principal. However, one evening before the appointment, Raj Sahab was having a drink with some unit members in the cottage garden. I was standing in a corner with a Coke in my hand, and suddenly in the presence of everybody, he took off on me, '*Ab main kal kya karunga? Tumhare saath jaunga college? Kya bolunga principal ko? Ki yeh bohot honhaar ladka hai? Jo fail ho gaya? Fail ho gaya aur honhaar ladka hai?! Meri zindagi yahi hai kya? Chintu jab fail ho gaya tha,* Campion School *mein toh mujhe ek* trophy *donate karni padi thi taki usko aage padhne dein. Tum bhi aise hi ho. Sab bacche aise hi hain.*'

The next day, he came with me to the college and, I remember, it created quite a stir. Everyone was wondering what was Raj Kapoor doing on the campus? Meanwhile, we went and met the principal and the principal said, 'No, I'm sorry, I can't pass him.' Even after a lot of convincing by Raj Sahab, his decision was final.

To compensate for our unsuccessful attempt with the principal, he took me out for lunch to Nanking and told me, 'Forget it! What will you do by getting a certificate? Because the way you're working with me, and what I'm seeing in you, I don't think you'll be needing any degree or certificate.'

That was all the confidence I needed. He went on to become my mentor, a father figure and a friend who guided me through life, professionally and personally. All I wanted to do was come back to the studio for more and more, every day. I was happy solely in learning everything there was to learn about films from the man himself. In my time at RK, I learnt how to run the projectors in a theatre, how to thread the reel, how to work a camera, how to record the sound, how to edit; in fact, I was put through the entire gamut of filmmaking. Raj Sahab, to me, was a genius. I had never thought that it would be possible for one man to have that kind of 360^0 knowledge of cinema.

Raj Kapoor was the puppeteer who deftly manipulated the strings of the script, dialogue, music, technique and visuals. He had given me a deeper understanding of filmmaking that stayed with me forever.

RK STUDIOS: A FOUNDATION FOR CREATIVITY

THAT SMALL PIECE OF land in Chembur called RK Studios housed the one man who was the epicentre of Indian cinema – Raj Kapoor. The sanctity of space the studio offered to learn the craft had me completely mesmerized. It was a revered place that would go on to give me my best experiences and lessons. RK was not only my place of work, but my place of worship.

It had a magnificent and awe-inspiring appeal to it. On entering RK, one would see a huge logo of a man standing with a violin in one hand and a woman bent in his arms, symbolizing the romance and music in Raj Kapoor's brand of cinema. This posture had become the logo of RK Films and Studios when *Awaara* was released. It was designed by the eminent designer M.R. Achrekar and painted by the renowned and respected Shri Balasaheb Thackeray.

The logo is said to have been inspired by the iconic scene in *Barsaat* in which Nargis ji runs towards Raj Sahab, who is standing with a violin in his hand. Raj Sahab then catches her in an embrace and bends her backwards to strike an instinctive and intimate pose. This classic scene was inspired, as all creative pursuits need inspiration, by a painting that Raj Sahab had seen in Stuttgart. The painting is of a man holding a violin wrapped in a passionate embrace with a lady who is bent backwards and is leaning against a piano. This painting was made by the French artist, René-Xavier Prinet, who was himself inspired by Leo Tolstoy's novel *The Kreutzer Sonata* in which a violinist falls in love with a pianist and kills her when he realizes that she doesn't love him back.

Below the logo, one would come across a huge statue of Lord Shiva. Raj Sahab was a believer of Shiva. On every mahurat (auspicious launching) of a new film, his father, the illustrious Prithviraj Kapoor, would pray to Lord Shiva. Though Raj Sahab did not have a very stringent belief in any particular religion, he had faith in the one God and strongly respected all religions as they were different manifestations of the Almighty.

There is a colourful story behind how RK Studios came to be. When Raj Sahab decided to make *Aag*, he had only ₹13,000 with him. He confided his plans of producing his own film to Vishwa Mehra ji (Mama ji), who was his close confidant from Prithvi Theatre. The film needed the help of a lot of people – makeup men, actors and dancers who were all working in Prithvi Theatre at that time. It was a collective effort of all the people employed at Prithvi Theatre that brought his dream to life.

In those days, it was crucial for a filmmaker to be tied up with a studio since the studio had a covered area to put up the set and also provided for the cost of the set. Having a studio also meant having sound equipment, a sound recordist, an editing room, cameras and much more.

Raj Sahab, driven by the madness of making a film, decided to tie up with a studio called Eastern Studio which was owned by Mr Lakhani. Raj Sahab wanted to have superior technicians in his films and had acquired the services of V.N. Reddy who was a very eminent cameraman. The production of *Aag* cost them ₹3,00,000 which was a huge sum of money at that time. Raj Sahab was confident that he would make a profit out of this film since the story had great depth and his vision would hit the bull's eye. However, the film got critical acclaim but didn't do well at the box office. Despite the financial setback, Raj Sahab decided that he would make another film.

Mr Lakhani had assigned Allaudin Khan, or Khan Sahab as we called him, an assistant sound recordist, to take over the designation of chief sound engineer. Though Raj Sahab had wanted to work with professionals who were experienced and technically sound, he was forced by Mr Lakhani to utilize the services of an assistant. Much to his dismay, Raj Sahab had no alternative. He decided that he would personally train Khan Sahab to become the most sought-after sound engineer in the industry.

In the shadow of Raj Sahab's guidance, Khan Sahab rose to the height that was expected by Boss. Mr Lakhani was upset that Khan Sahab was now being offered more lucrative jobs, and to create a stumbling block, he enforced the terms of his contract, further refusing to allow Raj Sahab to use Khan Sahab as a sound engineer in his next film. This prompted Boss to break ties with Mr Lakhani and help Khan Sahab in getting his contract nullified by the court and find another studio for his next film. People tried to persuade him to not be so stubborn and just go with the flow but he refused. He said, 'I will not compromise on my choice of a technician.'

Raj Sahab decided to make *Barsaat,* for which he signed up Roop Tara Studios, owned by iconic K. Asif, who welcomed him with open arms. He needed to raise finances for the production since the regular financiers were not keen on investing money into a producer whose last film was a commercial 'cold turkey'. Thus, Raj Sahab decided to take help from his father Prithviraj Kapoor, who magnanimously helped his son to get back on his feet again.

Raj Sahab decided to shoot the song '*Hawa mein udta jaye*' of *Barsaat* in the picturesque valley of Kashmir, a location where no film had ever been shot, thereby enhancing the visual experience for the audience. Shooting in Kashmir was unheard of since it meant an exorbitant cost of transporting the entire cast, crew and equipment coupled with huge logistical problems related to travel and lodging.

Raj Sahab was not willing to compromise on giving his audiences a breathtaking visual experience. He decided that he and Jal Mistry ji, the DOP of the film, would somehow reach Kashmir and shoot random shots of the landscape with a stand-in and the same would be juxtaposed with shots of the actor that would be executed in Mahabaleshwar. To lighten the burden of carrying a bulky camera that required electric power to run, he bought an Eimo camera – the only portable, battery-operated, 35mm camera of the time. This purchase was in fact Raj Sahab's first step into fulfilling his dream of owning a studio.

While making *Barsaat,* for which he had distributors and a financier, he started working in more films as an actor since that would generate more money which in turn would be used in fulfilling his ultimate dream. His next step came in the form of purchasing a sound truck, a necessity that housed all the sound recording equipment. Even after he built the studio, the sound truck remained a permanent fixture. The third step was his buying a professional 35mm camera, the Mitchell NC. These possessions stemmed from his passion for filmmaking and created the necessary stepping stones to owning a studio.

After the unprecedented success of *Barsaat,* he decided to assign Radhu Karmakar as his DOP for *Awaara.* Radhu Sahab had started his career in films with *Kismat Ka Dhani,* in Kolkata, followed by *Jwar Bhata, Noukadubi* and others. His mastery in shooting night sequences and his technique of high contrast lighting had brought him tremendous acclaim. These were his assets that drove Raj Sahab to employ his services, and the association between the two lasted up to *Ram Teri Ganga Maili*.

Asha Studios was contracted for the production of *Awaara*. Raj Sahab had planned a sequence in which Nargis ji enters a pond wearing a swimming costume. Although most films were shot on a set in a studio, for this particular scene, he would have to go to a swimming pool at the NSCI Club to shoot. Nargis ji had reservations about wearing a swimming costume on a location with too many people around. To appease Nargis ji, he dug up the ground of the studio, without prior permission, and created a pond for the purpose of the shoot. Raj Sahab was severely reprimanded by the studio owners for not seeking permission and demanded a whopping compensation of ₹80,000. He instantly reimbursed the studio but was very bitter about it and told the studio owners, 'It is not the money I paid that upsets me, but being dictated to seek permission for my creative pursuits does not gel with me at all. I am never going to shoot in this studio again!'

He shifted to Shrikant Studios for further shooting but the need for his own studio was growing stronger by the day. Adjacent to Shrikant Studios, there was a two-acre piece of land that Raj Sahab wanted for constructing his own studio. The land would cost him ₹1,50,000 and he did not have this large sum of money at that time; however, he was a man who was devoted to his art and saw the studio as a natural extension to his creativity. He managed to collect the required sum by working relentlessly for other producers and put in a lot of hard work and persistence. He even borrowed money on hundis (promissory notes) and eventually bought the land to build his RK Studios.

Building the studio led to problems in his household. Krishna Aunty would say, 'How long will we live in a rented house? Invest the money in a house.'

To which he would reply, 'I will…I will buy a house. But I need to have a studio first. Only if there is a studio will I be able to earn enough money to buy a house. Let me build the studio and you don't worry, eventually, I will buy you a house…'

A lot of blood and sweat went into building the studio of his dreams. Raj Sahab started working for *Awaara* at RK, but at that time there was no roof. The shooting would take place only at night to avoid daylight. During the making of *Awaara*, on a stormy night, the set got washed away due to the absence of a roof. This led Raj Sahab to invest in building a roof.

Once the studio was rebuilt with a roof, Raj Sahab became greedy. He now wanted an editing room and a preview theatre where he could edit and watch his films. So, he built an editing room and an adjoining theatre on the roof of the administrative building. For the theatre, he put wooden supports on the sides and stuck gunny bags together because of which it got the name, 'Gonpath Theatre'. Seating was on a couple of benches strewn around.

Raj Sahab could then finally finish *Awaara*, which turned out to be a raving success. Due to the successful turn-in of the film, he earned enough money to transform RK into a proper functional studio. He had finally put all the pieces together. *Awaara* led to other successful movies and it was only when he started making *Sangam*, that Gonpath Theatre was finally converted into a brick and mortar theatre. He also bought the adjacent Shrikant Studios after the success of *Sangam*, to further expand RK.

RK was the fulcrum for Raj Sahab's creativity to grow. A lot of movies have been shot there. The studio had four stages, stage number one being the most important as it was the first sound stage to be built by him. Many eminent filmmakers used to shoot at RK. Raj Sahab used to come out in the evenings to go around the studio, visit and exchange pleasantries with the units that were shooting at the various stages. It was considered an honour by other film units to be visited by and interact with him. I would tag behind him and had the privilege to watch L.V. Prasad, Manmohan Desai and other such masters at their shoots. These visits strengthened my knowledge base and I consider myself blessed to be able to learn from the greatest filmmakers of our times and gain knowledge from these masters.

RK also had a costume department, which had costumes starting from the time he shot *Aag*, that kept expanding with each new movie. If you went there, you'd see the costumes of Nargis ji from *Aag* and *Barsaat* as well as Raj Sahab's shoes from *'Mera joota hai Japani'*. We could pick up anything and use it for his own films. Unfortunately, with the fire in RK that stage burnt down and they lost this whole legacy which was absolutely priceless.

Raj Sahab continued innovating and adding equipment to the studio as time progressed and technology advanced. Not only did this keep the studio going with the pace of the generations, but it also kept the people working in the studio satisfied and happy. Raj Sahab had great value for his technicians. He had a bunch of very competent people working for him and he treated them like his family. They were his family.

Raj Sahab used to have a big celebration every year on Holi at RK. It was a grand, coveted affair. The industry and his friends would come there after 2.30 p.m. The idea was that after celebrating Holi with their friends, people would come to the studio to enjoy as a unit of the film industry. They would all be singing, drinking and making merry. Raj Sahab wanted to create RK into a foundation for creative people where one could come, sit around and discuss creative ideas.

For Raj Sahab, filmmaking was a celebration, and one could see the pleasure he derived from this in his eyes. He would sit and talk to all the people. He had this great quality where he would talk to people to understand them and also get inspired.

Raj Sahab's very capable son, Randhir Kapoor, Dabboo Sahab as he was called, was a very good friend of his father's; he was there to monitor the progress and to assist his father in any area that required his help. Dabboo Sahab continued the legacy created by his father and made sure that RK went down in the history of Hindi cinema as a cornerstone of creativity and filmmaking.

TRIMURTI

RAJ SAHAB ALONG WITH his most trusted technicians – Radhu Sahab and Khan Sahab – constituted the 'Trimurti', the Holy Trinity of cinema: the creator, his eyes and his ears.

Needless to say, they were indispensable to Raj Sahab. The three of them had worked together throughout the golden period of RK and were integral to the magic that happened within the walls of the studio. They developed a strong professional and artistic bond, shared creative inputs and also fought over creative pursuits. Raj Sahab encouraged them to experiment and with his masterful guidance, the results they achieved were remarkable.

Radhu Sahab's work in *Awaara* was exceptional! Black-and-white photography was very difficult and required painstaking attention to detail since the play of light and shade created the visual impact the director envisaged for the film. Radhu Sahab was a master at fulfilling that aspect. He was a stickler for achieving the director's vision and worked at his own pace to reach perfection. Generally, when you asked a DOP how much time lighting a particularly complicated shot would take, he would be conservative and say, maybe an hour, but when Radhu Sahab would be asked the same question, 'Five hours minimum' would be his reply.

When *Awaara* was screened at international film festivals, filmmakers sat up to take notice of his brilliance. Sir Alexander Korda, the iconic international film producer and director, was completely enamoured by Radhu Sahab's work. He suggested to Raj Sahab that when he made the shift from black-and-white to colour, he should have Radhu Sahab train under the master cinematographer, Jack Cardiff, which Radhu Sahab did before embarking on *Sangam*.

The visual quality of *Sangam* makes it one of the most memorable films. During the shooting of *Sangam* at the Ambala airfield, Raj Sahab had organized for 100 Gnat aircraft to be lined up alongside the tarmac, for the unforgettable shot of Vyjayanthimala ji running alongside the aircraft that was being flown by Raj Sahab. When Raj Sahab arranged the shot, Radhu Sahab asked Boss without hesitation, 'You think we could move all the aircraft 1 foot back?' I presume the creative eccentricity of Boss had trickled down to his creative team, too.

Khan Sahab was a master technician and had a great sense of humour. We had a theatre in RK where we used to dub. Dubbing is the process wherein dialogue, which has already been recorded, is recorded all over again and transposed onto the previous dialogue to eliminate the noise in the former. Dubbing theatres are supposed to be soundproof. There shouldn't be any sound penetrating from the outside and a clear dialogue track should be obtained. The recordist is supposed to watch the film playing so as to make sure that the dubbed sounds compliment the expressions of the actor and at the same time the sync and quality of the dubbed sound is perfect.

The dubbing studio at RK wasn't soundproof; in fact, there were all kinds of noises that were heard! The noise of machines running and banging from a factory situated four buildings away, traffic on the road and various other sounds were distinctly heard. High-end microphones, as used in a dubbing studio, would pick up all the noise and made it difficult to isolate.

The sound truck, where Khan Sahab would monitor the sound, was at the other end of the studio! One had to walk approximately 400–450 feet to the other side to get there. Thus, he had no visual contact but when we used to hear the sound, it was somehow brilliantly put together! Such was the talent that Khan Sahab possessed and he landed up with the Filmfare Award for best sound recordist every time an RK film released.

There were other people who made the crew of RK. Back in those times, films were shot mainly on sets that had to be erected from scratch and the backgrounds physically painted. The aesthetics involved were of massive dimensions and Raj Sahab would always have a detailed and specific visual in mind.

In *Awaara*, he needed sets of the slums, and also the exterior and interior of rich houses, courts and streets. In the fabulous 'dream sequence', which he had conceived, the sets involved surreal images. Keeping in mind the complexity of the sets, he approached Achrekar Sahab, the designer of the famed RK logo, to bring his vision to life. The art director in Achrekar Sahab was reluctant to dabble in films, but the perseverance and obsession for the art of cinema of Boss made him accept the job and the rest is history.

There were other people in the studio like Harish Dada, who was an electrician, today known as the gaffer. Harish Dada was an elderly man and had worked at RK since a long time. He and Radhu Sahab got along very well. When Raj Sahab would give Radhu Sahab a shot and tell him, 'This is what I want', Harish Dada would start lighting the background without Radhu Sahab having to tell him. Harish Dada did the basics and Radhu Sahab would come in and make final adjustments if needed. Raj Sahab at times would give directions to Harish Dada directly, '*Harish, yeh* area *jo peeche hai use thoda* dark *karna hai.*'

A trolley is used to move a camera on rails that have to be set up evenly on level ground so that the trolley moves smoothly. Raj Sahab had a carpenter called Bapu Katkar, who had a unique backstory. When they were shooting the song '*Bol Radha bol*' in *Sangam*, army-surplus smoke canisters were used to create fog. Bapu Dada, with his mop of jet-black hair, was assigned to open the canisters. Unfortunately, one opened up and blew into his face. When the smoke cleared, his jet-black hair had gone grey!

Bapu Dada was a master at setting up the rails for a trolley shot. It was simple to set up a trolley on hard and even ground, like at a studio, but in the outdoors, on uneven land, it was virtually impossible to have a smooth trolley. This is where Bapu Dada's expertise came in. Irrespective of the location or the terrain, he would set up the smoothest trolley rails that would enable the trolley operator to move without any effort. Raj Sahab wouldn't shoot without him and even when he went to Amsterdam to shoot some scenes for *Prem Rog*, he took Bapu Dada with him. Raj Sahab's influence on my work involved a fair amount of camera movement and I would avail of Bapu Dada's services for all my films. His passing away created a void and after that, every time I needed to set up a trolley shot, I would remember him and say a silent prayer for his soul.

We also had Om ji, Om Prakash Mehra, who was the production incharge at the studio; he was like a CEO and had his own quirks. He would come to the office every day, open up his payments diary and enter his name followed by – paid ₹500 to self. When I asked him about his peculiar habit, he readily told me, 'Listen, I take ₹500 for myself every day because my salary is too low. If I don't take this amount from the accounts myself, I'd take it in ways Boss would not even realize; I'd skim it off the top. I am a very honest man and dishonesty is something I detest.'

I think we attract the kind of people in our circles whose quirks are as odd as ours. Thus, it wasn't surprising to see the kind of people who worked with Raj Sahab. Om ji and Raj Sahab had a particularly strange relationship. Both of them were extremely fond of drinking and when they used to get high, they would invariably fight. At times, Raj Sahab would catch Om ji and throw him out of the studio and at other times, Om ji would catch Raj Sahab and throw him out! Seeing this unique behaviour, one watchman at RK was always confused and could never decipher whether Raj Sahab was the boss or Om ji was the boss. Late one night, Raj Sahab visited the studio and the watchman didn't allow him in. The confusing discussion that followed is the prime evidence of the unusual relationship Raj Sahab and Om ji shared.

Raj Sahab: 'Why aren't you letting me in?'

Watchman: 'I can't; Sahab has ordered me to not allow anyone in at night.'

Raj Sahab: 'Listen, I own this place! I am Sahab!'

Watchman: 'You don't and you're not Sahab!'

Raj Sahab (losing his patience by the second): 'Who is Sahab then?'

Watchman: 'Do you see the man right there? He is Sahab.'

He was pointing at Om ji because he was convinced that Om ji was the owner of the studio.

In spite of the push and pull in their relationship, they had a lot of trust in each other and Om ji was very efficient. He was excellent at his work, which explained why the two of them worked the best together.

Then we had a gentleman called Harish Bibra who was Raj Sahab's secretary. Such was Harish ji's nature that when the world was celebrating the landing of Neil Armstrong on the moon, he asked me if I knew the postal address of the White House.

I was puzzled and asked him, 'Why?'

He said, 'I want to send a telegram to the President of the United States of America to congratulate him on the landing of the first man on the moon. I will sign it "from Raj Kapoor".' I wanted to ask him if he thinks that the President would know who Raj Kapoor was but the confidence on his face made me keep my words to myself.

Harish ji's quirks have given us unforgettable memories. When Raj Sahab wanted Vyjayanthimala ji for his film *Sangam* and kept waiting for her reply, Harish ji sent her a telegram with the iconic words '*bol Radha bol sangam hoga ke nahin*'. The incident remains a classic memory of RK and became the introductory lyrics, *mukhda*, for an iconic song.

S. Kalachandra, referred to as Kala ji, was the chief assistant director. Kala ji had quite an interesting backstory. He came to Bombay, now Mumbai, with a friend from Madras, now Chennai, in the hopes of joining the film industry as an assistant director. So, the two of them went to meet Raj Kapoor. Raj Sahab had wrapped up the filming of *Aag* and was then working on *Barsaat*. They met him through someone and asked him about potential opportunities. Raj Sahab, as straightforward as he could be, told them, 'Look, I can only take one of you in the crew because there isn't enough space for both of you.'

On interviewing both, he found Kala ji to be the one he should take on as an assistant. Kala ji's friend was very upset and burst into tears. Since the friend was also a dancer and in dire need of a job, Raj Sahab got him a job at Prithvi Theatre.

Kala ji spent his whole life as an assistant at RK, and his friend, L.V. Prasad, became one of the major filmmakers of that era and a Dadasaheb Phalke Award winner. In fact, Raj Sahab played the protagonist in Prasad Sir's maiden Hindi film, *Sharada*. Raj Sahab used to playfully lament that his judgement had gone completely haywire when choosing between Kala ji and Prasad Sir.

Raj Sahab was extremely well informed and ran his own version of a secret service agency. He always knew what was said behind his back. Mama ji was his constant companion and instrumental in helping him set up the studio in the RK Secret Services. Mama ji used to revel in gossip and would carry the news of the day to Raj Sahab along with 'breaking news' as it occurred. He was assisted by Revati, Raj Sahab's personal valet. When Revati ji was not around the Boss, he would be lurking in all corners of the studio only gathering information. When the Boss would wake up in the morning, Revati ji would press his legs and tell him about all that he had heard and seen on the day before. Raj Sahab used to love the gossip he received from Mama ji and Revati ji. We were always afraid that 'fake news' had been passed on to the Boss. To appease Mama ji, who also considered himself to be a great actor, we would praise his acting talent to any extent to keep him happy. Revati ji, of course, used to be happy with the tips we used to give him.

As strange as every member seemed, the crew came together to make a marvellous team. The crew members were people Raj Sahab trusted and treated like his own family. He knew that they were the right people for him as they would assist him in delivering precisely what he wanted. His unwavering faith inspired me to realize that he would like and appreciate my work if I delivered according to his sensibilities, and the only way to learn more and more was to understand and deliver what Raj Sahab cherished.

DAMBARA NIGHTS

DAMBARA JI, AN EXTREMELY helpful, good-hearted and jolly human being, was the studio's head projectionist. Under instructions from Raj Sahab, Dambara ji took efforts to determine that I become proficient at operating the projector because of which there were times when I was able to run previews independently. A master at his work, he was also the in-house 'matka' bookie, a completely illegal, but national gambling system. I was extremely fond of him and enamoured by the stories he told, especially those concerning the Gonpath Theatre and the glorious past of RK. I spent a lot of spare time in his cabin where, apart from hearing his stories, I would also smoke on the sly.

The preview theatre was adjacent to the editing room and was conveniently accessible to view any edited sequence. When not being used for editing, it served as an in-house preview theatre, dubbing studio and as a venue for an in-house magical experience, 'Dambara Nights'.

Dambara ji had made a collection of Raj Sahab's iconic and favourite scenes from his films. The Dambara Nights involved the screening of this selection which reflected Raj Kapoor's creativity. It was strictly a private affair, limited to Boss and his assistants.

Boss had a policy of never touching alcohol when he was working. However, once in a while, when he was tired after a gruelling day of editing and needed to relax, he would sit in the theatre and his man Friday – aka

Revati ji – would bring him a bottle of Black Label (his favoured whisky) and then, it would turn into one of the Dambara Nights.

Dambara Nights usually commenced at around half past ten at night and by the time they would wind up, the clock would have struck around four or five in the morning. They would go on with the unique and unconventional approaches to visual narration with beautiful melodies filling the wee hours of the morning.

What unfolded before my eyes during these nights was the sheer spectacle of content, form and technique vis-à-vis cinema, and a magnitude I had never imagined or seen on celluloid before. The other assistants present would be enjoying their drinks, but for me, it was far more fulfilling than simply entertainment. It was an opportunity to learn seated in the first row of a masterclass.

The screening would start with *Aag*, Raj Sahab's first film, opening with the scene in which his newly wedded wife sees his burnt face and is powerfully impacted by it. Followed by *Barsaat*, which included the song '*Mera lal dupatta malmal ka*'. It would then play out several fragments of *Awaara*: the scenes of the protagonist's turmoil, his confrontation with his father, the scenes of romance with Nargis ji and, quite importantly, the dream sequence. Following this was Raj Sahab's favourite scene from *Shree 420*, where he is sitting alone with a pack of cards and there you see his sleight of hand and expertise in card-sharping, which eventually Nadira ji discovers and further influences him to turn into a greyer character. There were the songs he loved, '*Ichak dana bichak dana*' and '*Ramaiya vastavaiya*'; sequences from *Aah, Boot Polish, Jagte Raho, Jis Desh Mein Ganga Behti Hai, Sangam* and *Mera Naam Joker*.

Dambara Nights included a song from a film called *Sargam*, which was not produced or directed by Raj Sahab. The song in question here was, '*Main hoon Aladdin Aladdin Aladdin; mere pass chirag-e-cheen*' and featured Raj Kapoor as an actor and the extremely talented lady Rehana, who happened to be my father's foster mother in Calcutta, now Kolkata. The film was directed by P.L. Santoshi, the father of the iconic director Rajkumar Santoshi. This song in his cherished collection was a tribute to P.L. Santoshi.

Raj Kapoor was a great teacher. What he told me the day I joined him – 'I have not opened a school' – was a lie! Watching his spectrum of work and gaining knowledge from his experiences made him a fine teacher. He was extremely sharp which gave him the capability to understand emotions and expressions, which, as put by him, was the greatest asset of a director.

During one such Dambara Night, Raj Sahab was enjoying his drink and so were my other colleagues. I was too young to consume alcohol (although I did smoke; I regret it to this day despite having quit a few years ago). I would stand in a corner, eyes fixed on the screen, intently watching the spectacle, my head bursting with questions and craving to obtain answers for them. Suddenly, Raj Sahab told Dambara ji to stop the screening and the lights came on.

Then the following conversation ensued. He asked me, 'Why are you looking so bewildered and confused?'

I replied, 'No, I'm fine, Sir. Just a little lost.'

He said, 'It seems like you have questions for me but are afraid to ask. [I was quiet, my head hanging low.] Remember, if you want to attain knowledge, never be afraid to ask. The creator of the scenes that you are watching is me. That makes me the only person who can answer your questions and, believe me, I would be happy to do so. I promised Kali Mai [that's the term of endearment he used for my mother who was a Bengali] that I would impart whatever knowledge I had, provided you wanted to gain that knowledge.'

Encouraged, I asked, 'Sir, was there a particular reason to execute the dream sequence you filmed in *Awaara* on such a huge magnitude – the variety of sets and the mood of all three parts in the song?'

He replied, 'The character I played was a tramp, a downtrodden human being who had never experienced the big life. So, when he dreams about his lady love calling out to him, he places her in a surreal ambience, which is much larger than anything he has ever imagined. It is a spectacular setting where a man of his stature would dream about a utopia, but would finally encounter the demons of his past – a much larger-than-life, grotesque and frightening atmosphere. His hope, his efforts in attaining his love and his fears are all translated into this dream, each being more and more spectacular than the last.'

This explanation of what transpired in his creative mind made my day! Dambara Nights became awe-inspiring for me because of his narratives. At times, Raj Sahab would say, 'Run that scene, let me show it to Rahul.' The brilliance of his motivation behind his technique would astonish me each time, especially because I was hearing it straight from the creator's mouth. Every action and every reaction hit me with the unparalleled depth of Raj Sahab's work.

Similar questions regarding his technique and thought behind a particular moment kept popping out of my head and he kept replying. Dambara Nights were the closest I had got to exploring his inner mind and the magnitude of his obsession with music, dialogue and visual art. He adored all of his films and it was a joy to see this adoration. The event would go on for about five to six hours at a time but those hours breezed by easily since I was watching true gems of cinema.

After the first schedule of *Bobby*, Dambara Nights saw the addition of the scene where Rishi Kapoor (Chintu) meets

Dimple Kapadia for the first time at her doorstep where she has accidentally smeared her hair with some *besan* (gram flour). That sequence would always give me goosebumps, whether it was while shooting, editing or watching it. The innocence of a young girl and the infatuation of a boy for her, due to her simplicity, was the true moment of 'love at first sight' for me. A moment that I don't think has been surpassed in cinema!

I told Boss that this girl is a fantastic actress. He immediately grabbed my hair in his fist and snarled at me, 'So now you're raving about her performance but when I auditioned her, you and all the other imbeciles like you were extremely disappointed after seeing her audition and tried to dissuade me from casting her. According to your minds, casting her was a fatal mistake. Idiots!'

He walked out of the theatre to the strains of '*Jaago Mohan pyaare jaago*' in the background. To me, it seemed that the words were being sung for an 'idiot' like me, who had disagreed with Dimple Kapadia as the choice for the lead role in *Bobby*.

I guess that was the reason that he was 'The Raj Kapoor' and me, a mere mortal!

THE OBSESSIONS AND ECCENTRICITIES OF THE GENIUS

Raj Sahab had a whimsical and eccentric side to him which would shine when he used to be around his films, food or his favourite drink. These were his three obsessions that made up his eccentric personality. These eccentricities had a deep-rooted relationship with his films, as were all his actions.

His obsession with his drink – Johnnie Walker Black Label – was one nobody else could beat. In fact, once he would have a drink, all work would stop regardless of the schedule. He was convinced that he was the only man in India who drank genuine Black Label because he had bought his bottles on his trips abroad. He would buy his bottles on each trip and they would all be stocked in his personal cupboard to which only he had the key. In fact, when he passed away and they opened his personal cupboard there were only bottles of Black Label to be found and nothing else.

Once, I was at his place and he pulled out a bottle of Black Label and then Revati ji brought another bottle of Black Label which was placed in front of me. I thought it was strange that there was one bottle in front of me and another in front of Raj Sahab. So, I asked him, 'Sir, why two bottles?'

'Look, the Black Label I drink is genuine.'

'Are you giving me spurious alcohol to drink?'

To which he answered, 'No, no. I have brought this Black Label from my trips to England. Your bottle, I bought in Bombay from the bootleggers and I paid a 1,000 bucks for it. But I'm not sure if it's genuine. So why should I take a chance? You have this Black Label, but I will not give you even a drop of my Black Label!'

His eccentricities did not end with his choice of alcohol but were spread over the entire spectrum of his personality.

RK had a CFO, Mr Raman, who had become a distributor of his films for the territory of Tamil Nadu. When he died, his son Babu took up his father's distribution office. Raj Sahab was fine with it until *Bobby* became a big hit and Babu didn't pay the profits to Raj Sahab and he was pissed off about it.

One night, while coming back from town, Raj Sahab suddenly burst out, 'Driver, *ye gadi ghumao aur* Raman Sahab *ke ghar chalo.*' The car headed towards RP Masani Road, the film fraternity area of the past, where prominent figures like Prithviraj Kapoor, K.L. Saigal, K.N. Singh and many more stayed. Babu stayed in the adjoining lane, and it was past midnight when the car stopped outside Babu's house.

Raj Sahab got out of the car and shouted, 'Babu, Babu!' repeatedly until Babu came out running. Hearing the commotion outside, all of Babu's neighbours came out to watch the drama that was about to unfold. Babu came out in a half-asleep state, dressed in the traditional South Indian attire – a mundu (a half-lifted lungi) and bare-bodied with a huge tilak on his forehead.

He came rushing out and Raj Sahab didn't waste a moment to start firing him, '*Mera* Bobby *ka* profit *kahan hai*?'

Babu quickly responded, '*Mere paas* safe *pada hain*!'

But Raj Sahab wasn't having any of it, '*Tumhare paas hai, mere paas kyun nahi hai? Woh paisa mera hai, tumko rakhne ka kya haq hai*?'

Babu answered nonchalantly, 'I will give it to you, Sir. *Hum dega, kal dega aapko.*'

Raj Sahab stared at Babu for a few seconds and the next moment he pulled off Babu's lungi and Babu was left naked, trying to cover his manhood.

'*Kal subah paise lekar aao aur lungi lekar jao*,' saying this to Babu, Raj Sahab turned around and left Babu stark naked surrounded by his neighbours having a hearty laugh.

One night, at around three in the morning, I was woken up by my neighbour saying that Raj Kapoor was outside playing with the stray dogs. I went out looking for him but couldn't find him. I thought he must have left for home because his car wasn't parked anywhere around. I was about to return to my precious bed when I saw his car come into the lane, driven by his trusted chauffeur.

As if the night wasn't puzzling enough, I asked him, 'What happened? Where is Sahab?'

He said, 'Sahab Bandra *se jaa rahe the aur unhone bola ki* Rahul *ke ghar par lo. Toh main yahan par le aaya aur voh gaadi se utar gaye aur kutton ke saath khelne lage. Phir voh paidal chalne lage aur mujhe bole tum gaadi lekar jao mein* Chembur *paidal jaoonga*!'

I realized that Raj Sahab was probably angry with the chauffeur, so I asked him, '*Tumne roka nahin*?'

'*Main gaya unke peeche, par jab unhone dekha toh ghoom ke, "Get out! Get out!" chillate huye meri taraf bhagna shuru kar diya. Maine dar kar gadi ghumai aur yahan par wapas aa gaya*.'

I told the chauffeur, 'Look, I think he's annoyed with you. Don't worry, you go home and let me take my car and go around the neighbourhood. I will definitely locate him and drive him home.'

As I was driving around the neighbourhood, I saw Raj Sahab standing at a bus stop. I stopped the car and asked him, 'Sir, what are you doing here?'

He replied snarkily, 'Waiting for a train! Idiot, what does one do at a bus stop? He waits for a bus! Stop asking me stupid questions!'

'Why do you have to wait for a bus?'

'I will only go back by bus. I also have money to buy the ticket.' He took out a couple of coins and flaunted them.

I sighed and tried to dissuade him, 'You know buses don't start till five-thirty in the morning, and right now it's only quarter past three. Come sir, I'll drop you.'

He wasn't having any of it and screamed, 'I'll wait till five-thirty, but I will go by bus only! Go away and don't show me your face! You have been sacked!'

I burst out laughing and said, 'Since you have sacked me, you can pay me that bus fare but I will drive you myself.'

Anger and irritation bubbled inside him as he picked up a pebble and threw it at me while I was in the car. So, to cool him down, I drove around the block and came back to the bus stop. He wasn't there!

I couldn't tell where he might have gone but my instinct told me that maybe he would have taken a cab home, so I drove towards Santacruz. The usual route was from Kurla or Dadar because, at that time, there was no Dharavi Road. I believed that he must have taken the Kurla route so I drove towards there. Going towards the Santacruz subway, I overtook a taxi with three people sitting in the front seat, and as I passed, I just casually glanced inside the taxi and was surprised to see that Raj Sahab was the third occupant! He was sitting in between the driver and his companion, with his arms slung around their shoulders and a *gamchha* tied around his head. I drove up to them and heard that he was singing a song I had never heard him sing before, '*Sun sahiba sun, pyaar ki dhun*'.

Eleven years later, this song was recorded and featured in the movie *Ram Teri Ganga Maili*.

I did not stop the taxi and followed it instead to ensure that he reached safely. Once Raj Sahab reached his house, he got out of the cab, said his goodbyes, embraced them and walked away without offering them their fare. So, I asked the guys, 'What is your bill?'

They were thrilled and they said, '*Arey* Sahab, Raj Kapoor *gaadi mein baith gaye, toh bill kahe ka*?'

Anyway, I went home after that and in the morning, I got a call from Revati ji saying, 'Sahab *ne bola hai aap ghar pe aa jaiye aur khana ghar pe hi khana*.'

Once there, Raj Sahab asked me, 'I wanted to talk to you about the silver jubilee celebration of RK Films and Studios, which we are planning to have. What should we do?' During the course of this conversation, I didn't mention the previous night, but when he realized that I was not going to, he brought it up himself, 'Did I come to your house last night?'

I didn't reply.

He smiled and said, 'I know I came to your place. I know I stood at the bus stop and that I came back in a cab and I even know you followed me. So, did you pay for the taxi? Tell me so that I can pay you back.'

I declined, 'No, I didn't pay for the taxi. They were very happy that you sat in their taxi and didn't accept the money I offered.'

He asked, 'How did they like the song?'

This was his creative genius. Regardless of the events that transpired that night, he remembered every moment since it centred around his work. Even after consuming alcohol, he never rambled incoherently. Everything he said revolved around his foremost obsession – cinema.

Lunch was laid out and in between enjoying the hearty seven-course meal, he suddenly stopped eating, washed his hands and innocently said, 'Oh! What a terrible mistake I have made. It slipped my mind that today is *amavasya* and Krishna had instructed me to fast and refrain from eating until seven in the evening. It's shameful that I overlooked religious diktats. Anyway, I made a mistake and I'm sure God will also forgive me for this.' He dived back into devouring the seven-course meal all over again without any regret but constantly reprimanded himself for breaking the fast!

The affinity that the Russians had with Raj Kapoor was unapparelled. Once *Awaara* caught the fancy of the Russians, Raj Sahab's films became a hit not just in the USSR but in most communist countries. I have seen this for myself. I went to Tashkent in Uzbekistan with Chintu and Dabboo Sahab in 2007. Our flight landed in Tashkent at around 3.30 a.m. and it was freezing cold. All the guys at the airport, the traffic staff and the helpers, were humming the songs '*Awaara hoon*' and '*Mera joota hai Japani*', which over the years had become part of wedding rituals in the USSR, and this obsession has carried on to the CIS countries also. The whole area had a number of 'Raj Kapoor' clones and Raj Sahab considered himself to be one of them.

There is a very interesting incident that comes to mind. Dabboo Sahab and Chintu had a friend who used to work at the US Embassy. He was called Jerry Kirikano and was present for a party at Raj Sahab's house. Raj Sahab had been drinking; he got a little emotional and said to Dabboo Sahab and Chintu, 'You know my sons have come here after a long time.' He was sitting on a swing reminiscing the days of the past and told his children, 'Come here, sit on your father's lap. You know you haven't done it in a long while.'

Now, Dabboo Sahab and Chintu were obviously embarrassed. These were two grown-ups who were being asked to sit on their father's lap at a social gathering. So, they didn't really react but this full-grown, huge, American chap ran and sat on Raj Sahab's lap saying, 'I'm also your son. I'm like Dabboo's and Chintu's brother and you're also like my papa.'

Raj Sahab looked at him and then pushed him off his lap. 'How can you be my son? You're an American and I'm a Russian and we don't get along!'

Raj Sahab hated pretentious 'sadhus and sants' trying to preach their religious agenda and make money. His faith rested in the Almighty only. There was a famous godman at that time (I don't want to take his name), who had just started his practice. You see, all godmen use PR promotion to become famous and lure innocent people into becoming their 'bhakts'.

Raj Sahab was invited by a local police inspector to a sermon recital conducted by this godman. On reaching the venue, we were greeted by the organizers who did everything to make us feel comfortable and asked us to sit in the first row. Raj Sahab looked around and asked, '*Kursi kahan hai*?' Everyone else was sitting on the ground or on *gaddas* but Raj Sahab wanted a chair and demanded, '*Do kursi lekar aaiye*.' Since I was with him, I also got the privilege to sit on a chair!

The sermon was underway and they were serving *sheera* as *prasad*, which Raj Sahab noticed and said, 'That *sheera* looks nice.' He seemed more interested in the *sheera* than what the godman had to preach. He couldn't wait for the *sheera* to come around to him so he told me, 'Go and call the guy serving it and tell him to come here first.' So, I went and told that guy, 'Raj Kapoor is calling you.' His eyes twinkled at my words and he immediately brought one big vessel full of *sheera* and small bowls for us to eat in. Now Raj Sahab, being the 'foodie' he was, picked up the whole vessel and ate up all the *sheera!*

Then the organizers came up to him and gave him a garland, saying, '*Aap jaa ke Baba ji ko ye pehna dena*.'

Raj Sahab stayed put in his chair, happily enjoying the *sheera*. So, I told him, 'Sir shouldn't you go up and garland him.'

'Look, I'm Raj Kapoor. This man wants publicity. He will get up himself and come and garland me.' And believe me when I say it, that's exactly what happened! The godman himself came to Raj Sahab and put the garland around his neck. A 'double whammy' had been scored. The fraudster godman got his photo-op and Raj Sahab enjoyed the *sheera*!

Raj Sahab had an elephant's memory and if one had said something nasty about him or committed an action that did not appeal to him, he would never forget. Suddenly, after any number of years, he would remember an incident and reprimand you, and he had no qualms about doing that publicly.

When he made *Mera Naam Joker*, Gulshan Rai produced a movie at the same time called *Johny Mera Naam*. As you can see, the title of Gulshan Rai's film was very similar to *Mera Naam Joker* and it was released earlier, and became a very successful film. *Mera Naam Joker* didn't do very well and there were a bunch of jokes made about the similarity of the two titles and the fate of the films. After four years, Raj Sahab made *Bobby,* which was a runaway hit. One of those days, he was invited to a party where he caught hold of Gulshan Rai and said to him, '*Kyun, maine* Mera Naam Joker *banayi toh tunne* Johnny Mera Naam *bana li? Ab maine* Bobby *banayi, toh tu kaunsi film banayega*? Tobby?'

One evening, at his farm in Loni, after the day's work, he was sitting with the unit and having a drink. Through that evening he was being very nice to me and complimenting me about my capabilities as an assistant director, but for me, it was a 'red flag' being hoisted. I told Chintu, 'Look, Boss is being very sweet and nice to me, I'm sure I must have screwed up somewhere during work today, or, considering his memory, even two years back. I can't fathom what he is upset about, so

I'm going to sleep before he pulls me up and I'm "paraded" all night.'

As I got up and walked towards my room, I realized that Raj Sahab was walking behind me. I quickened my pace and he quickened his pace too. I ran into the room, jumped onto the bed and pulled the blanket over my head. He followed and entered the room, 'Wake up! Wake up! Wake up!' His volume kept increasing with each 'wake up'. I refused to acknowledge him and just pulled the blanket tighter around me. 'Stop pretending that you are asleep. I know you're not! You have to wake up and listen to me,' and he started shaking me. The shaking got more and more violent but like an obstinate 'SOB' I refused to come out of the blanket. So, he just sat on the bed next to me and said, 'Fine! I will sit here all night and keep shaking you. I want to see how long you can avoid me.' This carried on for most of the night and at around four in the morning, he finally got up and said, 'You are fired! I don't want to see you from tomorrow,' and he walked out banging the door behind him.

The next morning, I was on the set. He came in, we exchanged pleasantries and work carried on without any mention of the night before. He asked me, 'Did you sleep well?'

'Very well, Sir' was my reply.

'Good' was his response.

Towards the evening he called me and said very lovingly, 'Look, you need to pay more attention to your work. A week back, you couldn't remember one dialogue that I wanted to add in the scene and I had to shoot the scene without that dialogue.'

I replied, 'I am sorry, Sir, but I'll see to it that it doesn't happen again.' He patted my back and said, 'I'm glad that you are accepting your folly.' Till date I don't remember that forgotten dialogue!

Around 1979, I was in Loni to discuss the script of *Biwi-O-Biwi* with Boss. One evening, Naresh Kumar, a well-known producer and director, walked in and I was asked to leave the room as he wanted to discuss a matter personally with Boss. After about two hours, Naresh Kumar left and Boss sent for me. As I entered his bedroom, he was looking fresh and had a huge smile on his face. One bottle of Black Label was brought by Revati ji along with two glasses. I realized that it was some kind of special announcement since he had decided to share his personal bottle of whisky with me. 'You are going to be very happy to hear that Naresh Kumar has signed me for his film and is paying me ₹2,00,000 as my remuneration,' he said removing an envelope and pouring out the currency notes. 'This is the signing amount of ₹25,000 that he has given me!'

'Congratulations, Sir.'

'Did you hear me or not? A signing amount of ₹25,000 and remuneration of ₹2,00,000!'

I just smiled and he screamed, 'You have no reaction. Only Raj Kapoor is paid this kind of money and you, like a jackass, have no reaction. I think the shock has been too much for you to bear!'

I replied, 'Sir, last week Chintu signed a film of Manmohan Desai for a remuneration of ₹4,00,000 and in my presence, he was given a signing amount of ₹50, 000.'

'Chintu has made a fool out of you! It must have been just ₹10,000 and he must have added Monopoly notes to impress you. I know actors like him, they are available to anybody for a remuneration of maximum ₹50,000 and in any case that is what they are worth. Only an actor of the stature of Raj Kapoor can command such terms!'

The Delhi premiere of *Mera Naam Joker* was organized by the Naval Officers Wives Association. When we had the premiere there at night, dinner was hosted by the then chief of naval staff. It was attended by many eminent personalities and officers. Drinks were served, obviously, including Black Label, and the bar was being handled by a senior officer. After two servings, only the unit people and a few outsiders were left. The drinks that were served after most guests had left was premium Indian whisky. The moment Raj Sahab had a sip of that, he realized that his favourite drink had been replaced. He called the officer and fired the hell out of him. He said, 'You must be doing this because you got a quota from the government which you put into your cupboard. And you're going to sell it in the black market and make money out of it. You think we are fools that you'll get away with serving us Indian whisky? I'm going to file a complaint because you deserve to be court-martialled for serving fake whisky!'

During the shooting of *Bobby* in Pahalgam, I remember a similar incident but concerning a reputed general this time. We had just come out victorious from the Bangladesh war and the general was one of the principal officers involved. While we were shooting, the general came over to meet us. He was very happy to meet Raj Sahab and see him work. So, Raj Sahab played the song *'Beshak mandir masjid todo'* from *Bobby* sung by Narendra Chanchal. The lyrics were partly in Hindi and partly in Punjabi. The general was also Punjabi and he greatly enjoyed the song when he heard it. But after the song finished playing, he said, 'Raj, this is a Punjabi song, will people understand it?'

To which Raj Sahab said, 'Sir, this is cinema and normally in cinema, you understand things because it goes with the situation in the film. You may not know the language but the visual unfolds the context.'

To which the general said, 'No, no, I don't think people will understand it.'

Raj Sahab was about to lose his patience as he gritted through his teeth, '*Nahin. Samajh jayenge sab.*'

The general further rebutted, '*Nahin, mere khayal se nahin samjhenge.*'

So finally, Raj Sahab said, 'Okay, I'll think about it.'

With the end of that discussion, the general bid adieu and Raj Sahab escorted him to his car. He opened the door for him and the general sat in the car. Raj Sahab then closed the door and turned around and said, 'Now a general will tell me how to make a movie? Idiot!'

Later that night he called me out and said, 'Let's go to the army mess, I want to meet the general. I want to tell him that he is responsible for so many of my children dying in the war. They have died because of him. And he will tell me how to make a film when he doesn't know how to fight a battle! What right does he have to tell me how to make a film?'

Raj Sahab would often take things for granted. During *Bobby*, we were driving around, taking random shots of nature for the film. We passed an army checkpost and came to an area that none of us had seen before. Going ahead, we reached a barricade and the soldiers manning it told us that we weren't allowed to cross it and go ahead. So, Raj Sahab got down from the car and said, '*Mera naam* Raj Kapoor *hai.*'

The soldier had already recognized him and said, '*Kamal kar rahe hain.*' He touched his feet and continued, '*Aap ko kaun nahin janta? Aap utre kyun* car *se*?'

Raj Sahab wouldn't let this opportunity go. He replied, '*Nahin beta, woh kya hai ki mujhe* Bobby *ke do char shots lene hain yahan par. Mujhe border pe shoot nahin karna hai* but I like the area around it.'

The border was only 20 kilometres from there which is why it was a restricted area. The soldier said, 'I'm sorry, I can't let you in like this.'

Raj Sahab said, '*Theek hai*, no problem. Go to your commander, whoever he is, and tell him that Raj Kapoor is here.'

He said that with a voice full of pride. He also added, 'Also tell him that Raj Kapoor needs two four-wheeled car to drive us over there. Tell him I'm going up to the border to shoot.'

I was a bit concerned about his blatant request. I didn't want us to get into trouble with the army. I went to Raj Sahab and told him, 'Sir, at least go and ask him about this yourself.'

But Raj Sahab shut me up with, 'No, he will come, you all don't know my power.'

And the commander really did come out, greeted us and arranged cars for us to go to the border. We drove up towards the border and took our shots. We didn't go to any sensitive spot but he asked the commander nevertheless, if we could go up to the Line of Control and see it.

The commander readily agreed, 'Sure.'

I can't explain what an amazing feeling it was. It was a vast border, stretched out as far as our eyes could see. All the *jawans* were waiting for us because they had been informed over their wireless radio that Raj Kapoor was coming. They had arranged their own celebration with flowers and had made some pakoras and samosas for us to gorge on.

We sat with them and they explained how the whole area worked. They showed us the 'No Man's Land' and told us how the Pakistanis lived on the other side like we lived on this side. It was all very fascinating to see. In about half an hour, we bid our adieu to them but they said, 'Sir, please wait. We told the Pakistanis on the radio that Raj Kapoor is here and they are coming across to meet you.' We were delighted to meet them too. We waited a little longer and two Jeeps with Pakistani soldiers showed up. They were exhilarated to meet Raj Kapoor in person and had brought jalebis and mithai with them so that they could feed us. It was a great, great feeling to be there.

Raj Sahab's obsession apart from his work and drink was food. He was the foodie of RK and he turned us all into one as well. He had an eating routine which he followed every evening. He would leave from the studio at 6 p.m. sharp and go to Chembur Station. There was a pani-puri wala outside from where he would to eat pani-puri. Next to that was a South Indian restaurant, where he would go and have a dosa and a medhu vada. They used to make and serve the medhu vada only in the mornings but because Raj Kapoor used to come every day, they made it especially for him in the evenings as well. Then he used to go to a third restaurant nearby to have a filter coffee.

There was no way this routine could be broken or altered. In fact, if he had to meet people and it would have to be at that particular time, he wouldn't give up this evening routine but would ask them to join him. Imagine you've come to meet Raj Kapoor and you're standing on the street eating pani-puri while talking to him.

The meals at RK, which used to be laid out in the studio, were a huge affair. It could be called a meal for the kings because it literally was. Let me elaborate on the spread – there used to be one chicken dish, one mutton, one fish and over and above that we used to have a crab or a prawn and something else in chicken, like liver or kebab. Plus, there would be various types of dals, vegetables and three *meethas*. We would all sit together with him and all eat the same food.

We, at RK, were the only unit who used to be served high tea at 6 p.m. This was very nice of Raj Sahab because when you're working all day, you obviously feel hungry. The high tea was a very elaborate meal by itself! Raj Sahab called it a 'tiffin' which included a dosa, a vada, sambar, sandwiches, rolls, a jalebi or some *meetha* every day. This was during the shooting days, on editing days this meal would be even more elaborate.

During the final editing and up to the negative cutting of the film, Raj Sahab would turn vegetarian and wouldn't drink. This was when we had to start putting in longer hours. We would start working by 9.30 a.m. and would go on till whatever time he wanted to go on. And he would be the first to reach in the morning. Another interesting thing about these editing days was that before we commenced work, we would all assemble in the projection room with a paper and pad to decide the menu for the day – all three meals and an evening high tea. Practically an hour and a half was spent collecting everybody's views on the menu for the day.

Someone would suggest, 'Sir, Ghatkopar *mein ek* restaurant *hai jismein* dal *badi acchi milti hai.*'

Raj Sahab would say, '*Likho.*'

Someone else would say, '*Achha*, Thane *mein ek* restaurant *hai jahan* mutton *bohot sahi milta hai.*' That would be written down too, and it would go on and on until the whole menu was decided for the day.

He used to love the biryani from a restaurant called Coronation at Grant Road, next to Novelty Cinema. That would definitely make it to our list and then the list used to be divided, spread across lunch, evening tea and dinner.

We'd also decide what to eat for breakfast the next day. Just eggs for breakfast wasn't enough and the spread could rival any one of the fancy 5-star breakfast buffets today. Arrangements were made to assign cars that would go to various locations at varying times to pick up the food so that we all had 'hot food' to eat. Raj Sahab was also very particular about the snacks that were laid out in the evening with tea. It was a ritual that RK had started and then it spread over the whole industry. The entire day would be spent working and eating delicious food, and to have a foodie as a boss meant that apart from learning the ropes of filmmaking, I also turned into a foodie and my waist showed it!

Raj Sahab loved experimenting with food as well. I have seen him take a pav, put butter in the centre, pick up a jalebi and turn this concoction into a sweet jalebi sandwich! I was flabbergasted at seeing this and said, 'Sir, how can you eat a jalebi sandwich with pav and butter?' He looked at me, nodded his head in agreement and dipped the sweet sandwich into tomato ketchup and ate it up!

Raj Sahab was also fond of going to the races, and this was driven, not by a passion to gamble but by his obsession with food. He strongly believed that whatever he had, he was willing to gamble only on his films. He went to these races because of the snacks that they served at the race course. He would sit on the lawn of the Pune Race Course with seven or eight other friends and they would order sandwiches and chicken patties. When the race was about to start, they would get up to go to bet but Raj Sahab would stay behind. He would pick up the sandwiches, open the bread and eat up the filling, then close the bread and carefully put it back on the plate so that it looked like an untouched sandwich. He would later blame the waiters for serving them empty sandwiches! The fate of the chicken patty used to be similar. Seeing this really surprised me and he looked at me and said, 'What are you staring at? I'm dieting, you know. I'm leaving out the carbs.'

When Rita and I got married, the *pheras* happened in the morning and Raj Sahab was there, of course. He was very angry about the food because everything served was only vegetarian. He let Rita's family know how upset he was about it, 'Who told you that you have to serve only vegetarian food at a wedding? *Agar saath mein* chicken *ho toh shaadi nahin ho sakti kya*?'

We didn't organize a reception because I refused to sit on a stage like a fool, and arranged a dinner for about 200 close friends just outside my house. When Boss came, it was a shock for Rita and other guests. Raj Kapoor walked in with a tiffin! Seeing Raj Kapoor in a kurta-pyjama with a tiffin in his hand, a shocked Rita asked, 'What is Raj Uncle doing?'

'He has brought an empty tiffin with him because he will pack up the food and eat it at home.' He went to the kitchen area, tasted the various dishes and packed the ones he liked.

Raj Sahab then asked me, 'What about my whisky?'

'I've kept aside 12 bottles of Black Label, which have been sourced from 12 different suppliers. I have not opened them yet and kept them aside for you to sample and decide which bottle is genuine.'

So, he took me to the bar and told a friend of mine attending the bar, 'Pour me a small sample drink from all 12 bottles in different glasses.' Raj Sahab had a sip from each of them and finally decided that the fifth bottle was genuine. He then pulled out a plastic bottle from the pocket of his kurta and poured half a bottle of whisky into the plastic bottle, closed it and told his driver, '*Yeh gadi mein rakhna*.' And he told my friend at the bar, 'Keep this aside, this one's only for me. You will not give this to anybody else.'

While we were working on *Biwi-O-Biwi*, Sanjeev Kumar opened a restaurant in Bangalore, now Bengaluru. He was a sweet guy and as fond of eating as all of us. He invited Dilip Kumar and Raj Sahab to be chief guests at the opening of the restaurant. Obviously, the press had gathered around, clicking photographs and asking questions. Both Dilip Sahab and Raj Sahab spoke about the food and that it looked delicious. Food was laid out for them but both of them got up saying, 'We'll see you later.'

Confusion set over the entire crowd and Sanjeev Kumar asked them, 'Aren't you going to eat lunch?' They had come for the opening of a restaurant after all.

But without any regard, they answered, 'No, no, the food here looks very good but you know there is this restaurant in front called RR. The food there is amazing and we rarely get a chance to eat there.' They then got up and left to eat at RR. I honestly felt that it was rude of them but this is how Raj Sahab was. In fact, when he came back from Bangalore, he also had a tiffin with RR's food in it. When both he and I were shooting in Mysore for our films, *Prem Rog* and *Biwi-O-Biwi* respectively, he would have his car go to Bangalore all the way from Mysore to pick up dinner from RR.

In Bombay, he loved to go to town to this place called Wayside Inn. He'd always sit at the centre table there and the cooks would all come out to greet him. They would all slap his back and say, '*Raj, kaisa hai? Bahut time ke baad aaya.*' Seeing his chemistry with them, we learnt that he had been coming there since he was a child and the cooks were the same old guys from his childhood. The restaurant had a typical British menu. When I asked him why that place was dear to him, he told me, 'You know, there is a reason why I come here often and why I sit at this particular table and chair. This is the place where Dr Ambedkar sat and wrote the Constitution of India. I sit here so that it can inspire me to do constructive work.'

He used to love this place at Flora Fountain called Marosa. It was a typical, small cafe where you sat at a table and would only be asked if you wanted tea or coffee. Without ordering, they would bring you a British tiered serving stand containing sandwiches, chicken patties, chicken cutlets and scones. One could eat whatever they wanted and they would be billed according to how many of those assortments they had eaten.

Raj Sahab used to love that. Just like what he did at the race course, he would open up the sandwiches, eat up their filling, put the bread slices together and place them back on the serving dish. So, when Raj Sahab was billed, the owner would actually open the sandwiches to check because he knew what Raj Sahab usually did. It was one of his favourite places and he would go there regularly.

Raj Sahab also had an affinity towards Pune. He loved going there and he did a lot of shootings there as well. He was simply infatuated by that place. He would go there at the drop of a hat. He even had a farmhouse in Loni, which was a mere 14 kilometres from Pune. He had a very nice house there because of his frequent visits and he had to gradually expand the house to accommodate the entire unit. Raj Sahab also managed to fit in an editing room in the house because he would often edit there. This was also an extension of his obsession. He wanted to make this place into a kind of a film hub.

Raj Sahab loved travelling to Pune by the Deccan Queen, a train that even today leaves from Mumbai for Pune at 5.10 p.m. and returns from Pune to Mumbai at 7 a.m. It's basically a working man's train. This enables people who live in Pune to come to Mumbai in time for their offices and go back. The drive from Raj Sahab's house in Chembur to Pune would take the same amount of time the Deccan Queen would take to go from VT to Pune. Raj Sahab would drive an extra hour and a half to get to VT and travel by the Deccan Queen, the reason being his undying love for the food offered on the train.

Mind you, it was an assorted menu. There used to be samosas, baked beans on toast, railway cutlets, his most favourite keema pav and pastries. He'd want to travel by train just because he would get to eat these delicacies and we'd obviously accompany him.

The train had a canteen car and he used to sit there and be eating most of the way. He wouldn't only eat the food on the train, he would eat from each platform of the stations the train would stop at. And trust me when I say that he was obsessed with going to Pune by the Deccan Queen. So much so that after travelling all the way from Chembur to VT if we would miss the train at VT, he'd say, 'No, let's go to Karjat and catch the train.' We'd drive to Karjat and if we missed the train at Karjat too, he'd say, 'Let's go to Lonavala and catch the train.' He just had to board the Deccan Queen and sometimes it would be that we would finally reach Pune by car in our attempt to chase it.

One night, after the end of our shooting schedule in Pune, he decided to have a party for the unit which went on till 6 a.m.; everyone was in a great mood and high on alcohol. He suddenly said, 'I want to go back by the Deccan Queen because I want to have breakfast on the train.' So, I booked him a seat on the Deccan Queen. The train had compartments with seats that were aligned in the direction opposite to how the train would move. Suppose the train is going to Mumbai from Pune, the seats will face in the direction that's heading towards Mumbai and vice versa for going to Pune.

On that morning, Raj Sahab came to the station. I took him to his seat and as my luck would have it that compartment had the seats facing the other way. He stopped there and said, 'I'm calling the police.'

I was astounded by his sudden reaction and went on to ask, 'For what?'

He looked at me and started shouting, 'You're kidnapping me!'

I had no idea from where had he come up with this, 'Why would I kidnap you?' I tried to reason with him but he just wouldn't listen.

He said accusingly, 'You're not taking me to Bombay. You're taking me somewhere else. The train's seats are facing the other way. Tell me where am I going?'

I patiently asked, 'Sir, why will I take you anywhere else?'

He refused to listen and said, 'No, you are! Otherwise, why would the train face the other way? You are trying to kidnap me and I will not fall into your trap!' In reality, he just wanted to go back to Loni and sleep.

His obsession for Pune extended beyond the place to the food there. There was a place called India Coffee Centre on MG Road where we used to go. Raj Sahab used to order cold coffee and a club sandwich for himself. This was his patent order every time we went there. Then there was this place called Good Luck and he loved the biryani from there. He would always call for it. There was also Dorabji, where he would go to especially eat their famous Parsi food. He also had a favourite Chinese restaurant called the Chinese Room in Pune like he had Nanking in Bombay. We would travel 14 kilometres from Loni to come and eat at the Chinese Room.

Once, he decided that he needed to lose weight and got himself admitted into a nature cure clinic which was situated at Uruli Kanchan, a mere 12 kilometres from Loni. I thought I would visit him on a weekend and I did.

Raj Sahab had rented a cottage that was at a far end in the woods away from the main hubbub of the centre. I went to him, feeling grim that he had to stay like this but when I saw him, he looked like the happiest person. He welcomed me with open arms, 'Come, Rahul, have some tea.' Revati ji was with him who made some tea for both of us. As we sipped on our tea, Raj Sahab asked, 'How are you? What's happening?' and we made small talk.

Soon it was around lunchtime and I decided I should leave, 'Sir, I shall leave now.'

He said, 'Why? Have your lunch and go.'

I was very worried to have lunch because I knew that they gave a minuscule quantity of bland food to eat, so I told him, 'Sir, I can't. I believe these places give one *gobhi* for breakfast, lunch and dinner.'

He smirked and said, 'Listen, Raj Kapoor is inviting you for lunch...'

A villager from Pune came on a cycle with a bag. He had paper plates and bowls along with him and he delivered our lunch. On opening the packets, I saw that it was food from the Chinese Room!

Raj Sahab wasn't allowed to eat food from outside but he had managed to get food smuggled in all the way from Pune. He was possibly the only man in a nature cure clinic where instead of losing weight, for which he was admitted, he had put on 3 kilos by the end of his stay.

His obsessions were one aspect of his personality but his work was his passion. It was what made him Raj Kapoor. When he was shooting the song '*Mera joota hai Japani*', he decided to shoot it in Panvel. Going all the way to Panvel was a big thing at that time. He wanted to shoot there because he felt that the sky would have better clouds. In black-and-white photography, the clouds in the sky made it more picturesque.

So, the team went to Panvel, only to be met by a clear sky. They decided to go further ahead and in the process they reached Pune. Raj Sahab wasn't happy with the scenery there either so they went further ahead and after five days, they reached Ooty. He had left for Panvel and had reached Ooty! He could go to such lengths chasing a beautiful background for one song in a film. His passion towards the art drove him to no bounds.

After that, whenever Raj Sahab said that he will shoot in Pune or someplace else, a truck would travel with food and other necessary tools for cooking along with the whole unit because he would want to stop anywhere and stay the night. We had all heard this story which is why during *Bobby*, while shooting the climax, he said, 'Rahul, let's go shoot this scene on the Bombay-Nashik road.' He wanted to capture the scenic ghats.

I replied, 'Sir, you are saying you want to shoot on the Bombay-Nashik road now but ultimately you will say that let's go and shoot it in Pune. I know that. You will say let's go from Pune to Mahabaleshwar and shoot on that ghat.'

He refuted that and said stubbornly, '*Nahin, nahin*! I've decided that we'll shoot there. We'll go for a three-day shoot, get everything ready.'

So, I did but I also told the unit, 'Listen, he says it's three days but I'm pretty sure it will be longer; knowing him, we will ultimately land up in Pune.' And that's what happened. We went and shot the first day. We stayed at the Dwarka hotel.

Then in the evening, he told me, 'I'm not really happy with the location.'

I said, 'Sir, I've already made arrangements for us to go to Pune.' Our trip was supposed to last three days but we came back after sixteen or seventeen days. This is the way he would work.

Raj Sahab's obsession for cinema extended beyond the boundaries of India. He loved movies like *The Bicycle Thief* and Hitchcock films. We had all read *The Godfather* and were very keen to know how the movie had turned out. Raj Sahab was in New York when the film released and he had stood in a queue for five hours to get a ticket for the 'first day first show'. When he came back to Bombay, he spoke to us for over two hours, only talking about *The Godfather*. By the time he finished narrating the whole movie, it was as if we had watched the entire film. He remembered each and every sequence and scene – how it was executed and how the characters spoke.

When we used to edit at RK – be it a song or a particular scene – he used to send me down to the stages there. He would say, 'Call everybody to come and see this.' And of course, it was a great opportunity to see the work of the master. At times we had to run the song twice because we couldn't accommodate so many people at once. He would screen and watch it with everyone else. He had a sharp eye. He would easily spot where the audience felt that something was not right.

After watching the final cut of *Mera Naam Joker*, the general consensus of the unit was that Raj Sahab should reduce the length of the film. He had a profound reply, 'The film I'm seeing is the complete film the way I look at it and the way I want to narrate it. At this point, I cannot pinpoint even a single frame that can be reduced so this is the version that will be released. However, when the film releases on Friday and when the paying audience comes out of the first show and pass any adverse comments on the film, is the day that I will also realize that portions should have been cut out. But by the time I realize this, it will be too late then. Remember the filmmaker is not the king, the audience is, a reality that every filmmaker has to live with. Trying to repair a film after its release is pointless.'

The kind of knowledge there was to be gained from Raj Kapoor was truly unparalleled. He was a very good teacher. He didn't believe in attending schools or following particular curricula to learn filmmaking, but believed in practical training and grasping the techniques employed by your teacher. He believed that a teacher enjoyed teaching a student who strived for knowledge.

WORKING UNDER THE MASTER

While learning under Raj Sahab, I was determined to reach a stage where I could pre-empt what he wanted in a shot that he was contemplating at that moment. That would be the day of achievement for me. So, I started paying keen attention to his actions. I tried to learn his way of going about shooting a scene and later his technique of editing it. These were lessons learned gradually.

The foundation of his school of filmmaking was based on the fact that we were making a 'motion picture'. Raj Sahab had explained to me, 'What we're making is a motion picture. If I have to just tell a story, I would write a book but a motion picture requires "motion". Now, this motion could mean camera movement or actor's movement or a combination of both. These aspects add life to the narration of the story.' He'd say, 'Whenever I'm shooting, I try to keep the motion in mind. Not that I'd do it all the time, but as much as possible. It makes the sequence more interesting and this way you have the audience glued to what's being depicted.'

At RK, we had access to a theatre and I would go there to watch his older films and observe the camera movement in various shots. These shots were unique as they must have been very difficult for people to understand during execution; however, when all the shots were put together, one realized how the shots were smoothly woven into the narrative. He used to say, 'Whenever you shoot, keep the camera angles simple. Don't complicate your shots leading to a visual narrative that complicates the mind of the viewer. Every shot should seamlessly flow into the next thereby forming a smooth narrative.'

I was very eager to see the magic that was being created through the lens of a camera, but I had heard stories that some cameramen would give a kick on the arse of any assistant who asked to see through the camera. Which is why, though worried, I conjured up the courage to ask Radhu Sahab during the shooting of *Mera Naam Joker*, 'Dada, can I look through the camera?'

He simply said, 'Of course you can but I want to know why do you want to look through the camera?'

To which I explained, 'I want to try and understand how Raj Sahab has arranged a particular shot. This way I can see what is going on in his mind.' Radhu Sahab smiled and said, 'Go ahead.' The teaching process was not limited to Boss alone, but extended to the 'Trimurti' throughout my assistantship.

I looked into the camera and would request one of the assistants to replicate the actor's movement as Raj Sahab had explained to the actor. I wanted to understand the impact of the artist's movement, camera movement (if any) and why this shot was framed in a particular way.

Later, I came to know that Raj Sahab had asked Radhu Sahab, 'What was Rahul asking you?'

Radhu Sahab had replied, 'Sir, he was asking if he could see the shot through the camera.'

Raj Sahab had said, 'I'm glad you encouraged him. It's good that he's learning these things.'

Raj Sahab was very happy that somebody was making the effort to learn and understand the way he made his films. As a teacher, he had this great quality in him – if you asked him a question, he would really go through a long, detailed explanation and take pleasure in explaining things to you, unlike most people. And if you made a mistake, he would sit and explain to you what went wrong. He was undoubtedly a teacher to envy and also had definitive guidelines which helped in character building.

The circus had shifted to Delhi so that became our next filming location for *Mera Naam Joker.* This meant that the whole crew had to go to Delhi to finish the shooting schedule. I had been to Delhi accompanied by my parents during school vacations but this time I was going as a unit member unaccompanied by any family member. We were to travel by the Janta Express and I was the only unit member whose parents came to see him off. Okay, I was not sixteen as yet, but it was still very embarrassing!

Later during the schedule, my father had come to Delhi for a few days for some work and came to visit me. The next thing I knew, when we came back to Bombay, Raj Sahab was very angry at my father and met my parents personally.

He told them, 'Do you know that almost everyone in my unit has a father and a mother? Did you think about it? You thought you should go to the station to see your son off? For what? There were 200 people who went. Why did those people not get their parents? They didn't, because that's not right. What you did was wrong; he's working! Rawail Sahab, you said you had come to Delhi for personal work, but you did not! You had come to meet your son, I know that. Don't do these things if you want him to grow up and become a responsible and independent human being.'

For Raj Sahab, the word 'compromise' did not exist as far as filmmaking went. During the edit of *Mera Naam Joker*, he said, 'I need three shots of the exterior of the big top. I know that we do not have these shots so Rahul, find out where is the circus based right now, go there for a day and take these three shots.' The circus happened to be in Bhopal and the journey to and from Bhopal took four days and the shooting less than four hours. This was not the end. I was sent to different cities five more times to shoot one or two atmospheric shots of the circus that he required in the edit.

The one thing I learned when I was a junior assistant was that you should keep an open mind about the kind of work you are given despite your position in the hierarchy. Don't say, 'Because I am the third assistant, I will only do this.' If you do things beyond your role, it is going to show your enthusiasm and will eventually help you move ahead.

I was a junior assistant until *Bobby* came into the picture. The night before the first day of the shooting of *Bobby*, Joshi ji and Mhatre ji, Raj Sahab's assistants, quit and the assistants remaining were just Kala ji and me.

Boss called me and said, 'Shooting starts from tomorrow and Joshi and Mhatre have suddenly quit. Do you think you and Kala ji will be able to carry the load?' (Kala ji had been with Raj Sahab since *Barsaat*. He had somewhere, along the line, accepted the fact that he is always going to be there in the same capacity as he had been for so many years. He was an elderly man and everyone respected him for that and humoured him.)

I replied, 'Don't worry, Sir, our work will not suffer.' And that is how I was promoted!

A little later a tragedy fell upon us, our production in charge, Om ji, passed away. It was very unfortunate and that left us without a production head as well. However, we were in the middle of shooting and Raj Sahab didn't want to stop, so he asked me if I would take on production duties in addition to my job as an assistant director, to which I readily agreed.

When we shot the first schedule, the then editor's assistant, Kabre ji (Raj Sahab was the editor himself) had also left along with Mhatre ji and Joshi ji. The rushes were all piled up and hadn't been edited since we were trying to find an assistant editor. There was no digital at that time which meant that sound and visuals were in separate pieces of film and both had to be matched together. Then the shots, since we shot in random order, had to be placed in the correct sequence; at least that was the way Boss worked. Added to this was the task of choosing the takes since there were multiple takes, about six or eight takes per shot. They were all loaded into reels and projected in the screening room. Kala ji used to sit with a book that you had to prepare for him, dictating what scene number it was, what shot number it was and what take number it was. The film had to be made, and there was no assistant editor there to help in lining up the shots.

The first schedule we shot was Pran Sahab's house and the second schedule was the exterior and interior of Prem Nath ji's house. When we were shooting the scene of Pran Sahab visiting Prem Nath ji's house, Raj Sahab lamented, 'I wish I had edited the scenes from the first schedule since they lead to this scene.' Later that day, I went to the editing room after the shooting was over, picked up the rushes and started matching the sound and putting the shots into order. This process took me four evenings after shooting and when it was ready, I went to the set and talked to Raj Sahab.

'Sir, first schedule rushes are ready for the edit.'

Raj Sahab was surprised, 'How come they are ready, they haven't been synchronized and laid in order?'

I said, 'Sir, I have completed it all.'

He asked, 'The whole thing?'

I replied, 'Yes, Sir.'

He instinctively embraced me. This gesture brought tears to my eyes. For the first time, I felt like I had earned my living.

We went to the editing room after two days. The reels which I had assembled were all there and believe me I had screwed up in a lot of places. Before Raj Sahab could react,

Kala ji burst out saying his favourite Telugu line, '*Yendera edwa re, lenja kudka*!'

Raj Sahab burst out laughing. He asked me, 'Do you know what this means?'

To which I said, 'Yeah, but I'm too embarrassed to say it out loud.' I simply stood there staring at the ground.

Kala ji then interrupted, 'It means that you are a stupid idiot. You're a bloody fool and son of a bitch...'

I was genuinely embarrassed and Raj Sahab was still laughing. He told Kala ji, 'Don't say this to him, we should appreciate his effort and teach him where he made mistakes and what he could have done better.' When one's work is appreciated by their teacher, it is the greatest honour they can ask for. That is when I realized what he meant to me.

That was 1971 and I had started in 1968. In the three years of being paid ₹72 every month, that was the first time when I received ₹350 instead. I was ridiculously excited that my salary was now five times what it had been.

I went to thank Boss and said, 'Thank you, Sir', to which he replied, 'Thank you for what? Listen, son, you are paid for the work you do, and you should be paid much more. You always earn more when you work diligently and honestly. The increment is an incentive for you to work harder and be rewarded accordingly.'

After getting the increment, I pampered myself. For the first time, I took a taxi from RK to my house. There was no Dharavi Road at that time which meant that we had to take the long route via Dadar or Kurla and the taxi fare would cost an arm and a leg – ₹3.25! A king's ransom which a serf could hardly afford to pay!

During my first film itself, I had experienced and collected all kinds of incidents and memories, the type which would count as valuable and funny anecdotes. One funny incident that comes to my mind is when we were shooting the song *'Jeena yahan marna yahan'*. We had a set of rings put up for the song. If you remember this scene from the film, there was a lot of festivity going around. The focus was on Raju, the protagonist, but the background involved 30 dancers going around in circles. Raj Sahab wanted a shot of the dancers going around from a low angle. When the rehearsal started, with Boss looking through the camera, and the dancers began with their dance, Raj Sahab suddenly caught hold of one of the female dancers and commanded, at the top of his lungs, 'Dress dada, *chaddi pehnao isko*!' Red flushed on her cheeks as she looked thoroughly embarrassed. This is the type of man Raj Sahab was. He never felt a twinge of embarrassment. He was always straightforward and blunt, no matter what the situation was.

Raj Sahab's knowledge of cinema was extensive and his quality of grasping nuances was unparalleled. In 1972, he was heading the jury of the International Film Festival of India, which was held in Delhi. He took me along so that I would get an opportunity to see films from various countries. About 20 minutes into the film, without fully understanding the spoken word, he would decipher it from the visuals alone and whisper to me where the film was leading to, what would be the ultimate endeavour of every character and where the film would twist in a different direction. Almost 95 per cent of the time, he was spot on and it used to give him great pleasure if the film deviated in another direction than what he had envisaged. Boss had a huge armoury that contained 'weapons of mass creation' and, as and when the need arose, he would use these weapons or create new ones.

Raj Sahab has given me a deeper understanding of filmmaking which will stay with me forever and now I think I'm ready to share it with the rest of the world.

LESSON 1: CONCEPTS AND INSPIRATION

RAJ SAHAB WOULD ALWAYS make sure that his movies would impact the audience in such a way that would leave an indelible mark. Most of his films have some kind of social message that he wanted to propagate to the viewers for which he would draw inspiration from the world around him. Once he had zeroed down on the concept, he would surround himself with all types of stimuli – films, radio, books and even comics. *Prem Rog*, for instance, was initially a radio play written by Kamna Chandra. Raj Sahab had heard it and contacted her and asked her to narrate the same play to him. While hearing her narration, his mind triggered him to mentally visualize the narrative, thus influencing his decision to turn the radio play into a film. When he was being narrated a script or a story, he was not 'hearing' it but 'seeing' the same.

These days, most filmmakers, writers, etc., are attuned to reading a script, but believe me, hearing a script helps you connect with the emotions of the writer or director, who is narrating, since the narration will always contain their emotional connect with the film.

Sangam was a story idea taken from Hall King's novel *The Manxman*. Inder Raj Anand, the prolific writer, had read that book and narrated the idea to Raj Sahab who got inspired by the plot, took up that story and changed the background and the characters to be more relatable to the audience. It was a very intriguing romantic film. The movie showcased a brilliant conflict – the misunderstanding between a husband who believed his wife had been with his friend.

It was for the shoot of *Sangam* that for the first time, a filmmaker had stepped out of this country to shoot all over Europe. This was his way of connecting to the common man through the story with the added visual pleasure of travelling abroad through these characters. In those days, it was not easy for everyone to travel abroad, but they could see these sights of Europe through a screen sitting in the comfort of a theatre and this is what Raj Sahab made possible with *Sangam*.

Talking about the artistry of his films, I thought the concept behind *Satyam Shivam Sundaram* was a great one. The movie shows a man who falls in love with a voice, just the voice without having seen the person behind the voice. Raj Sahab was inspired by Lata ji and her voice and that is where this story came from. I have seen Lata ji sing and it left me completely enamoured; an indifferent face with an enchanting voice. This combination of voice and face came to become the concept behind *Satyam Shivam Sundaram*.

Raj Sahab drew inspiration from forms that were probably simple ordinary thoughts to others. One such inspiration was for *Ram Teri Ganga Maili*. He was taken by poetic words in the epic poem Ramcharitmanas, which means 'lake of the deeds of Ram', and was written by Saint Tulsidas. The poem describes a scene from Ram's journey to Chitrakoot when he halts at Prayagraj and meets a boatman. When Ram expressed his pleasure at seeing devotees atoning their sins by taking a dip in the holy Ganga, he was told by the boatman, '*Ram teri Ganga maili ho gayi, papiyon ke paap dhote dhote*', which indicates that washing the sins of men have soiled the Ganga. These words impacted Raj Sahab and led him to want to make a symbolic film that critiques the duality of society but he did not have a story that would justify this thought.

This concept as a foundation for a film was weighing heavily on his mind and had turned into an obsession. The obsession flowered when he went to Delhi to attend a wedding, where Ravindra Jain was singing a song for the audience. The first few words of the song were, '*Ek Radha, ek Meera; dono ne Shyam ko chaha. Antar kya dono ki chaah mein bolo? Ik prem diwani, ik daras diwani*'. Raj Sahab immediately walked up to Ravindra Jain and asked the orchestra to stop playing the song. He said, 'I was inspired by a scene from the epic poem "Ramcharitmanas" to form a foundation of a film but alas I did not have a story to build on that foundation. Today, the words of Pandit Ravindra Jain's song have given me the building blocks to strengthen that foundation.' He removed some money and handing over the same to Ravindra Jain, said, 'Pandit ji, this is a token signing amount as you are going to be the music director of an RK film titled, *Ram Teri Ganga Maili*.'

The original actor who played the tramp and scaled enormous heights in popularity was Charlie Chaplin and Raj Sahab was highly inspired by him. He had told me, 'I'd gone on a film delegation to Montreux in Switzerland, and the delegation was invited to meet Charlie Chaplin. It was a major fanboy moment for me to be able to meet the "Tramp". When we got there, I got the chance to spend some time and talk with Chaplin. After we'd dispersed, most of the people in the delegation – Bimal Roy, Radhu Karmakar, Dev Anand and Nargis ji – commented, "You both sound so alike, your way of talking, your thoughts and your characteristics..."'

Raj Sahab as an actor had adopted the Chaplinesque character of the tramp. The people of the Soviet Union, the Eastern Bloc countries and China especially related with the tramp and this infatuation led *Awaara* and *Shree 420* to attain cult status.

I had been to Tashkent in 2007 along with Dabboo Sahab, Chintu and Nitin Mukesh for a series of shows that were dedicated to the Legend. I was introduced at such shows as a one-time assistant director of Raj Kapoor. Once, we went shopping in the local market and there was a big crowd that had gathered to see Raj Kapoor's sons and close acquaintances. Amidst them, there was an old lady who came up to me and asked, 'Were you an assistant to Raj Kapoor?' I had an interpreter who translated her question to me.

I replied, 'Yes.'

Her whole demeanour changed at my answer; her eyes were sparkling as she said, 'That means you have touched him.' I found that a little odd but still replied with a yes. She immediately held my hand in her own and started crying and kissing my hand. Seeing her and her reaction, I burst into tears. I had never experienced anything like this. Even now, when I think about it, I feel like one of the privileged people to have been associated with a man of that stature.

Awaara had a great narrative – the story of a father and son who are separated in childhood and how the child grows up and adapts to the circumstances he has been brought up in. It is not a question of what's '*khandani*' but it is about how you have been brought up. The circumstances made Raj (the protagonist) what he became; although there was the inherent simplicity that stayed with the character. So, it became a conflict between his genes and circumstances. 'Raj' is not repentant of the fact that he is downtrodden. It was one of Raj Sahab's strengths to imagine these characters – powerful regardless of their fate – and portray them that way.

In *Shree 420*, the protagonist was a happy-go-lucky chap, with a great sense of humour, a great way to keep himself alive and kicking. He is shown this way from the beginning through the song, '*Mera joota hai Japani*'. His simplicity allows him to get manipulated by Nadira and the villain, Nemo, who speaks a dialogue, '*Isme fayda hi fayda hai*', which entices the simple character into a life of deceit. When the materialistic gains start creeping in, he not only stops caring about the woman he loves, but also stoops down to cheating those simple people who had helped him in his life, people who supported him and considered him family.

Raj Sahab believed in one thing, '*Dekho, beta, ye jitne bhi lakhpati* [millionaire] *hain, inhone paise mehnat se nahi kamaye hain. Inhone koi na koi* fraud *kiya hai, nahi toh yeh itne ameer admi nahin ho sakte*. This is greed. *Aur itne bade ho gaye hain, par inka lalach khatam nahin hua. Inke paas abhi sab kuch hai, par abhi bhi yeh aur* fraud *karte hain.*'

Raj Sahab wanted to send a strong social message through *Boot Polish* that portrayed children who lived on the streets of Bombay. It was based around their triumphs, their tribulations, how they feel, how they react to situations and the irony in their lives. They have everything going, but how circumstances stop their lives from really going ahead. The characters played by children were similar to that of the tramp but had varying points of view which drove straight into the hearts of the audience and showed them the reality of life on the streets of Bombay, a life that Raj Sahab had observed minutely.

Jagte Raho was a very interesting commentary on the dual nature of society. The story follows the events of a single night where it shows a beggar and his greed for just a glass of water. He went to a building to satisfy his greed and is labelled a thief by the people living in that building. The protagonist was not materialistic; he just wanted water, but in pursuit of his greed for necessity, he discovers that all those who called him a thief were bigger thieves themselves.

Jis Desh Mein Ganga Behti Hai was directed by Radhu Sahab, Raj Sahab's cameraman, and dives into a different stratum of society. Before getting into the concept of the film, let me give you a little trivia about it. The time when Raj Sahab produced *Jis Desh Mein Ganga Behti Hai*, Dilip Sahab produced *Ganga Jamuna* and Sunil Dutt produced *Mujhe Jeene Do;* it was a strange coincidence. The three big heroes produced three dacoit films but all three films from the same genre were poles apart from each other. All three were dramatically different and were directed by Bengali directors – Radhu Karmakar, Nitin Bose and Moni Bhattacharya. The coincidence was that all three films were actually directed by the actors themselves!

Coming back to the content of *Jis Desh Mein Ganga Behti Hai*, the protagonist finds himself in the midst of dacoits. Raj Sahab wanted to explore this unrepresented territory of the dacoits living with their families; they were also slaves to their destiny like any other human being and were led by circumstances to provide for their family through their wrongdoings. Raka, the leader of the dacoits played by Pran Sahab, was a man who knew what he was doing was wrong, but his destiny had brought him into this life. The protagonist finally convinced him to surrender, pay his debt to society and live a more fulfilling life.

Raj Sahab believed that even when people are going through hardships in life, they should project a smiling face so others don't realize their pathos but see a smiling world around them; the philosophy behind the life of a joker – the show must go on! This philosophy is what Raj Sahab followed when he made *Mera Naam Joker* based on his inner thoughts and dreams.

Raj Sahab read comics with a passion. He found great narratives, stories and plots in them. *Archie* comics inspired him to make a story about young love. He was quite taken by the characters of Archie and Veronica and how the class difference between them doesn't affect their love for each other which is what he adopted for the story of *Bobby*.

All of Raj Sahab's films had diverse stories to tell which came from a vast variety of sources. Converting these stories into films came from a great understanding of cinema. He designed characters who would aptly fit into the narrative. Telling the story and using the characters cinematically is another lesson.

LESSON 2: PREPARING FOR THE SHOOT

As a director, Raj Sahab paid very close attention to what was shown on the screen, how it was shot and how it came across to the audience. He believed that the audience's experience was all that mattered and he worked towards making impactful films that had some of the most unforgettable scenes. From showing the beautiful valleys of Switzerland to the colourful and lively circus, Raj Sahab's films were larger than life which was owed to his technique. I was very glad to have been a part of this process and learn how to handle a camera, the lighting, arranging shots and everything else that contributed to the process of shooting.

Raj Sahab also worked in a time when motion pictures changed from being filmed in black and white to colour. Since most of his earlier movies are in black and white, there was a lot of importance given to tones and cinematography during the shooting of those. The difference between black-and-white cinematography and colour is that in black and white, the DOP had to create all the images to have different tones which were not there for films in colour. If this was not done and it was just black and white, there would be no difference in the picture. So, to create a difference between the background and foreground, they'd have to really light up the sets that way so that shadows were created. I had once asked Raj Sahab a very stupid question, 'Sahab, when you made these films in black and white, did you really have to bother about the clothes that the actors were wearing?'

He said, 'What do you mean?'

I said, '*Jo kapde pahente hain*… it's all black and white. So, it shouldn't matter.'

He replied, '*Tum mere ko samajhdar lage the, tum toh bewakoof ho*. Of course, we had to because the whole image you're seeing, that differentiation between the foreground and background, that's all created because of different colours and textures. It was definitely far more difficult.'

Mera Naam Joker was to be shot inside the big top, a location with a huge expanse, and the team was not able to get enough lights to light up the whole location. To achieve the same, additional arc lights, a bright light produced by generating an electric arc across two electrodes, brute lights, more powerful than an arc light and powered by 225 amps DC and 10 KW tungsten lamps were specially imported at an exorbitant cost. Even this was not enough and a higher rated ASA film negative was required. An ASA (American Standards Association) rating relates to how quickly the film reacts to light which, in turn, dictates the amount of light needed to illuminate the given expanse. As the ASA went higher, the requirement of lights came down. The last I remember working on celluloid, we had come up to using 400 ASA. But during the time of *Mera Naam Joker*, only 16 and 32 ASA rated raw films were available in India; 64 ASA rated raw films were available in the world but they were not being imported into India by Kodak, because no filmmaker asked for it! So, Raj Sahab struck a deal with Kodak to import raw negative rated at 64 ASA. Raj Sahab left no stone unturned when it came to delivering the visual that he had encapsulated in his mind.

This brings me to the preparations for the scenes and the shots. There is a process that each director goes through before actually shooting a scene. There are various types of shots, a trolley shot, a close-up, a zoom shot, and each scene is made up of a collection of such individual shots. The director at his discretion makes a decision depending on the impact of the scene that he or she wants to create.

The next thing the director needs to decide is the camera lens that he would use for the shot. The camera lens varies depending on the focal length of the lens. This is very important because every shot has its own depth of view and depth of field. Let me make it simpler; depth of field is what determines what is the minimum and maximum focal point of a lens. That is, how many feet away will the character be and stay in focus and this depends on the lens the director is using.

Something which is believed to be a fallacy is that one can take a close-up only with a 75mm lens and a wide shot has to be 25mm. Raj Sahab did not believe in this. He believed that you can take any shot with any lens; it depends on what you want the shot to look like. When he used to shoot outdoors, it would be in a way that the viewers saw the beauty of the location. If he took a closed lens, he would start losing the background because it would go out of focus. Raj Sahab would take even the close-up shots with a lens that had a shorter focal length so that audience could see the vista of the backdrop as well. He had to be very careful because, with a wider lens, the shot could get distorted.

The focal length, apart from the standard prescribed measurements, also depended on various factors that could change. There is a manual called *American Cinematographer Manual*, which is like a bible for all DOPs. It lists out the prescribed focal length of every lens based on a mathematical calculation. However, one could change the focal length depending on two things, the first one being the ASA rating of the film negative. The higher the ASA, the higher the leeway you would get with the focal length. The other thing that the focal length depended on was the

F-stop. The F-stop is a mathematical calculation of how much light is being absorbed by the film negative through the lens. The depth of focus can also be altered depending on the amount of light that is coming in and for that, you need to change the F-stops. Now the thing about the F-stop is that it can be changed but the difference between the current number and the next consecutive number is wider apart. Let's say if there is a lens that has an F-stop 2.4, the next F-stop that it can go to will be 4. After 4, the next F-stop would be 11. They do not move in a mathematical progression.

One could refer to the ASC (American Society of Cinematographers) manual to find out the correspondent F-stop for their preferred focal length. Usually, people like to shoot with a full open, which is about 2.4, so that they have more depth of field or if they require more depth in the frame, they could go up to an F4. The F-stop would need to be increased depending on the depth of field required. For example, if one went for a focal length from the closest to camera being 2 feet and the furthest from camera being 8 feet or 10 feet, then for that particular lens, they can refer to the manual which will tell them what F-stop they have to use. Raj Sahab used to love experimenting with the lens and different depths for different shots. Thus the ASC manual was revered.

Raj Sahab was very fond of using this particular technique which he called a 'pan-focus shot'. The shot would have one character very close to the camera and the other character at a fair distance away and he needed both of them in sharp focus to create a dramatic effect. Since the F-stop would be different than normal, lighting would at times take hours.

I remember this scene in *Shree 420* when he comes to meet Nargis ji after having played cards. He has got money in his hand and he is drunk. In that scene, he is far away from her in a full figure shot whereas she is very close to the camera in a big close-up – that's a pan-focus shot right there.

There was one in *Bobby* too; the famous scene when Pran Sahab has called Prem Nath ji to his house. They are speaking and Pran Sahab is accusing Prem Nath ji of belonging to a lower stratum of society and how he will never be able to match up to him. Prem Nath ji is in front of the camera in a very big close-up and Pran Sahab is standing quite far away in a full figure. The reason Raj Sahab did this was to show Pran Sahab as a very shallow man as compared to Prem Nath ji. By this expression, that shallowness came across along with the hurt on Prem Nath ji's face which was seen better by the audience. Such shots were designed around the way Raj Sahab perceived them.

As mentioned earlier, Raj Sahab strongly believed that we are making a motion picture and it should have movement! Either the characters are moving or the camera is moving or when the characters and camera movement is required to be static then a character's expression – eye movements, lip movements, etc. should be incorporated and this keeps the whole narration alive. He'd say, 'If there is to be no motion, we should not be making a motion picture but writing a book.' Although comic books, like he rightly said, have this great quality – though they are individual frames but sometimes when one reads them, one could feel that the characters are moving along the frames.

Raj Sahab was well attuned with this sense of movement and in using the trolley. 'A camera moving on a trolley,' he said, 'was the biggest responsibility of a director, because the trolley shot is changing the visual perspective of the audience.'

Raj Sahab rarely used the zoom shot and he was very clear on one thing that the zoom and the trolley were two different shots. The zoom is taking the character closer to the audience, the whole narration was from the audience's point of view. With the trolley, on the other hand, the director was taking the entire audience to the character and this is done to enhance that experience. In a trolley, you are going towards the actors, so you emphasize on something. The zoom is the characters being pulled towards the audience, so the emphasis is on the character.

This is why I used a lot of trolley shots; I just don't know if I was sensible or not. In fact, many actors, Sunny Deol, Anil Kapoor and others, used to make fun of me, '*Arre, ek* miniature shoot *karna hai, ek* trolley *lagao,* Rahul *ke liye ek* trolley *bhi chahiye hogi.*' They did this because they probably did not understand the use of the trolley!

Sometimes, even the technicians got annoyed with me, a very senior sound guy once told me, '*Kya, jab dekho tum* trolley *lagate ho*!'

I replied saying, '*Arre bhai*, it's my film. Why do you get annoyed about this?' But they always did, regardless of the fact that the value of movement was something I had learnt from the Master.

The actor's responsibility also increases with a trolley shot because when the trolley starts moving, he or she can't fumble anywhere because it brings the audience closer to them. I think that's a sign of a good actor, one who can handle all that. In fact, when and where the trolley starts and ends is something that the director has decided and they need it to be done in a particular way.

I remember when I was shooting *Kuch Khatti Kuch Meethi* with Chintu, I had to get the camera to start trolleying into his close-up when he had to say the dialogue while sitting on a sofa. I told him that when the dialogue finishes that's when the trolley will end. We had rehearsals but ultimately the trolley is being pushed by human beings, so they cannot come to the exact place every time. Although, when we took that shot, everyone on the set was very impressed because as the trolley was coming close to him, Rishi Kapoor, who was a great actor no doubt, adapted the speed of the dialogue so that the trolley stopping and his finishing the dialogue was exactly at the same time. He was giving exactly what the director wanted. Now, this was a training that he had also received from Raj Kapoor.

Along with the trolley, there was also a crane that moved the camera up or down. In those days, there used to be a weekly magazine about films called *Screen*. Every director wanted a photograph of his sitting on top of a crane published in it; it was a status symbol for them to use a crane. Me, I was shit-scared of the crane because you've suddenly gone up 20–25 feet, with your legs dangling mid-air. We had even heard of accidents on cranes and I learnt that you don't have to necessarily use it. We used to go shooting outside with Raj Sahab and a crane never went with us. People would say, '*Arre* crane *nahi leke aaye tum saath mein?*'

I would reply, '*Arre baba, agar* Boss *bolte hai ki nahi le jana hai, toh* why should we carry extra luggage with us?'

Another aspect of shooting that Raj Sahab paid special attention to was the sets. He was very particular about the details, such as the characters, the clothes, the sets and backdrops, etc., and wanted them to be perfect. The colours or tones he required would be discussed with Radhu Sahab according to what kind of visual atmosphere he was looking for. Raj Sahab used to create the ambience for his sets very well. That was a period in which films were all shot on sets, not locations. Even if there was a street, you'd have a set and Raj Sahab used to go in for a lot of detail.

If you go back to his film *Shree 420*, the street where Nargis ji and he are walking during the song, '*Pyaar hua ikraar hua*', is a complete set. There were small details which he got Achrekar Sahab, the art director, to add for him, such as the electric train passing by on the set was a miniature train, hooked onto the set at a distance. Since it was a night scene, it got mostly covered, but it was all done for the details.

Then, even in *Bobby*, though it was shot on location, the little fishing area outside Prem Nath ji's house was a set and the sea was painted in the background. To get the feel of waves, there was a wooden contraption with the ebb of waves painted on it, which used to be turned around manually. So, in the shot, the audience can see it behind. It was crazy, but to create that atmosphere that these things were there, it was put in.

He put a lot of detail into his scenes. Raj Sahab was one of the few filmmakers whose house sets used to have a floor, too. Till quite recently, people never put flooring on sets, they used rubber mats or linoleum pieces and never bothered about it. Raj Sahab's sets always had flooring, because he knew it would be seen at some point or the other, and it would add to the whole aura and the atmosphere.

At times he would require a ceiling and I realized that this could create a problem for lighting the set so I asked him, 'Why do we need a corner-to-corner ceiling? Will it be seen?' He looked at me, 'There you go asking your stupid questions again. If I'm insisting on a ceiling, obviously it is not to stop the rain from coming down, it is going to be seen when I shoot.'

I had asked yet another stupid question but this is how I learnt.

These aspects were something that contributed to his process of preparing for the shoot. But the shoot is where the actual magic happened. It used to be a delight for me to watch Raj Sahab work because not only did I get to learn but I also got to watch him bring those performances to life. To see how he orchestrated the entire crew, the actors and the camera, singlehandedly! Now let me take you to a regular day on set.

LESSON 3: THE SHOOT

THE ENTIRE FILM IS broken down into scenes, and every scene consists of various individual shots. Raj Sahab would not only 'see' the entire film but would also 'see' the scenes. This is where his strength was.

When shooting a scene, Raj Sahab believed in one thing – every scene is a story in itself. Every scene has a three-act structure like a film, so every scene has a start, middle and end. Directors have their own method of shooting, some people do storyboards, where all the shots are broken down and sketched by the director or the storyboard artist. Raj Sahab never did a shot breakdown; his process was rather ingenious. He believed that the most difficult aspect of a scene was the first shot. To get the first shot in place, one needed to convey a lot of things to the audience, so as to establish the scene.

He believed that a scene, at its beginning, has to establish three aspects. First is the location; where is the scene based? This isn't told but is shown. For example, a dialogue goes, '*Arre, hum* Ratan ji *ke ghar aa gaye*?' but this dialogue proves useless because why should it be said? The audience has to be able to understand that the character is at a location, and that should be shown at the beginning of the scene. The second aspect is to know which characters are present in the scene. Directors should establish this in a shot or two; within two shots, they have to establish who are the characters in the scene. He also believed that if a scene is supposed to have three prominent characters, but the shot requires only two of the actors to be there as they are the only ones contributing to the shot, then the third actor should be removed rather than have them stand there and do nothing. He said, 'If they are in the shot then the audience expects them to say something and contribute to the shot.' The third and final aspect is the placement of the characters. Who is going to be where? For the characters to come to where they are to their final placing would all depend on how Raj Sahab wanted to treat that scene. He had to make a pattern visualizing who is on the left and who is on the right. He had these things in his mind and he knew why he was placing them in particular places.

When Raj Sahab was preparing the shot, he had a mental narration about how he wanted the shot to be played out. It was a very good habit; in fact, I had tuned myself to this habit so much so that I even narrated a script without referring to any material. I formed this habit while working with him because when he asked me to narrate a scene's dialogue, instead of fiddling with papers every time, it was better to be adept with the narration and Raj Sahab appreciated that. He used to also ask me or one of the other assistants to narrate the script to the actors. Although he did not need to do this and generally no actors asked him, but he would want to allow the actor time to prepare and think about their scene and dialogue.

Before beginning the shoot, Raj Sahab would look around the set or the location and he would ask me, or any other assistant, to narrate the dialogues to him. So, while I would be narrating the dialogue, he would be listening to that narrative and his gaze would be fixed directly on my face.

I was curious about this so one day, I asked him, 'Why do you keep staring?'

'Because while reading the scene, you may have something in your mind, like how you are interpreting the scene or how it's playing out in your mind. That shows on your face when you are narrating. The way you narrate the dialogue will tell me how you are looking at it, whether you want an emphasis at one place or not. Although that is for me to decide, but I have a reference that this is the way you looked at this scene.'

After I would finish narrating the scene, Raj Sahab would look around the set and then he would stand up and say, 'Okay narrate it again.' When I would narrate it the second time, he would be looking around the set or the location and then he would say, '*Ek baar phir suna do.*' When I would narrate it to him the third time, he would be moving around the location from place to place.

This used to happen from the first shot itself; he would move from place to place and then he would say, 'Alright!', like he'd made up his mind, and go on to explain the shot to Radhu Sahab, 'This shot starts here, the actors are placed in [x] position.' For example, he would say, 'Chintu will move from here, Prem Nath will be sitting here and Dimple will be sitting here. Then Chintu will move to Dimple and this is how the first shot will take place.'

He would then go ahead to tell us the way he had imagined the entire scene. He'd say, 'Okay, after this, somewhere I come to this shot and there is a close-up here and...' It would go on till the end of the scene. He would work in great sync with Radhu Sahab. By the time he was done narrating the shot and the positions, Radhu Sahab would have started 'lighting up' for that shot accordingly.

Raj Sahab had once commented, 'People shoot in various ways. I'm not commenting on what is right and what is wrong. I can only comment on what I think is right. Normally directors want to finish all the shots from one angle, so that the placement of lights does not have to undergo frequent changes. They follow one axis of the camera, finish all the shots in a scene from that one axis. They then shift to another axis and the lighting will be done for the new camera position. This non-linear pattern of shooting will undoubtedly save them a lot of time, however, I staunchly believe this system of working compromises a director's creativity.'

Therefore, Raj Sahab would first work out the scene mentally and shoot the first act of the scene in a quasi-linear manner. Since this would always have a twist, Raj Sahab would provide an opportunity for the actors to express their thought patterns as to how their performance should unfold leading to the next act. He would fine-tune their suggestions and based on the performances, a new blueprint for the second act would emanate. Now the process would repeat, to take the scene to its conclusion and he would again adopt a quasi-linear system to achieve the same.

The leeway to mould a scene at the end of each act was open not only to the actors but also to every single technician. Raj Sahab had this one quality that he would listen to everyone, 'You tell me anything you want, but to listen to it or not is my choice.' A quality that made him stand apart from others.

He looked at all the aspects while taking a shot, where would the junior artists be positioned, special props be placed, and add various artefacts that would enhance the scene.

Most directors today repeatedly shoot the same shot from multiple angles and then give the material to the editor to decide which angle should be used and intercut with other angles. For Raj Sahab, this was an absolute 'no-no'. He taught us that you not only have to decide where your shot starts and where it finishes, but also the angle best suited to that particular shot. 'You can't just arbitrarily take shots from all angles! When you have already seen the scene in your mind's eye how can you just suddenly say that oh, let me take it from this angle also! This shows you have no confidence in your vision.'

Apart from certain cases when he might want you to extend the cue in the edit, Raj Sahab's takes were fixed; it starts with this dialogue and ends at this dialogue and this is the angle from which it has to be shot. And it never changed. Cameramen also are more comfortable with shooting with just one camera so that the lighting is done according to that one camera only. Multiple cameras compromise the lighting in a huge way as there is a very likely chance of one camera being seen in another. This can lead to compromising with the ideal placement of light.

Patchwork is done by a lot of directors, where you've shot the scenes and you need to add a close-up or a shot to patch it in and make the scene smoother. Raj Sahab never did that. He would sometimes take an additional silent close-up of a character in the scene. According to him, this was his insurance, but that silent close-up always found its way into the scene inadvertently. If he did patchwork, it would mean shooting a completely new scene, not just adding patches to it.

There were certain moments in a scene in *Bobby* in which Raj Sahab insisted on the movement of the actors being exactly what he had in mind. He would tell me sometimes, 'Rahul, *yeh jo* scene *kal* shoot *karenge na,* I need to get this moment where Chintu holds Dimple's hand like this.' He would think of the moment in complete detail; although, where would he use it, nobody else would know. Once a scene was shot, he would say, 'Okay, we've come to that moment.' He would look really happy then because he would have found the place of the moment exactly the way he had visualized it.

Movement is something that he really used a lot, and very sensibly, which is something I picked up from him. Raj Sahab had a unique technique, 'Use movement or sound to distract.' In a scene, he would want the audio to also establish the location; what is the kind of ambience of the location? Suppose they were shooting on a farm; the audio and movement would be used to establish where within the farm is the scene taking place. Then, the next scene could be anywhere, it didn't have to be in a chronological order, it could be a scene that is 20 scenes away. So, he would have to start again and this is something I had to learn as a director. Normally, directors have the whole screenplay written but Raj Sahab didn't. Jainendra Jain wrote the dialogue, but the exact scene, what is the movement going to be, Raj Sahab had all of that in his mind.

There was a scene in *Sangam* that really blew the wind out of me. Once Raj Sahab started the misunderstanding bit, his entire visual focus was based around a 'triangle' between the three main characters. By triangle, I mean three people standing in three corners, and this composition, which left the impression of a triangle, was maintained until the climax. A series of shots that we called a 'trilateral shot'. The climax of *Sangam*, I think, is one of the most brilliant sequences ever filmed.

If Raj Sahab was at a position in the room then Vyjayanthimala ji was standing diagonally opposite to him and Rajendra Kumar Sir was standing diagonally opposite to her, to form a triangle. The three of them stood in the formation of a triangle which was maintained throughout the scene. While speaking, if Vyjayanthimala ji walks towards Raj Sahab, he replies and walks away from her. It was to keep that triangle going and he kept it going for about nine minutes! Those nine minutes were really something; they were brilliant and have stayed in my mind since. This was the kind of importance he gave to movement and position.

The integral ingredient in the visual narration is the actor whose movement, reaction and expression of speech are controlled by the director. This aspect, of which Raj Sahab was in complete control, needs to be spoken about in much more detail.

LESSON 4: ACTORS AND THEIR PERFORMANCES

'THE MOST DANGEROUS THING is make-up,' Raj Sahab once told me. 'The moment an actor, including myself, puts make-up on their face, we transform ourselves from Dr Jekyll to Mr Hyde; from the "gentle" into an "egoistic beast", who believes that they are superior beings and everyone else is beneath them.'

He added, 'Even when I just acted in a film, I demanded and got paid a huge amount of money contradictory to my belief that actors do not deserve this kind of money! The actors also believe that they know more than the director about how the film needs to be told. Even I have extensive boxing bouts between Raj Kapoor, the director, and Raj Kapoor, the actor. However, rightfully and invariably, the director always wins!'

The belief that any good director can make any person 'act' was a fallacy according to him. 'A director is not a magician who just waves a wand and any person starts performing. A director can only help an actor take their performance in the right direction and give nuances in line with the character. The basic effort and belief in the character has to come from the actor.'

'One who is a good conversationalist will generally be a good actor.' This was Raj Sahab's outlook about the characteristic of an actor. He believed, 'Acting is not a cakewalk, it is an extremely complex and difficult task. The actor needs to be a person who has the power of grasping the characteristics of the person he is going to play. Actors need to have a very sharp mind; for every shot, they have to keep in mind the movement, their exact position, and certain shots require the actor to move exactly to the mark as instructed by the DOP. Their physical gestures, movements and positions should not interfere with the light assigned to another actor and their dialogue should not, unless instructed by the director, overlap and/or disturb the other actors in the shot.'

Raj Sahab believed that the performance of the actors was the vital ingredient of a film since they were the conduit for telling the story. He had all the characteristics of a character firmly entrenched in his mind. The upbringing, the circumstances he or she lived in, the influence of their parents on their lives, the strata of society they belonged to, the love and/or the hatred for other people and their philosophy of life. He would explain to an actor, in the minutest detail, the intricacies of the character and expected them to remember and emote within the barricades of such intricacies.

Raj Sahab, while shooting a scene, liked to give a certain amount of creative freedom to the actor provided it was acceptable to him. 'Actors are basically insecure and selfish creatures; when hearing a script or a scene, they only look at themselves and are not bothered about the flow of the script and how their performance would impact the film.' An actor has to always remember the trajectory of his character and the impact it has on all the other characters and finally on the script as well.

Raj Sahab used to tell a great story. Sir Laurence Olivier was one of the greatest actors ever. He worked in a film called *Marathon Man* with Dustin Hoffman. Sir Laurence Olivier played a dentist who was an ex-Nazi officer and had, before escaping at the end of the Second World War, pilfered exquisite diamonds from the Nazi's looted treasury, and Dustin Hoffman's dead brother knew where the dentist had hidden the said diamonds. There was a crucial scene where Hoffman is strapped onto a dentist's chair and Sir Laurence is trying to extract the information which the dead brother had. The process of extracting that information was chilling and sent shivers down the viewer's spine. The dentist uses a drill to create cavities and expose the nerve in Dustin Hoffman's teeth and thereafter starts poking a 'sickle probe' into the cavities!

Next, a scene after this grotesque torture, where Dustin Hoffman comes back to consciousness, was to be filmed. In preparation for the same, Hoffman, who was a 'method' actor, subjected himself to extreme physical and mental torture by staying in a room without any light and surviving on sparse food and minimum water for five days. By these actions, Dustin Hoffman had achieved the 'look' he wanted to portray in the film and reported on the sets, but as the camera started, he fainted and had to be moved to a hospital. Sir Laurence went to see him at the hospital, with a bouquet of flowers, and said, 'Son, next time, just "act".'

This statement of Sir Laurence Olivier was what Raj Sahab completely believed in.

Method acting was something he did not believe in, he believed in spontaneity. 'An actor is somebody who "acts" and not one who goes home and prepares himself for the role, like getting tortured for days. An actor is one who can switch in and out of a character the moment a shot is over.' Raj Sahab himself was a spontaneous actor. There was a snippet from his acting days that Dilip Sahab had told me about once. 'You know when I did this film *Andaz* with Raj Kapoor, we had the shoot at 10 a.m. I used to be on the set at 7 a.m. because I wanted to read the scene, understand it and prepare myself for it until the shot was ready. Raj, who was shooting all night, from 7 p.m. till 6 a.m. for *Boot Polish*, would come to the studio after his shoot and go to sleep in the make-up room. Then, when the shot was ready, an assistant would wake him up. He'd get up, he'd wash his face and while washing his face, he'll tell the assistant to read the scene out loud for him. He'd be getting ready and have the scene narrated once or twice to him during that time. I used to think it's going to be a cakewalk for me as a performer to overshadow him. But the moment he started performing and the shot was complete, the whole unit would stand up and clap for him and nobody clapped for me though I had put in a lot of energy rehearsing the shot. This is the difference between a "method" actor and a "spontaneous" actor.'

With Raj Sahab's influence and training, Chintu turned into one of the most underrated but brilliant actors that the industry had. Kajol, like Sanjeev Kumar, Shahrukh Khan and a host of other actors, is a 'spontaneous' actor. Chintu and I would share snippets about different people. I will not name any actors but there are some who would say, 'Oh, I was so emotionally drained doing this particular shot.'

Then, there are people saying, 'Oh, that script was so scary that I would not shoot after six in the evening because the unit was so scared!'

There was an actor at one time, he played a deaf character in a film and I saw the film at the premiere. There, I asked him if he found it difficult to play a deaf character. He replied, 'Yes Sir, you know, I used to put cotton in my ears so that I couldn't hear anybody and the expression of being deaf would stand out.' I just blurted out to him in retort, 'Thank God you're not playing a homosexual in the film!'

There was another actor who said that she was playing a beggar in a film and during the close-up shots, she used to stand barefoot in the sun so that her expression would be correct with her feeling the heat!

Raj Sahab considered that all actors had their own assets and liabilities. Assets are inborn habits that a person is very comfortable with and liabilities are some of their awkward habits that they can't change. He would say, 'As a director, you have to work around the actor's liabilities and see to it that the liability comes off on-screen as an asset.' The responsibility of a director, according to him, is to see what the actor is not comfortable with and shoot in such a way that when the audience views the performance, they are left extremely impressed.

Raj Sahab had a Rasputin-like hold over his actors; he would cast a web around them and they would be completely mesmerized by him and strive to deliver their best with all sincerity and honesty. He would explain to the actors the smallest details like where he wanted their hands to move or how to hold a prop in a particular fashion. Also, the actor would be put through the drill of emoting as he had decided for the particular shot. If an actor said that he was finding the dialogue spoken along with a particular movement, which Raj Sahab desired, difficult, he himself would perform that shot for the actor to see how the dialogue and movement gelled with each other, 'If I can do it, so can you.'

This reminds me of an incident during the shoot of *Mera Naam Joker*, where he wanted an actor to climb the steps leading to the top where the trapeze artists stood and say the dialogue while climbing. The actor responded that it wasn't possible for him to do this as the climb was quite scary and to speak at the same time would be impossible. So, Boss just walked up to the rope ladder and started climbing and saying the dialogue. The actor rushed to him when he was on the third step and said, 'Sir, I'll do it, please don't go up further. I'm very sorry to have said no to you in the first place.' Raj Sahab patted the actor's back and came over to us and asked,

'Did you guys really think that I was going to climb? No chance, I was so scared; thank God the actor decided that it was not fair for me to climb.'

Prem Nath ji was a very peculiar person. A great actor, but obsessed with himself and believed that every shot which he gave was brilliant and could not have been done better. While taking a shot during *Bobby*, as soon as the shot was completed, Prem Nath ji went ballistic, 'What a great shot I have given! All the other actors belong to the municipality!'

Raj Sahab agreed with Prem Nath ji that it was a great shot, but suddenly he turned to me and said, 'Oh! You didn't like it, why?' I did not know how to react because I had never said anything and Prem Nath ji was staring at me as though he was ready to wring my neck.

Raj Sahab said, 'Tell me what you think the problem is.' He then bent close to me and started a whispered conversation with me:

'Sir, I never said that!'

'Just shut up and whisper anything to me, pretend like you are explaining something to me.'

'Sir, the way Prem Sir is looking at me is extremely scary and I feel that he might just hit me!'

Throughout this conversation, Raj Sahab had a very serious look on his face and he turned to Prem Nath ji and said, 'You know Prem, let's do one more take. Rahul feels that when you spoke your last line, it didn't carry the weight it should. Though I don't agree with Rahul, let's shoot another take to humour him.'

'Raj, you are listening to this municipality assistant director?'

'Come on, Prem! He's learning and I think the best way he's going to learn is when he sees the rushes and realizes how wrong he was!'

The shot was repeated, Prem Nath ji did put emphasis on the last line and Raj Sahab, by firing a gun over my shoulder, got what he wanted!

This same ploy was used again by Raj Sahab in another shot. Prem Nath ji stomped up to me, held me by the collar and said, 'You bloody municipality, every time I give a fantastic performance, you don't like it for some reason. Why?' I was shit-scared and sure that he was going to strike me, but I had no reply. Prem Nath ji just walked away in complete disgust and Raj Sahab, along with the rest of the unit, was in splits of laughter.

Boss said to me, 'I'm sorry but I wanted the correct expression which I finally got. You know Rahul, I'm a very selfish director.'

Raj Sahab was very sweet and patient with his actors, more so with the female actors. He believed that a director had to be in love with his leading lady to enable him to bring out the right emotions, but at times he used unconventional methods to convince them to see his point of view. There was a well-known female actor who was working with Raj Sahab on a film; in those days she was in a relationship with Mehmood, a very successful actor. There was a scene in the film where she walks into an adolescent actor's room while he is changing, sees him from the back, butt naked, screams and leaves the room. The actress knew from the very beginning that this scene was a part of the film, but finally when we came to the point where it had to be shot, she refused to do so. Raj Sahab was taken aback that she should refuse when he had come so far with the film. He tried his best to convince her and even explained to her that the adolescent kid was just like her little brother and the scene was not to titillate the audience, but she was stubborn and said, 'No!'

Boss just blurted out, '*Tumne kabhi* Mehmood *ki gaand nahi dekhi hai kya*!' The lady was just quiet and staring at Boss's face. He was relaxed and lighting a cigarette and I, along with the unit standing around, was finding it very difficult to control my laughter.

The lady just got up and said, 'I'm ready for the shot, let's go and do it.' The director finally got his way.

When he was acting and directing at the same time, Raj Sahab also had this unique ability to realize whether his performance as an actor lived up to the expectation of the director. When he worked as an actor with other directors, he paid rapt attention to what the director wanted and delivered a performance exactly as was required. The director in him never interfered with the directors' work.

While shooting his own film, the director in Raj Sahab would be paying attention to the actor's performance including his gesticulations, expressions and movement, how the junior artists, if any, were moving in the background, how minor characters moved and while orchestrating all of this, sometimes his fingers would be tapping a table in a rhythm. He was mentally playing the background music that he would require for the particular shot. He was counting the beats, deciding where he wanted the music to swell or the music to play low, and if he wanted a gap in the narration so that the music can rise. The man was thinking one step ahead. This takes me to the next lesson which is Raj Kapoor and his music.

LESSON 5: RAJ KAPOOR'S MUSIC

MUSIC WAS AN INTEGRAL part of a film for Raj Kapoor and carried great weight in the impact of the visual narration of a film. He had an acute sense of music without being a trained musician. One could call him a musician, an arranger of the musical score or an accomplished music conductor. He built situations into his script so that a song would never seem out of place and also carried the story further. He had a unique gift of making sure that his music directors were creating the right music for the atmosphere that was being depicted. While hearing a script, he would suddenly gesture to the writer to stop narrating and his eyes would be focused on any one object; when asked whether there was any problem, he would reply, 'Look, this is a perfect place for a song.'

His mind would be working on a song from the time he finalized the situation for the same. He would, at times, hum something which he had mentally created and his daughter, Ritu, would play his composition on the piano. The song '*Jeena yahan marna yahan*' from *Mera Naam Joker* was one such creation.

Raj Sahab had a knack for introducing unique elements into his songs. The song '*Awaara hoon*' has one such element. The words of the song are; '*Awaara hoon…awaara hoon… gardish mein hoon, aasman ka tara hoon.*' The words '*awaara hoon*' are always followed by two bars of music, which are played by a combination of the clarinet, the mid-flute and his favourite musical instrument, an accordion. What makes this song unique is that anyone trying to hum the song cannot do it without humming the two bars of music as well, '*Awaara hoon, ta tara tum…*'

He believed very strongly that the sign of the popularity of a racy number was when that song was played by a 'Nan Khatai band', the traditional band that plays in baraats at Indian weddings. 'The nan khatai band will only pick those songs where a player of a minor instrument, the triangle, also has an involvement since he is being paid for his services by the band!'

When I started working with him, during *Mera Naam Joker*, Shankar-Jaikishan were the music directors. The lyrics were written by Shailendra ji and Hasrat Jaipuri ji. Raj Sahab would sit with Shankar-Jaikishan at their music room in Famous Studios at Mahalaxmi, along with the lyricists and the iconic 'voice of Raj Kapoor', Mukesh ji. It did not matter if the song was written by Hasrat Jaipuri ji or Shailendra ji and sung by Mukesh ji or not, they were all part of a gifted ensemble composing a song, under the guidance of Raj Sahab.

I went with him to the music room for a music session and was awed on seeing the entire gifted ensemble in one room. I saw the process of composing a song wherein they would fight with each other, abuse each other and even come to blows, all for no personal reasons but the creation of a memorable song. They were intellectuals dedicated to music.

For the circus episode in *Mera Naam Joker*, Raj Sahab wanted a romantic song (unfortunately the song was not used in the film due to length constraints) with the Russian heroine, Kseniya Ryabinkina. The concept was based around the words, 'Da (yes in Russian), *haan keh do*'. Immediately, Shankar ji and Jaikishan ji started humming various melodies which would suit the situation and the song according to them. This was done only between the two of them, while

Raj Sahab was discussing the concept he would need in the *mukhda* and *antara* (stanza) with the lyricists.

Finally, the music directors said that they had composed a melody that would suit the romanticism that Raj Sahab required. Shankar ji, playing the harmonium, sang the melody with dummy words and I almost passed out!

The melody had dummy words that were downright obscene, '*Da haan keh do, ki ch*** phat jaye. Da haan keh do, ki l**** ghis jaye.*'

Raj Sahab and the others had no adverse reaction to the obscene words and went on to discuss the lyrics for the melody, '*Yeh jo hissa hai, "ch*** phat jaye", isko kar do, "dil mil jaye" aur "l**** ghis jaye" ko "gul khil jaye" aise gaa ke sunao.*'

So, the words were changed accordingly. The gang of geniuses did not flinch at the dummy words but were immersed into giving birth to an evergreen melody. This may sound unbecoming to some of you, but this was the process of evolution for them.

Raj Sahab firmly believed that a song worked only if it was a part of the screenplay and had to be picturized and performed in an apt manner. Though songs are rendered by playback singers, the actor needs to lip-sync to the singer's voice when the song is being picturized. He insisted that the actors do not just move their lips to match the voice but they should literally sing the songs at their loudest volume.

The actors would be embarrassed at times and say, 'Sorry Sir, I sing very badly and completely out of tune.'

Raj Sahab's explanation to the actors was, 'Your singing prowess does not concern me, but only when you actually sing will the camera see the movement of your facial muscles and your vocal cords belting out the song, thus, uplifting the performance.'

We have seen and still see, most actors who only move their lips to the playback, but the accomplished actors actually sing to the playback. While watching a song this difference is very evident. In recent times, a great example of the proper rendition of playback was Anushka Sharma singing in *Bombay Velvet*.

While picturizing a song, Raj Sahab always paid attention to the fact that the actors should not be 'out of character'. We sometimes see that the performance of the actor is completely detached from the character they are playing. In fact, before a song was to be recorded, Raj Sahab would insist that the singer, be it Lata ji, Mohd Rafi, Kishore Kumar, Asha Bhosle, Mukesh ji or every single playback singer whom he worked with, go to the music director's place and hear the melody.

He would then go ahead and explain the story of the film, the situation of the song, the actor who would be singing the song and the character description of the role being portrayed to them.

He coaxed the playback singer to put all his or her passion into rendering the song and therefore expected his actors to do the same.

A choreographer was involved in the picturization only if the song required dancing. He himself had great knowledge of classical dance which he had acquired without any formal training, but when required, he would seek the assistance of well-known classical dance gurus.

The song, '*Ye pyaar hua, ya kuch aur hua*' from *Prem Rog* was choreographed by Shri Krishan Maharaj. Earlier, in *Bobby*, the choreography, for the song '*Main shayar to nahin*' was assigned to Salome Aaron Kapoor, a renowned dance teacher.

Raj Sahab's conviction of incorporating songs into a film came from his firm belief that a song would convey much more than a verbose scene. He had a great quality of weaving the songs into the script. He would never let a song emerge as an extraneous detail. The situation for a song had to have a natural progression into a scene. In *Sangam*, the song *'Main kya karun Ram, mujhe buddha mil gaya'* flowed very naturally out of a situation where the husband wants to go to a nightclub in Paris but the wife doesn't want him to go and to prevent her husband from going to the nightclub, she herself performs a 'nightclub act' in the confines of their hotel room. A great situation for a naughty song during the honeymoon of a couple.

For Raj Sahab, 'milking' the correct emotion of a situation through a song was a great asset. *Jis Desh Mein Ganga Behti Hai* had a song, *'Hum bhi hain, tum bhi ho, dono hain aamne samne'* in which Pran Sahab, who played the dreaded dacoit, sings a stanza of the song, '*Hai aag humare seene mein, hum aag se khelte aaye hain*'. It was Raj Kapoor's way of expressing the emotional turmoil of the character through music.

Similarly, in *Sangam*, '*Dost dost na raha*', was an insight into the turmoil of the three principal characters – Sunder, Radha and Gopal. Likewise, in *Bobby*, the situation for the song '*Ghe ghe ghe ghe ghe ghe re sahiba*' was a wedding celebration taking place in Prem Nath ji's locality. Chintu has come to invite Prem Nath ji to his house to meet his father. The celebration is underway and the dialogue of Chintu talking to Prem Nath ji is heard over the song, and the last dialogue which Prem Nath ji speaks is seamlessly connected to Prem Nath ji's singing, '*Na chahun sona chandi, na mangun heera moti*', the philosophy of Prem Nath ji's character. This was an example of how the Master wove music into the narration by having a situation for the song tailored for a scene.

Raj Sahab wouldn't bother about the number of songs in the film. What he was bothered about was the context. The song was supposed to have a context within the story and that's what mattered to him the most. *'Ghe ghe ghe ghe ghe ghe re sahiba'* and *'Jhooth bole kauwa kaate'* were two different songs but they were woven together to make one song. Chintu and Dimple singing '*Jhooth bole kauwa kaate*' was an extension of the happiness and excitement of the young lovers following the invitation from Chintu's father. Thus, the songs joined as one was relevant to the situation and this did not disturb the audience nor did they complain about the song being too long.

I had heard the words '*Jhooth bole kauwa kaate*' from him in 1968, the time I joined him as an assistant. He had come home for dinner and at that time, I heard him telling my mother, '*Kali Mai, jhooth mat bolna, jhooth bologe toh kala kauwa katega*!'

Then he hummed, '*jhooth bole kauwa kaate*'. I heard him humming the same song at various times but it finally found its way into *Bobby*, which was conceived and shot in 1972! He had finally found the right situation to place this song that had been composed by him.

Similarly, in 1972, when we had gone to shoot *Bobby* in Kashmir, we were invited for dinner by the owner of the houseboat that we stayed in and he had organized the performance of a local Kashmiri singer along with three musicians for our entertainment. That evening, the local singer sang a folk song which had the words, '*sun sahiba sun*'.

Raj Sahab got very excited on hearing these three words. The next day, he called me and said, 'All night the three words "*sun sahiba sun*" haunted me and this morning I came up with a tune for a song using those three words.' He sang the song which stemmed from his inspiration, '*Sun sahiba sun, pyaar ki dhun*'. The song, hummed by him in 1972, finally found its way into *Ram Teri Ganga Maili* in 1983!

When Raj Sahab had launched *Bobby*, he was still contemplating about the music director for the film as the genre would require extraordinary music. Laxmi ji and Pyare ji along with Anand Bakshi ji came to meet Raj Sahab, 'We were informed by Mukesh ji that you had not finalized the music director nor the lyricist for *Bobby*; we were very excited and requested Mukesh ji to arrange a meeting with you, hence we are here with a song that we have composed and are sure would fit in your film.'

Raj Sahab asked them, 'How can you compose a melody and write the lyrics for a song when you don't know a thing about the characters?'

They replied sheepishly, 'Sir, Mukesh ji narrated the entire story to us and asked us to prepare a song especially for the film, though we had also composed a song keeping in mind that if ever Raj Kapoor called us for a film, we would sing this song for him.'

Raj Sahab laughed and said, 'In that case, first sing me the song that you had made on your own and not for *Bobby*.'

That particular song was '*Ye jo public hai, ye sab janti hai*'. Boss appreciated the song and asked them to sing the song that they had composed for *Bobby*. They then sang '*Hum tum ek kamre mein band ho*', and Raj Sahab stood up and clapped. He was completely ecstatic about the composition and lyrics. That is how Laxmikant-Pyarelal and Bakshi ji were assigned for *Bobby*.

Unfortunately, the other song '*Ye jo public hai, ye sab janti hai*', which had been composed specifically for Raj Sahab, could not be used as there was no 'situation' for the same in *Bobby*. It was eventually used in *Roti*, which was a Rajesh Kumar-Mumtaz film directed by Manmohan Desai.

In the song, '*Hum tum ek kamre mein band ho*', there is a line '*hum tum kahin ko jaa rahen ho, aur rasta bhool jaye*'. While the rehearsals of the song were going on, Raj Sahab was visualizing how the song would look like on screen. He suddenly told Laxmi ji that he would like to shoot these particular words at a crossroad and he required Lata ji to sing an *alaap* over the interlude leading to the words.

Laxmi ji called Pyare ji and after a small discussion Laxmi ji said, '*Yeh aalap is* music *ke upar aa nahin sakta hai. Aap chahen to* interlude music change *kar dete hain*.'

Raj Sahab said, '*Nahin* music interlude *bohot accha hai issi par yeh aalap gavane ki koshish karo*.'

Laxmi ji and Pyare ji said, 'Raj Sahab, *nahin aa payega*.'

Raj Sahab said, '*Main karke suna dun*?'

Lata ji, who was also present at the rehearsal, turned around and said, '*Laxmi inko gaa ke sunane do*.'

The interlude music was played back and at the desired moment, Raj Sahab sang the *aalap* to perfection. Laxmi ji and Pyare ji were dumbstruck and Lata ji had a smile on her face. Pyare ji finally spoke, 'Raj Sahab, I'm considered a very gifted music composer but what you have done has made me hate myself for not being able to add the *aalap* so easily.' He bent down and touched Raj Sahab's feet and said, 'Sir, I need your blessings and hope one day I can reach your level of understanding music.'

There is a piano piece called 'The Blue Danube' which Raj Sahab admired and loved. It is a beautiful piece of waltz composed by Austrian composer Johann Strauss II in 1866 and most beginners who are learning how to play the piano, usually learn this composition amongst one of their first lessons. It is extremely popular the world over; in fact, if you roam around the streets of Austria you will hear the tune being played by the buskers.

Raj Sahab truly loved this composition. It was stuck in his mind after Jaikishan ji played it for him on a violin and he insisted on using it in the song '*Chhod gaye balam*' in *Barsaat*.

People had stood up and clapped when it played and that propelled Raj Sahab to use it as part of a background score in all his films. It was given a standing ovation by the people in the Iron Curtain countries, the Soviet Union and the Baltic states. 'The Blue Danube' became synonymous with Raj Kapoor and it enhanced the romanticism and melancholy that was very much inherent in all his work.

Background music played an essential role in Raj Sahab's films. He used to spend a lot of time developing background scores as he believed that the right background score enhanced the impact of a scene. In fact, at times, Raj Sahab would silently be humming a melody, while the rehearsals for a particular shot were in progress. He would then give very specific instructions like, 'Now at this point, look down' or 'Here, at this dialogue I want you to give him an intense look of hurt'. These were the places where the background music, which he had mentally composed, would play, and at other times, as I have written earlier, his fingers would be tapping a rhythm, thus formulating the style of background music that would be used.

Background music used to be composed and, still is, executed by the music director and his arranger. At the recording studio, the final edited film is projected and the background music is composed on the spot. A practice that was not accepted by Raj Sahab since, for him, the background music was an essential part of the film.

He would first hear the composition and only if it lived up to his expectation, would it be approved for recording. Separate days were provided for hearing the compositions and for recording the same. He was also very particular that if there was a song in the same reel as the background score, the score had to be in the same *sur* or melody as the song or it would sound contradictory to the ears. His immense knowledge of music was also applauded by the music directors he worked with.

Every music director had his own method of laying the foundation for the background music. Jaikishan ji, who handled the background music of all Shankar-Jaikishan films, would have the film shown to him at the recording studio. He would start a count while his fingers would tap a beat on his knuckles from the point where the background music started till the point where it ended. The starting point would be marked 'XXX' on the film.

Pyare ji, who used to compose the interlude music and background music in all Laxmikant-Pyarelal films, used to require, apart from a marking of 'XXX' at the start of the background score, another marking 'CCC' at any point where a change in the background music was needed to enhance the score, and lastly 'OOO' at the end of the score. He would use a stopwatch to note all the changes and the length of that particular background score.

When the background score was being recorded, Jaikishan ji would start playing the score at the 'XXX' marking and the tapping of the knuckles would start again, and his changes came at points where it was required. Pyare ji, at the recording, would switch on the stopwatch and would conduct the orchestra and the changes would be monitored by him in sync with the stopwatch. His composition and the changes were 'bang on'.

By the time work on the background music of *Kal Aaj Aur Kal* started, Jaikishan ji had passed away. Dabboo Sahab was the director and I was working as his assistant. Shankar ji expressed his inability to compose the background score and said that his long-time arranger, Sebastian, would handle the same. This was completely unacceptable to Raj Sahab and he decided that he would compose the background music himself (this was also the point where Raj Sahab decided that his next film would have a new music director). This was at a juncture when the recording was to start on the same day and could not be delayed as the release date had already been set. Therefore, Raj Sahab needed to compose the background music to the satisfaction of the director, his son Randhir Kapoor, without any previous discussion about the same.

He asked his son, 'Dabboo Sahab, are you okay with this?'

Dabboo Sahab replied, 'Dad, this would be a great privilege and honour for me!'

An instrument which we had never seen, called a synthesizer, was brought by a musician to the background score recording. Raj Sahab, who had the unique ability to play any instrument though he was not a trained musician, saw the synthesizer and asked, quite puzzled, 'What is this thing that looks like an electrical piano?' The musician gave him a verbal account of the instrument and its capabilities. He looked at it and started playing one or two notes and then he pressed a button here and there and was quite amazed at the different tones which the instrument emitted.

Within 10 minutes, he was playing the synthesizer fluently. He realized what button to press for the sound he wanted to hear and also the automation capability of the synthesizer. Even the musician, who had brought the synthesizer, was fascinated to know about some aspects of the capability of the instrument that he himself was unaware of.

Raj Sahab's passion for music was such that he yearned to have a song recording studio built in RK and even bought a state-of-the-art recording console for the same. But, the ambition to set up a recording studio at RK did not materialize so he invested money in a start-up laboratory, Natraj Lab, solely because his dream of setting up a music studio would be fulfilled.

The first song of *Bobby* was recorded at the new studio, Natraj Labs, and Raj Sahab was very proud of that.

Unfortunately, after the recording, when he heard the track, he was completely dissatisfied and decided that the song needed to be recorded again at the old Famous Studios where all his earlier songs were recorded.

This move was quite a setback for the recording studio since one of the bosses himself had moved his song recording back to the old studio as the quality of the studio wasn't up to the mark. He summed up this unfortunate incident in two sentences, 'I am completely shattered by the failure of the recording studio, not because of the expense involved in recording a song again, but from the fact that my own music recording studio could not satisfy my own level of excellence.' For Boss, quality reigned supreme.

For the song, '*Aa ab laut chalen*' in the film *Jis Desh Mein Ganga Behti Hai,* Raj Sahab envisaged a gigantic collection of musical instruments to add the grandeur the situation in the song required. He consulted with Shankar-Jaikishan and they came to the conclusion that his dream song would require 60 chorus artists, 80 violins, 12 cellos, 4 double basses, 2 mandolins, 2 full Indian rhythm sections, 2 sitars, 10 brass trumpets, 6 side rhythms, and Lata ji and Mukesh ji to provide the playback. Alas, there was no recording studio big enough to accommodate this large orchestra. The Famous Studios had the capability of only using 4 microphones for the orchestra and 2 for the voices. So, Raj Sahab consulted with the inimitable recordist Minoo Katrak and they devised a unique method of recording the entire ensemble together, since in those days multitrack recording did not exist.

The entire chorus was made to sit outside the sound stage due to lack of space and the final recording was held at 3 a.m. so that there was no traffic on the road. In 1961, Bombay was a quiet city, in 2021 Mumbai is not!

The passion of the maker, the singers, the orchestra and the technicians was the order of the day.

His musical style and technique were such that even the esteemed director, Bimal Roy Sir, used the melodies from one of Raj Sahab's background music scores in the songs of *Madhumati*, which was one of Bimal Roy Sir's greatest films.

Raj Sahab's background music continued to inspire and feature in songs composed by generations after him. His musical flair has set a benchmark for Hindi cinema.

LESSON 6: THE EDITOR'S CUT

For Raj Kapoor, the entire process of filmmaking was sacrosanct and therein the editing room was the 'sanctum sanctorum'. Therefore, no one was allowed to bring shoes into the editing room and alcohol and cigarettes were strictly prohibited. This rule applied to his own use of the editing room as well.

Raj Sahab's process of editing would start in the projection room before it moved into the editing room. The exposed film was processed at a laboratory and resulted in obtaining the negative. A logbook consisting of the continuity sheets was maintained whilst shooting; these continuity sheets carried various bits of information about every particular shot, including the takes that were okayed by the director. The negative was sorted and all the okay takes were printed on positive film and resulted in obtaining a picture positive.

The negatives were handled sparsely to avoid any dust or scratches on the surface. Once the positive print was obtained, the negatives were handled in a sanitized room, with the negative handler entering the room without shoes and wearing gloves. The negatives could not be used on any machine and even the printers were specially designed for negative handling. Similarly, the okay takes of the sound, which were recorded on magnetic tape, were transferred onto a sound negative, and this sound negative was then processed and printed onto a sound positive for use in the edit.

Thus, there were two strips of celluloid, sound and picture, that were synchronized as per the clapboard. The clapboard, apart from having the scene number and shot number written with a piece of chalk, also had a piece of wood hinged on the top giving it the ability to emit a sound when clapped together. The frame containing the visual of the clap for each shot and the corresponding sound of the clap was used to synchronize the two celluloid rolls.

The synchronized sound and picture together constituted the rush print. Since the shooting was held over a number of schedules, at the end of every schedule, the rush print would be projected for Boss to decide on the best take of each shot that would find its way into the film.

Watching Raj Sahab decide on the best take initially created confusion in my mind as I found it very difficult to differentiate between the takes. Boss, being the best teacher a student could have, explained his whole process of selection.

'There are various factors that go into my selection. I have to see which take has the sharpest focus, the best performance, the correct movement of the camera and/or an actor, the frame, the junior artists, if any, their positions and any movement happening in the background. All these elements resonating in harmony decide the winner, but nothing happens in a utopian manner. It is very rare that all these elements will be perfect and generally there is some discrepancy, then my decision has to be made on picking not the ideal but the next best.'

Once during the projection, while Raj Sahab was selecting the okay takes, a Russian fan with an Indian friend, who spoke Russian, came to meet him. The friend was disturbing Boss by constantly jabbering loudly in Russian. When the lights came on, the Russian inquired through his friend as to what the editing process would be after this exercise.

Raj Sahab explained to him patiently, 'The okay takes will be taken to the editing room and assembled in chronological order and the beginning and end of every shot will be cut and the next shot will be joined. Once all the shots are assembled, I have to decide on the pace that would be right for the scene and accordingly add or subtract any shot to suit the pace that I require.'

The Indian friend butted in, 'Oh! So, the editor is like a surgeon.'

Raj Sahab, who was already irritated with him, replied, 'When I edit, I have the liberty of placing any scene at any place, unlike a surgeon, who cannot shift your organs from their designated position. So, I hope you understand that unlike a surgeon, I can't shift your brain to your ass and vice versa, though I wish I could!'

In the editing room, an assistant would sort out the okay takes and join them in chronological order as the scene required. Raj Sahab would view the reel of the sorted takes on an upright Moviola or a flatbed Steenbeck. Both these machines had similar capabilities barring a few exceptions.

The Moviola was an upright machine. The picture and sound had to be physically threaded on two different channels, about one foot apart, with the sync marks at the designated spots on the Moviola. The two channels could be locked to play in sync together or either one could be played individually as the situation required. One had a choice in playing the reel; one could either use an electric motor, which ran at exactly 24 frames per second or one could use a pedal to run the reel, much like a sewing machine, which would run at a variable speed depending on the pressure with which the pedal was pressed.

Raj Sahab preferred to use the pedal as it gave him the opportunity to stop the frame at a precise point. He would always stand next to the Moviola with one hand on a lever which, when pressed, would stop the film from running. This enabled him to mark, with a red china marker pencil, the frame that he would use in the edit. At times, with his hand on a steel plate attached to the Moviola, spinning as the film ran, he would suddenly hold the moving plate with his palm, thus stopping the film and marking the same. 'At times, when I use a lever to stop at a particular frame, the time taken for my brain to signal my hand to press the lever would result in a frame or two being missed, but when I stop it by holding the plate, my experience tells me that this movement is in sync with my brain sending out the "stop" signal.'

The Steenbeck, a step above the Moviola, was initially owned and used by only three people in the Indian film industry – Raj Kapoor, B.R. Chopra and the grand old man of the film industry, V. Shantaram. It was easier to operate since all the controls were on various buttons. The impulse triggered by the brain to stop the film and the action of lightly tapping the stop button were simultaneous. No motorized steel plate to hold anymore, and it was more comfortable since one could sit while operating this machine.

Anna Sahab, as Shantaram ji was called, was more comfortable sitting on a gaddi than on a chair. So, the legs of the Steenbeck were cut to bring it to ground level so that he could sit on a gaddi with *'gau takiyas'* while editing his film. Manoj Kumar Sir, who bought a Steenbeck much later, was comfortable using it lying down, so he had the legs of the Steenbeck cut to a level that allowed him to edit while lying on the bed. Three extremely gifted filmmakers, all three eccentrics!

Raj Sahab, with intense concentration, would play the shots on the machine and mark the first frame and last frame of each shot. The marked shots would be taken to the editing table. The centre of the editing table had a 9-inch-by-1-foot frosted glass with a tube light attached below. This light enabled him to see, with a magnifying glass, a particular frame. The sound and picture were loaded onto upright stands attached on one edge of the table and they ran over the frosted glass onto an instrument called a syncrometer. The instrument had a wheel and sprockets, and the wheel had to be manually rotated for the film to go forward or backward. The start marks of the sound and picture were loaded onto the syncrometer so that while he would be moving the picture and sound forward and backward, they would stay in perfect sync.

The start and end point of every shot was snipped using a specialized blade. In order to join the end of the outgoing shot to the beginning of the incoming shot, we had to use film cement, a transparent liquid. The picture and sound were on a celluloid base that had two sides – an emulsion side and the opposite side was a glaze side. Joining the shots meant the emulsion side being joined with the glaze side, and that was only possible by scraping off the emulsion from the outgoing shot. Every shot consisted of four sprockets, perforations, on both edges. When scraping the emulsion, one sprocket would be lost. After this the outgoing shot would be affixed onto the right part of the splicer, a two-part apparatus allowing the left part to be moveable upwards and the right part being fixed, and film cement would be applied on the scraped portion and the incoming shot was affixed onto the designated place in the left part of the splicer and lowered onto the right part. With the pressure applied, a joint between both the parts was 'cemented'.

The process of cutting and joining the shots, as marked by Boss, was done by an assistant. At rare moments, Boss himself would want to operate the splicer. At one such moment, he looked at a confused me and asked, 'Are you looking so bewildered because you can't visually differentiate between the glaze and emulsion?'

I nodded.

'Rahul, the best way to find out the emulsion side is to lick the film; the sticky side will be the emulsion. Try it now and show me.'

I picked up a piece of film and as instructed, licked it and one side was sticky.

I told Boss, 'You are right, Sir! This side is sticky and therefore this must be the emulsion.'

He smiled, 'You cannot be expected to keep licking the shot to find the emulsion. There are two ways, one is that the shiny side will always be the glaze and the non-shiny one will be the emulsion. Another simpler way is, the film print does not have a soundtrack now and the sound is played from another roll of celluloid, but on the picture roll of the rush print, there is a provision for the soundtrack to be printed when the final prints are to be made. Therefore, the emulsion will have a blank space provided for the sound, and that blank edge will always be on your left when looking at the image vertically.'

Raj Sahab was an avid reader of *American Cinematographer*, a magazine published in Los Angeles, which kept one updated on all upcoming technology and tools to assist in the filmmaking process. Raj Sahab had read about the tape splicer there, an apparatus which did not require one to use film cement while editing the rush print, but used Sellotape instead.

Raj Sahab called a friend in LA and a tape splicer was hand-delivered to him within a week. This turned out to be a big boon in editing – no scrapping of emulsion, no using cement and for the idiots like me, no licking.

The big advantage was when Raj Sahab wanted to extend the beginning or the end of a shot after the edit. When extending a shot, we had to be very careful in maintaining the 16 frames that make up one foot of film. Since the splicer required one sprocket of a frame to be scraped, re-adding just a single sprocket to the extended shot was physically not possible. Hence the three remaining sprockets had to be removed and replaced by a single white frame thereby maintaining the thumb rule of 16 frames = 1 foot.

After Raj Sahab had joined all the shots in a scene, the edited scene would be taken by him to view on the Steenbeck. From this point forward, Raj Sahab was like a man possessed! He would run through the scene and look out for any corrections that would be needed to make the transition of shots smoother. Such corrections would be executed immediately, viewed again and, if needed, corrected further till a smooth narration was attained.

Raj Sahab would come out of the room and light a cigarette and through the connecting door, have the entire edited scene run on the Steenbeck without any disturbance. He would, with sharp attentiveness, repeat this process many times. As always, the second or third viewing would have his fingers tapping or moving which would, to us, signify that his mind was racing, imbibing the emotional impact of the scene.

'Every scene, whether a romantic scene, a funny scene, a dramatic scene or a tragic scene, has its own inherent emotion', this was something which he strongly believed in and would ask for our reaction whether the scene worked emotionally for us or not. Raj Sahab had a keen eye for reading one's expression and while any one of us was expressing their observations, he would be listening intently but was also trying to gauge everyone else's reactions to what that one person was saying.

This exercise of critiquing the scene involved the individual participation of all the assistants present. After having heard the lot, he would make up his mind about which elements the scene required, which were extraneous and whether the tempo of the scene required a change.

He would come back to the Steenbeck and start making corrections by adding or subtracting frames from a given shot so as to smoothen the movement between the outgoing and incoming shot or increase or decrease the tempo of the scene.

At times he would pause the Steenbeck at a particular point and say that he needed a silent close-up of one of the actors in the scene. We had already used all the shots at various places in the scene and we did not have any 'insurance shot' that would suffice. He would then say, 'Get me the other okay takes of the shots we have not used pertaining to that actor.' We would refer to the continuity sheets to determine those okay takes. These were brought to the editing room and loaded onto the Moviola since the Steenbeck already had the scene we were editing. He would watch the same, and rarely, when this did not work for him, he would ask for any close-up of this actor from any of the scenes. He would run the other complete take from a different scene on the Moviola and when he found a silent portion that suited him, he would mark the beginning and end, remove that from the roll on the Moviola and replace only the picture from the point he had marked on the Steenbeck.

He did not bother about the fact that we had used this same shot earlier or that it belonged to a completely different scene and the actor was in a different costume! 'The audience will never notice that a shot is repeated or belongs to another scene provided that what they are seeing is engrossing and convincing. Their mind will only waver if you allow it to. This is the magic of cinema,' he believed.

After having corrected the entire scene and going through the process of viewing, observing, contemplating further changes and seeking reactions from the assistants, he would start again and go back to the Steenbeck for the second round of corrections. The spurt of corrections would carry on till he was completely satisfied with the scene. The finalized scene would then be projected in the preview theatre to get a sense of how the scene looked on a larger format.

The excitement of achieving the desired impact of the scene showed all over his face and the expression was something that cannot be explained. His whole persona changed and he was like a happy child who had been given a chocolate. In that extremely happy mood, he would go to the restroom leaving his packet of cigarettes and we, the four assistants, would whack a cigarette each and happily smoke them. By the time we had finished the cigarettes and stubbed them off, he would return to the editing room. We would be very proud that we had finished smoking before he came and we never got caught for the robbery until we realized that he was going to the washroom every time he was thrilled with the edit, purposely giving us the opportunity to whack his cigarettes!

Then he would go back to the Steenbeck to mark the next scene to edit and the child in him would turn back into the man possessed.

Raj Sahab always emphasized that cinema was an audio-visual medium; therefore, not only did the visual have to be structured correctly but the sound was also an integral element for a motion picture and had to be used diligently. When he would come across a situation, in the edit, where the two shots joined together would not flow smoothly, he resorted to the use of sound. 'This flow is not smooth at all, therefore, we need to divert the audience's attention from the visual for a fraction of a moment. You can't have a jarring disturbance as that could probably lead to their mind disconnecting from the scene. This is where your soundtrack plays a crucial part. A loud sound playing at the joint of the outgoing and incoming shot is the solution to the problem. You have to be very careful that the nature of sound, which you are planning to use as a decoy, blends with the nature of the scene.'

Normally, this would be an atmospheric sound but in the event of any atmospheric sound being out of place vis-à-vis the scene, you would need a music piece to start just a fraction before the actual joint. It is very natural that your audience's eyes are going to blink, hearing a loud sound and they are not going to realize where the jerk came from, but also remember, a loud sound is not created in a film by pushing up the volume but by a kind of momentary silence leading up to the sound.

For example, in the circus sequences of *Mera Naam Joker*, he would take the sound of a lion's roar and use it to camouflage the transition. This would be a sound that was an integral part of the atmosphere of the sequence and would not be out of place. I had asked him, 'What if this whole exercise does not suffice and the jerk is still there?'

'Then you live with the jerk!'

Raj Sahab possessed this unique skill; the perfect amalgamation of a director's vision and an editor's skillset. His expertise came to the fore when he dealt with the 'silence'. The narrative in a motion picture requires silence to enhance the impact of a shot leading to the overall impact of the scene. A silent pause between dialogues, or increasing or decreasing the length of silence before or after a shot, could change the emphasis of the scene. There are also scenes that do not require any dialogues but have an irreplaceable relevance in the narrative. Such scenes are envisioned by the director, and the shots are juxtaposed by the editor into forming a compelling narrative wherein dialogue is not required. Even background music or the deliberate lack of the same is a decision that could make or break the impact of the edited scene on the audience. The mental compatibility between Raj Kapoor, the director, and Raj Kapoor, the editor, was of prime importance in taking this decision.

In *Bobby*, there were a series of moments between Chintu and Dimple – walking along the seaside, Chintu watching Dimple playing badminton, both of them walking through this beautiful alley lined with Gulmohar trees, the iconic 'library scene' and many more. These were all silent moments where the romance developed between the lovers and the visual narration was entirely to the credit of the director and the editor. Since these sequences were never mentioned in the script, the only reference in the script was 'romantic montage between Raja and Bobby'.

All these sequences germinated in Raj Sahab's mind, and it was a continuous process wherein he would mentally conceive such a scene and shoot it the next day. One day, we happened to be shooting specific scenes from the script in Pune and he suddenly said, 'I think a great moment can be created in the library of Pune Club.'

The next morning, we were in the library to shoot a scene that had been conceived by Raj Sahab only a night before, and we had no written scene to rely on. The only detail given to us was, 'Dimple is studying in the library, seated adjacent to an elderly gentleman, extremely committed to reading. When Chintu comes in to speak with her, the elderly gentleman looks disturbed and Dimple throws Chintu out saying that he is not supposed to speak in a library. He goes out, finds a piece of broken mirror and uses the reflection of the sun to disturb Dimple and in turn the elderly gentleman gets irritated. We'll shoot this first thing tomorrow morning.'

I asked, 'Sahab, for the character of the elderly gentleman, is there any particular actor that you want me to get from Bombay?'

'No! In the evening, after the shoot, I was having tea with some friends and a Bohri gentleman, Mr Tayyab, happened to be there. He has a very interesting face and I had always thought that I would use him in some film because I was fascinated by his face. I was also sure that he would be a very bad actor, but I was fascinated by his natural expression of getting irritated when the horse he backed would lose at the races or he himself would lose any money. This scene's actual concept was based on my being able to utilize his character in a moment contributing to the progress of romance in the film. So, I have got a "non-actor" to "act" and I hope I can make people believe that he is a good actor.'

In the library scene, three different actions were taking place at the same time, without any dialogue. The light flashing on Dimple's face, Chintu using the mirror to flash the light and Mr Tayyab being disturbed and irritated by the gestures between the lovers. Raj Sahab used a hilarious technique to get a disturbed and irritated look on Mr Tayyab's face. The camera was facing Mr Tayyab while Raj Sahab sat behind the camera and nastily lectured Mr Tayyab about how his favourite horse should be called a donkey and he was definitely going to lose all his money and go broke because of that horse. Mr Tayyab was not aware that this was being shot; we used a Mitchell BNC, a noiseless camera, and while Raj Sahab's soliloquy about the atrocious attributes of the horse was going on, the camera was running to capture the unbelievable and horrendous expressions of Mr Tayyab!

Finally, the version which played out on film proved to be a masterpiece with great appreciation for the actor Mr Tayyab. Raj Kapoor, having worked with extremely competent actors, who in turn had become stars, also possessed the unique ability of turning non-actors into actors who down the line also became stars. Believe me, a breed of non-actors who never learn and always stay as non-actors become stars and are still hanging around and such people will always keep cropping up!

Raj Kapoor, the director, handed over a bunch of random shots, without a script or dialogue, to Raj Kapoor, the editor. He was now responsible for assembling the random shots and creating a semblance of sanity so as to convey a sweet and funny narrative, keeping in mind the foremost fact that the inherent emotion in the film was not to be disturbed. The only information the director had given to the editor was the start and end of the scene.

Raj Sahab started building a narrative from scratch and constantly kept making changes in the same. This process went on for about two days during which he also asked the assistants for their feedback on every narrative that he assembled. The acceptance or rejection of the feedback being his prerogative, he would, however, go out of the way to explain his reason if he didn't accept a particular suggestion. This was the mark of the wonderful teacher that he was!

Raj Sahab had in stock the background music of all the past films made at RK. He would always want a background score from his earlier films attached to the silent portion of the film that he was currently editing. 'The background music I want to put is temporary; the final background music will be recorded when the film is entirely complete. I require this temporary background music, not only for the edited rushes having a better impact, but also to serve as an example of the kind of background music that we would finally require.

With the number of silent portions and silent sequences, a judgement on the impact would be influenced in a great way with background music.'

When we laid the temporary background music track on the rush print, his approval was extremely essential. Once approved, he would ask for the silent sequences with the rough background track to be run on the Steenbeck. Here, he would make corrections so that essential joints in the visual coincided with a musical change to give the right impact, even though the music track being played was temporary and would be changed later.

'Music is also governed by mathematics. There are four beats of music in every bar and a particular number of bars are contained in the melody. The changes I'm making here are to act as a further guide for the final background music recording so that the changes of beats in the background score would not necessitate any change in the picture.

'If the musical beats or changes do not exactly synchronize on hearing the final background music, we will come back to the table and add or subtract picture frames to match with the beats of the recorded music without creating any "jumps" or visual disruptions in the picture. In case it is absolutely necessary to make the changes, irrespective of the jumps or visual disruptions, then the solution will only lie in recording a musical "bang" over the background music track and this would divert the attention of the viewer for a split second and make the visual disruption unnoticeable.'

This bang for the final mix would be placed in a separate but parallel track of the background music, giving Raj Sahab the flexibility of raising or lowering the volume according to his requirement.

The edit is also important for the song sequences. In a song sequence, if one character is singing and moving out of the frame in one shot and Raj Sahab wanted him to enter the frame in the next shot, he would not show the character exiting but would only indicate the exit through movement and have him enter in the next shot. The reason for this was that the music had already been recorded and the actor was a human being. Each time he exits a frame and enters another frame, the movement will never match, and it is not possible to add or subtract the music to match the entry-exit frames, as the song is filmed on playback which is a fixed factor.

I asked, 'Sir, what about the exit? Won't it look odd?' He said, 'In a song nothing is odd. Songs can be manipulated in various ways. There could be one shot at a certain location and the next shot could be anywhere else or there could be one shot at one end of a set and the next shot at the opposite end of the same set, and nobody would question how the location or the positions on the set changed. This phenomenon happens as the mind is hearing a continuous song and a change of shot makes the viewer oblivious to the last location.' Believe me, nobody notices!

At times, Raj Sahab would find it necessary to not only reduce the length of a song but also juxtapose two *antaras*. This required the soundtrack to be manipulated. Either sound had to be cut off so as to reduce the length or juxtaposed from point 'A' to point 'B' to swap the position of the stanzas. This required absolute precision as no glitch in the soundtrack would be tolerated. Raj Sahab would do this not by hearing the sound but by 'seeing' the sound. He would first hear the sound and approximately mark the beginning and end points for the reduction or the points of juxtaposition and then, the final cut was made in the sound not by hearing it for the precise point but by 'seeing' it. Since the soundtrack was a visual representation of the modulations, he would visually find the smoothest modulation, and cut and join accordingly thereby obtaining a smooth edited soundtrack.

In the editing room, Raj Sahab would not realize that other people were sitting around, and while watching the edited rushes and realizing that he had made a mistake, he would talk to himself, 'Raj Kapoor, you are an absolute idiot!' or use more explicit words. The really enjoyable time was when actors screwed up in any aspect of a shot, which happened, still happens and will keep happening for eternity. A barrage of abuses would be hurled towards the actor who was not present at that time. This led me to make it a point to bring debuting actors into the editing room so they can hear how they are being 'praised' for their performances.

A change in the decor of the editing room heralded the commencement of the final editing. The windows were masked with black paper and the clock was removed. Raj Sahab turned vegetarian, went off alcohol, started working longer hours and he would not enter the editing room with his watch and neither were any of the assistants allowed to wear a watch. This ensured that everyone involved in the edit had no sense of time since the edit would go on until Boss was tired.

Final editing is the process wherein all the edited scenes are finally assembled in order, vis-à-vis the creative discretion of the director but within the realms of the script. This essential exercise requires the ultimate finesse to give final shape to the narrative, thereafter not leaving any margin for a U-turn.

A huge contribution to the ultimate impact of the film was the tempo of the entire narrative. Raj Sahab concentrated completely on the same and would sometimes require changing a take of a shot and/or adding or subtracting frames to a shot and/or deleting an entire scene.

It was in this process that Raj Sahab would need a particular shot or cutting of an existing shot. His 'elephant's memory' would at times become quite a nightmare for the assistants. He would ask for a particular shot or cutting and we would spend hours trying to find it, somewhat convinced that this kind of shot did not exist, but finally finding it, realizing he was always right!

During the final edit of *Mera Naam Joker*, he suddenly asked, 'In the unused crowd shots, there is a mid-shot in which everybody is looking to the right of the camera, but there is one man in a blue shirt who is looking to the left of the camera. I want a 1½ feet, one second, cutting of that shot.'

We had approximately 50,000 feet and 6-hour long crowd shots of the circus, and two years after having concluded the circus shooting and having seen the edited film a number of times, the man remembered, in detail, that one stray shot!

The entire lot of assistants got down to looking for the shot he required. We had spent about seven hours going through every cutting. Boss called us to have a cup of tea with him, spoke about other sequences in the film but made no mention of the cutting we were looking for. As soon as we finished our tea, he said, 'You chaps must be really tired and it must be really late, so let's speed up things and find the shot quickly.' After about three more hours, an assistant called Verlikar, who had slept through the entire process, miraculously appeared with the shot!

We were all surprised and Kala ji was fuming. We realized that he had found the required shot very early, put it in his pocket, slept off and resurfaced at his own will with the shot.

Raj Sahab had this rule with regard to sound and reels. It was that no reel would start with a song or a portion where the background music was needed, and no reel would finish with a song or would finish with a background score still playing. During that time, the reels used to be loaded onto two different projectors and there used to be a manual changeover between the reels. A manual changeover required two different operators for two projectors. As one reel was finishing, the second reel had to seamlessly start on the second projector. Invariably, there would be a slight lag in the changeover from projector A to B, which was the reason why a song or a background music finishing or beginning with a wobbling sound due to the lag would greatly disturb the audience. Raj Sahab would not let this happen and that is why he was very particular about the reeling.

The other important thing, leading up to the final sound mix, was laying the sound effect tracks, incidental and other sounds, to create an overall audio experience in sync with the visuals, which when mixed with the dialogue and music formed a consolidated audio track. This included atmosphere sounds, birds, wind, traffic, etc., and sounds attached to the visual in the film, footsteps, passing cars, doors opening and closing, etc. This also involved the sound of animals either for the atmosphere track or in tandem with an animal seen in the scene, and there were plenty of these animal sounds required in *Mera Naam Joker*.

I was trying my hand at laying an effect track in the editing room when Raj Sahab walked in with Khan Sahab who said, 'In the song "*Ae bhai zara dekh ke chalo*", when the joker walks in to the ring along with a chap dressed as a lion and the words, "*kya hai karshima kaisa khilwar hai*", I think we need the sound of the roar of a lion over the music.'

Raj Sahab responded, 'Splendid idea, Khan Sahab! Rahul, the lion's roar, in the effect track, should be in the same *sur* as the song.'

This instruction from Boss flummoxed me. How would I be able to find a lion's roar in a musical *sur*? I spent hours and sleepless nights trying to find the 'in *sur*' roar of a lion. Finally, I gave up trying to find the 'musical' roar and did not put it in the soundtrack and mentally prepared myself to face Boss's wrath at the mixing.

When the reel was threaded for mixing and the song played through without the lion's sound, Khan Sahab stopped the reel and asked me angrily, 'You were specifically asked to put an "in *sur*" roar of a lion but it's missing!'

I sheepishly told him, 'Sir, I spent two days and nights trying to find a suitable musical roar but I'm afraid I couldn't.'

Raj Sahab also exclaimed angrily, 'You have ruined the entire effect that I wanted to create in this song!'

I could have burst out crying but instead replied with an exasperated laugh, 'Sir, I'm very sorry, but I honestly tried my best.'

Raj Sahab turned to Khan Sahab, '*Arre* our entire plan of pranking him has fallen flat. He is laughing and not crying as we had planned.'

And I burst out crying!

Like Dambara Nights would end with the strains of the song '*Jaago Mohan pyaare*', every session during the final edit would end in exactly the following manner:

Raj Sahab, 'Remove the black masking from the window.'

As the mask was removed, bright sunlight was seen, 'Oh, *subah ho gayi*! We have been working for practically 20 hours. I'm so sorry to keep you guys awake till this awful time and I promise you it will not happen again. I'm going to instruct one of the drivers to drive you guys back home, the last one to be dropped please relax and rest, but don't take more than an hour since you have to pick up everybody else and come back to the studio. Sorry for really pushing you guys.'

THE PHOENIX: RISING FROM THE ASHES

THE EDITING CONCLUDES THE lessons on the filmmaking techniques of Raj Kapoor. These lessons just scratch the surface; there is a lot more about the ingenuity of Raj Sahab that needs to be told. What better way of doing this than sharing my experiences, from the inception to the release of that trendsetting, iconic and cult film *Bobby*.

Mera Naam Joker had not fared well at the box office and Raj Sahab was extremely disappointed, but not disheartened.

He said, 'Every film is akin to a child for a director. A mother who gives birth to children, raises them to the best of her ability, with zeal and zest, so that every child would step out into the world with the singular aim to triumph in life. If she realizes that one of them is not as adept as the others and lags behind in the journey, she does not discard that child but holds the child closest to her heart. *Mera Naam Joker*, a film made with all honesty but one that did not connect with the audience is that child for me. I will never forget but hold it close to my heart, like my other films, or maybe closer. I have to rise like the mythical phoenix from the ashes and conquer the world!'

Stars like Rajendra Sir, Dharam ji, Manoj Kumar Sir, Padmini, Simi Garewal and Dara Singh ji had gone out of their way to adjust their busy work schedules for *Mera Naam Joker* since they were getting an opportunity to work with the master, Raj Kapoor. Stars used to be elated to appear in any film that he would make.

However, he believed, 'Stars do not make a film, only the right concept and narration is what catches the fancy of the audience. We had the biggest stars in *Mera Naam Joker*, but I could not bridge a connect between the narrative and the audience, even though the concept and narrative stemmed from my heart, so, I have another concept from the bottom of my heart that I want the audience to experience. A unique never treaded before path, a teenage romance!'

One day he called his entire team of finance, production and direction, to the cottage. Like an excited child, he told us about the new path that he had decided to pursue for his next film, 'I am making a sublime love story. Every love story inherently requires an opposition to the lovers, and our films have always used wealth, property or religion to be the fundamental grounds of opposition, but my teenage romance will not have any of these clichés; don't ask me what the grounds for opposition would be as even I don't know yet.'

In those days, it was very common for affluent households to have catholic nannies, since they spoke the English language and were inherently courteous, which is why they were employed as governesses to look after the children and in that process, they would influence the kids in their growth. This was a premise that appealed to Raj Sahab and was the foundation for the film. 'The parents of the boy would belong to an extremely affluent family and the girl would be the granddaughter of the ex-governess who brought the boy up.'

Kala ji commented, 'Raj Sahab, so the opposition to the teenagers' romance is going to be religion? This can create problems regarding religious sentiments.' Raj Sahab retorted, 'Not at all! What you are thinking of is a cliché but I am thinking of tackling a different opposition. The father of the girl, who is the governess' son, would be a very rich fisherman who lives the lifestyle of a fisherman, speaks in a very rough tone but with underlying simplicity, whereas the parents of the boy belong to that stratum of society that is very "pretentious" and "elitist". Although the girl's father possesses equivalent wealth to the boy's father, but his wealth has not made him forget his humble days, and therefore the bone of contention between the lovers will not be wealth or religion but upbringing!'

Raj Sahab had made up his mind that this film would herald the debut of Chintu, Rishi Kapoor, and he now required a new girl who had to be a good actor, very good-looking and fit into a catholic girl's persona.

Immediately, the financial controller of RK, Raman Sahab, jumped up and angrily opposed the idea, '*Kandum, Kandum!* Nonsense! Very bad! The story is good, but requires a lot of money to be spent and with Chintu debuting with a new girl, which distributor will give money for this project? For Chintu we will plan a small cheap film later on, but now, after the debacle of *Mera Naam Joker*, we immediately need a solid star cast so that we get money from the distributors and pay off our debts. Why don't you cast Dharmendra and Hema Malini as the lovers?'

Raj Sahab replied angrily, 'Dharmendra and Hema Malini to play teenage lovers? Raman Sahab, it looks like the debacle of *Mera Naam Joker* has made you lose your senses and I, who is most affected, have my mental faculties very much in place. I have earned the money to make this studio, prestige and respect because of me being a filmmaker, and money is the least concern for a true filmmaker. When I make a film, I eat, drink and obsess over it and as of now, I am only "living" this teenage love story. I will mortgage and sell all my possessions to conjure up the money to make this film and if this doesn't suffice, I will beg, borrow and steal to make this film. Take it in writing from me that my loss in a film has not deprived me of my talent nor have I lost faith in the same. I will make this film with all honesty and integrity and if this also fails, I will find money again to make a third film. So, after today, nobody in this room discusses the monetary aspects of the film.'

To raise finances for the film, he entered into an agreement with a large conglomerate, who made their initial money via Raj Kapoor's films and grew to be known as one of the richest Indian families in the UK. However, their agreements were known to be draconian and included the producer mortgaging his entire assets to them, and their wicked mindset ensured that they would finally be the owners of everything the producer had earned and still not be free from the liability incurred by him. Even though Raj Sahab knew about these dangers, he still borrowed from them at an interest rate which was exorbitant, compounded every three months and also created mortgages, in their favour, on all his assets! But this did not deter him from spending as much money as his heart deemed necessary for the film.

We started searching for a girl to play the lead. The number of screen tests we took was enough to drive us crazy; I don't even remember the exact number. Every second day, Raj Sahab would say, 'Rahul, *kal* audition *lena hai*.' He wanted to be there to audition every girl since only he knew what he was looking for exactly.

A close friend of Mrs Raj Kapoor, Munni Dhawan Aunty, brought a family friend, Chunnibhai Kapadia with his wife Bitti Ben and daughter Dimple, to simply look around and meet Raj Kapoor as Chunnibhai was a great fan of Boss. Munni Aunty had actually brought them so that Raj Sahab would see their daughter Dimple, as she was very keen on acting.

When they left, Raj Sahab asked me, 'What do you think of that girl?'

I replied saying, 'She's very good-looking.'

He asked, 'Do you think we should audition her?'

I had no choice but to agree with him as the very fact that he asked me whether we should audition her or not was a sign that he had already made up his mind to conduct the audition.

Raj Sahab auditioned her; the technical crew and Dabboo Sahab were also present at the audition. Though she seemed very keen, all of us, except Boss, thought that she was just about average but our opinions changed when we saw the audition on screen – she was good-looking but a bad actor!

Raj Sahab saw the audition thrice and said, 'I have found Bobby.'

Completely perplexed, I asked him, 'How come while watching Dimple's audition, you have thought about and finalized another girl called Bobby?'

'I have found Bobby which is going to be the title of the film and the lead will be played by Dimple Kapadia.'

We were dumbstruck and tried our best to dissuade him.

'Sir, I'm sure we can find somebody else.'

'Papa, she is okay but there are better girls we have auditioned.'

'Raj Sahab *aap ke* calibre *ki* actress *bilkul nahin hai*.'

He calmly heard all the complaints which we had and gave us a simple reply, 'What I see in her is what you people don't have the capacity to see. That's the difference between all of you and me.'

There was no point in opposing him further as he had made up his mind and my exposure to Raj Kapoor's cinema had taught me that the man is a 'magician', so, he would definitely make us realize what we had not seen in the audition.

The process of Dimple being launched in the film constituted her seeing every single film that Raj Sahab had directed so that she would be familiar with what he expected from his heroines. The script of *Bobby* was being completed by Raj Sahab in collaboration with K.A. Abbas and V.P. Sathe. Chintu and Dimple were being put through workshops and familiarization sessions with the technical crew.

Raj Sahab called in his technical crew and the actors to hear a preliminary narration of *Bobby*. It sounded great and we were sure that with all Raj Sahab's improvisations in the script, he would have a winner in his hands.

After the narration, when Chintu and Dimple had left, Khan Sahab said, 'Raj Sahab, *yeh* film Chintu *ka* launching pad *hai aur* Dimple *ka* role *bahut jyada behtereen hai, aur phir* title *bhi ek* feminine word *hai,* Bobby. *Aap ko lagta hai, yeh* Chintu *ke saath sahi ho raha hai*?'

Raj Sahab replied, 'Khan Sahab, I am making a film and you as one of my oldest associates know for a fact that when I make a film, I do not have any acquaintances, friends or relatives. The film stands above everything else. Chintu being my son cannot make me hamper the natural flow of the script or the title, but I assure you, Chintu, being the tremendous actor that he is, will rise above any debut that has ever been made.'

Raj Sahab wanted a fresh dialogue writer working in tandem with the fresh approach that he had envisaged for the script. There were various wannabe writers who Raj Sahab met and finally zeroed in on Jainendra Jain Sahab, a journalist and photographer for the *Madhuri* magazine. He was given a couple of sample scenes and Raj Sahab was very impressed with Jain Sahab's approach and use of the language.

This brought us to the final casting of the film. Pran Sahab's personality and the power of his performance made him the obvious choice to play Chintu's father, Mr Nath. For his wife, Boss needed a face and demeanour of a lady who would fit the character of an elite socialite, who partook more in kitty parties than responsibilities of the household. After going through various meetings and auditions, Sonia Sahni ji was finalized to play Mrs Nath. To portray the other character of Neema, a younger kitty party friend of Mrs Nath who needed to be extremely attractive, an extremely talented actress, Aruna Irani, fit into the character sketch that Raj Sahab wanted. The veteran, Durga Khote ji, was an actor in whom Raj Sahab had great faith. He told us that when the concept of *Bobby* took germ in his mind, he could only imagine her to play Mrs Braganza, Chintu's governess and Dimple's grandmother. This left only Mr Braganza, Dimple's father and Durga Khote ji's son. Now Raj Sahab said that like Mrs Braganza, he had also finalized Prem Nath ji for the role of Dimple's father when the concept had germinated.

All the actors who were cast in *Bobby* came to the studio and met Raj Sahab, who ran through the character sketch with them and they were all happy and excited about their roles. Prem Nath ji was the only exception. After Raj Sahab narrated the character to him, he said, 'Very good, but I need to hear in more detail as I have to tune up my character more. For this, you send the "municipality" writer to my shack at Versova tomorrow evening at five.'

Raj Sahab told me to accompany Jain Sahab for the narration but while saying this he kept laughing all the time. 'This man, Prem Nath, my brother-in-law, is verging on the brink of eccentricity and madness!' Laughing heartily, he added, 'I hope this meeting with Prem does not rattle Jain and he comes out sane and alive.' Raj Sahab was in splits of laughter.

On our way to his place, Jain Sahab asked me a peculiar question, 'Babbu Sahab, Prem ji *theek hain na*?'

I was surprised by the question and so I asked him, '*Theek hain matlab*?'

He replied awkwardly, '*Maine suna hai ki wo thode se jhakki hain.*' I had great difficulty controlling my laughter in light of what Raj Sahab had said. Jain Sahab carried on, '*Aaj milunga pehli baar. Maine itna suna hai ki unko zyada sawaal nahi puchna chahiye nahi toh who kabhi haath paanv bhi ghuma dete hain.*'

To scare him further, controlling my laughter with difficulty, I said, '*Maine bhi yahi suna hai,* Jain Sahab.'

'Babbu, *agar woh mere saath* violent *ho gaye, zara mujhe sambhal lena*!'

The moment we entered his shack, he curtly told Jain Sahab, 'Before you start narrating, I want to know what my character is.' This conversation was happening with Prem Nath ji sitting on a sofa, a strange-looking uniformed bodyguard standing next to him and us standing at the door! Jain Sahab said, 'He's a fisherman, but he is a very rich man. He lives a simple life in a cottage in the fishermen's colony, is very benevolent and does not like the vulgar display of his wealth. *Bohot hi munhphat aadmi hai, jo bhi sochta hai bolta hai* and people love him for that. He loves his rum and…' Prem Nath ji immediately said, 'Bond! Go to the wine shop and bring two bottles of rum.' Bond saluted his boss and marched out with Prem Nath ji imitating fanfare music with his mouth!

It was hilarious that the bodyguard with his frail physique was called 'Bond'. This chap had various insignias and a nameplate on his chest that said, 'James Bond, ADC to Prem Nath'. No wonder he wore a suit, which was definitely not stitched in Savile Row and he drove around in a two-wheeler scooter, not an Aston Martin!

Coming back to the scene in the shack, Prem Nath ji was playing the harmonium and singing some *raag* (Jain Sahab was standing as he had not been asked to sit) when the phone rang. Prem Nath ji was too engrossed in his 'off-key' singing and harmonium playing, so I picked up the phone and it happened to be Raj Sahab.

'*Kya hua*, Prem *ne sun liya*?'

'*Nahin, shuru nahin hua*.'

'*Shuru nahin hua*?' It had been a long time.

'Sir, wait *kar rahe hain. Kyuki unhone* basic character *suna aur* James Bond *se* rum *mangwaya hai*.'

'*Kya*? Rahul *kahin iss pagle ke saath tum bhi toh pagal nahi ho gaye? Aur* Jain *zinda hai, behosh ho gaya ya usne khudkhushi kar li*?' As usual, Boss was in peals of laughter and disconnected the phone.

When I came out from the telephone room, Prem Nath ji and Jain Sahab were not there, but James Bond was back and he said, 'Sir, they're waiting for you in the bathroom.' As he led me towards the bathroom, he was marching but this time playing the fanfare himself. It was a bizarre situation but I had never realized that the situation was going to get more bizarre. Prem Nath ji had stripped down completely and was sitting under the tap with a bottle of rum. Jain Sahab was sitting on the threshold of the bathroom, James Bond was standing in attention, his hand in a salute, and I was seated on a stool. A very surreal kind of atmosphere for a bathroom.

Prem Nath ji then turned on the tap so that water fell on his naked body and kept drinking the rum. According to him, he had created the correct atmosphere for Braganza's character and commanded loudly to Jain Sahab, 'Present Arms!'

Poor Jain Sahab could not understand what was happening and I whispered to him, 'Sir, please start narrating.'

When the narration finished, Prem Nath ji, suddenly jumped up, quite tipsy, since he was now consuming the second bottle of rum, and started running all over the house as well as in the lawn, mumbling about the nuances he would create in the character, his style of walking and speaking. Jain Sahab muttered under his breath, 'Babbu, *jab bhi* Prem Sahab *ko naya* scene *sunana hoga toh har baar yahi cheez hogi kya*?' He was really terrified and if I would have said, 'Yes!', what Raj Sahab had enquired about would have played out in real life, he would have given up the film, passed out or committed suicide!

When I went back to the studio and met Raj Sahab, I described the bizarre scene that had taken place, from the narration to his 'celebrating' his character. Raj Sahab didn't laugh but sighed, 'Well, we will all have to tolerate his bizarre behaviour, but what you should never forget is that he is a very, very talented actor, and like parents who handle naughty but extremely talented children, I will have to handle him with kid gloves.' So, the director, who would be the father figure for the newcomers, was now going to don the additional role of a naughty, talented child's father too.

The casting complete, the new talented leads in place and a script written, which we knew would keep changing as and when Boss's fertile mind would be further inspired, the film was now ready to commence shooting.

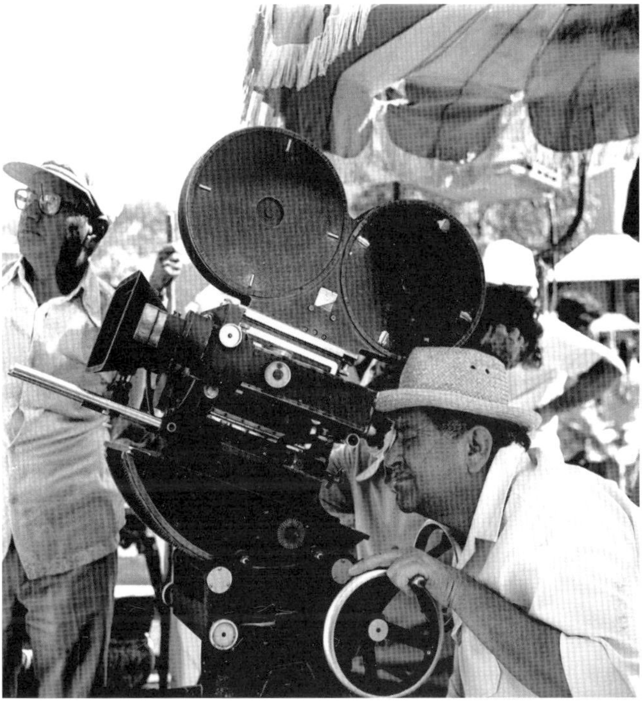

Raj Kapoor checking the frame through the Mitchell BNC camera on the sets of *Ram Teri Ganga Maili*.

The Master applying final touches to the make-up of Zeenat Aman.

Raj Kapoor instructing Lata Mangeshkar on the final notes of a song in *Bobby*.

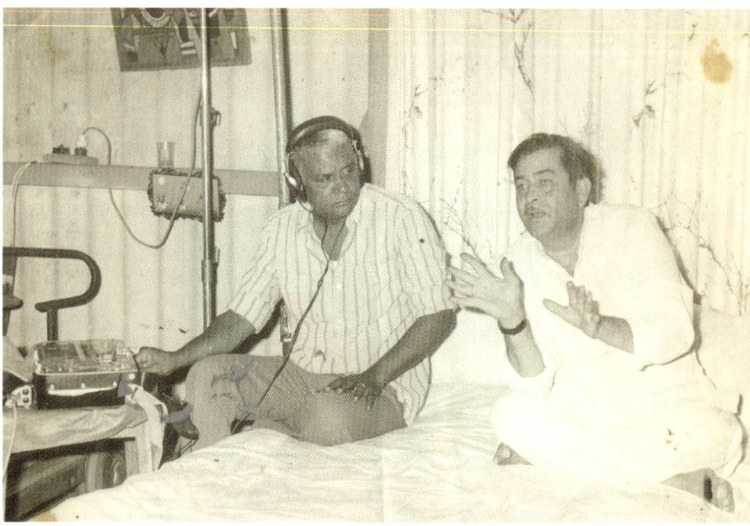

Raj Kapoor explaining a shot to the actors, while Allaudin Khan looks on.

Two great filmmakers in one frame: Raj Kapoor and Manmohan Desai.

On the sets of *Prem Rog*, Raj Kapoor explaining the nuances of the shot to Rishi Kapoor and choreographer Suresh Bhatt.

Shankar-Jaikishan and his 'music family' at the recording of *Jis Desh Mein Ganga Behti Hai.*

Raj Kapoor explaining the visual impact he requires to Radhu Karmakar and Shashi Kapoor.

Raj Kapoor enthusiastically playing a *dholak*, which was one of the various musical instruments he possessed an inborn talent for.

At the song recording of *Love Story* (from left to right): Rahul Rawail with Rajendra Kumar, Vijayta Pandit and Raj Kapoor.

On the sets of *Bobby*, Rahul Rawail assisting Raj Kapoor, who is demonstrating to Dimple Kapadia the gesture he requires.

BOBBY: EPISODE 1

THE SONG 'MAIN SHAYAR TOH NAHIN', figured in one of the early schedules of *Bobby*. The search for a lead actress had finished but the search for a 'voice' for Chintu was still on. Raj Sahab believed, very rightly, that a new face essentially needed a new 'voice', as this aspect would also give a fresh and unique outlook to the debuting actor. Various voices were auditioned by Laxmikant-Pyarelal but Raj Sahab, who himself possessed a keen sense of music, was very difficult to satisfy. Shailendra Singh, a student at the Film and Television Institute of India, was the voice that Raj Sahab chose, much to the disdain of certain people. Raj Sahab was certain that Shailendra Singh's voice would fit Chintu's persona and the character of Raja like a hand in a glove.

The shooting commenced on a grand set of a part of Mr Nath's house where Raja's eighteenth birthday was being celebrated. Raj Sahab wanted the whole ambience to be that of 'society' birthdays.

Raj Sahab told me to order a cake for the shoot from Mac Ronells, 'All the accessories at the shoot should look authentic, thus I want a chocolate cake which is 1 foot by 1 foot by 1 foot. We'll cut the cake for the shot and then distribute it to all the junior artists to eat.'

Raj Sahab kept adding expenses to the atmosphere without batting a lid. 'I need 300 junior artists, of which 200 would be females and one 100 males, all from the "Super A" category', which meant that the females would wear very stylish clothes and the males had to be in ties and suits. This would cost us a bomb! He further added, 'If they do not have very stylish dresses, sarees, salwar-kameez or ties and suits, go to the costume department and get suitable clothes from the earlier films and if need be, get some tailored.' This would add up to be an atomic expense!

As he came on the set, he saw me with six empty champagne bottles that I was filling up with a mixture of Limca and soda to make it look like authentic champagne.

'What are you doing? Is this what would be served in place of champagne at Raj Kapoor's party? If you want to save money, why spend even on Limca? Make the unit piss into the bottles! Cheapster!'

So, six bottles of champagne, the cheapest quality I could find, were ordered from a bootlegger, which almost led to me being fired again, 'Raj Kapoor serves only the finest quality of champagne in Magnum bottles.'

For the party sequence, we had to lay out snacks and I did what most people used to do. I had these small silver bowls filled with wafers and peanuts. It looked like the perfect party snacks but to Boss, it did not. 'I've repeatedly told you, this is a rich man's party. I don't want to see these *moongphalis* and wafers, I want the party guests to be served *pista* and *badam*.'

'Sir, *pista* and *badam* are very expensive,' I blurted.

'I want it! The expense is my prerogative for my film, how does it concern you?'

Normally, to avoid anyone eating the food or snacks that were provided on a party set, producers would spray insecticide on the edibles, thus avoiding replenishing the same and saving money. It was a terrible thing to do and Raj Sahab would rightfully never subscribe to this form of inhumane behaviour. (As a matter of fact, Shri Prithviraj Kapoor had fallen ill because, engrossed in his performance but oblivious of such evil practices, he had consumed a piece of adulterated chicken while he was performing in a shot for the film *Rustom Sohrab*.)

I was aware of the fact that Raj Sahab would want to see the junior artists nibbling at snacks in the party scene. I reluctantly laid out the *pista* and *badam* and added some *kaju* also. I quietly instructed the junior artists, '*Dekho, agar khana hai na, sirf thoda sa, bahut thoda, zyada se zyada do daane kaju khana, lekin pista aur badam ko haath mat lagana*.'

In the shoot, my mind was only focused on monitoring the fact that no *pista* or *badam* was being eaten by the junior artists and the consumption of *kaju* was limited to only two pieces.

Regardless of my warning, there were two junior artists who were just sitting having an animated conversation carefully eating only the *pista* and *badam*. I could have killed them! Even now when I watch *Bobby*, when that particular shot comes, all images in front of me are blurred and I can only see the *pista* and *badam* being devoured.

'*Jo* cake order *kiya hai, aaj shaam ko le aana, kal uska* shot *lenge*,' said Raj Sahab. I went to Mac Ronells at night to pick up the cake and was shocked when told that the bill for the same was ₹ 700. A princely sum in those days. So, I called up Raj Sahab and told him the exorbitant amount of money we were being charged for the cake. He was furious and said, 'Tell Ronnie [the owner of Mac Ronells] that he is fleecing Raj Kapoor and I will never in my life set foot in his bakery again!'

The next day on the set, the huge chocolate cake looked really appetizing and the junior artists, along with the whole unit, were looking forward to eating a piece of cake. Unfortunately, the shooting had to be put off for the day due to some unforeseen circumstances and the cake was stored overnight in Boss's air-conditioned office. The next day when the box containing the cake was opened, we saw, to the disappointment of everyone on the set, that rats had eaten most of it! We had to manage the shoot with only a small part of what would have been an exquisite cake showing in the frame, and immediately after the shot, it had to be thrown away. What a waste of money!

Raj Sahab's instant reaction after the cake was destroyed was, 'Rahul, ring up Mac Ronells and order an identical cake for tomorrow. The junior artists and unit were looking forward to tasting the cake and I would hate to disappoint them. So, tomorrow evening after the shoot, we will have a party for everyone and will also share the cake together.' He did not flinch at the thought of spending ₹ 700 again.

This was a lesson that the money being spent on a film was of no consequence to him, as long as the expenses incurred befitted the ambience and the narrative of the story he was telling, and further, the love and respect he held for all personnel associated with the production of the film. He wanted perfection and warmth from the unit hands as he believed that these were two important facets that contributed to the making of a film. Generally, a filmmaker who had gone through a major financial loss and had been abandoned by his permanent distributors would normally be wary of expenditure. But Raj Kapoor was a unique and rare human being who would fight every battle without finances bothering him as long as he had a good story to tell. He was a genuine filmmaker.

There was a moment that was etched in Raj Sahab's memory, from 35 years before *Bobby* was made. When he went to meet Nargis ji to offer her the role in *Barsaat*, her introduction to him was a moment that he had never forgotten. The impact of the visual when he saw Nargis ji stunned him, and he always wanted to recreate that unforgettable visual in a film and finally found an opportunity in *Bobby*.

The scene had Raja coming to the Braganza house, with an excuse that he wanted to meet his adorable governess but actually he wanted to meet Bobby, who he had seen in the prelude music leading to '*Main shayar toh nahin*'. Chintu comes to the door, rings the bell and the door is opened by the stunningly beautiful Bobby, whose hands are soiled with *besan* since she had apparently been cooking. As she sees Raja, she moves a strand of her hair that had fallen on her forehead and in the process smears the *besan* on her hair. He went through about 27 takes of the same shot, which meant Dimple washing her hair each time this shot had to be re-taken, and he patiently kept egging her on until he achieved what he was striving for; the unique innocence on her face, enhanced by the simplicity of the *besan* smeared on her hair. The impact of this shot is what I saw on the first day, first show of the release of the film. People were keen on seeing Dimple because apart from being Raj Kapoor's discovery she was Rajesh Khanna's wife. When she was first seen on screen, in '*Main shayar toh nahin*', there was a flutter amongst the audience; 'Wow!' 'She's beautiful!' 'So cute!' but when she was seen in the iconic shot, with the *besan* streaking her hair, people were on their feet and there was an extended standing ovation. This was the power of Raj Kapoor's visual narrative.

During this schedule, Prem Nath ji was due to shoot with us for the first time, and remembering what Jain Sahab had gone through was enough to frighten the poor man in anticipation of meeting Prem Nath ji again.

Raj Sahab, Jain Sahab and some people from the unit were sitting outside the shooting stage when Prem Nath ji entered. He was sitting in a convertible Buick, dressed in an orange dhoti kurta with strange religious embellishments, accompanied by four sadhus, with the blaring sound of so-called religious shlokas that had been written by him. Even the music accompanying his shlokas was his creation. His eyes were closed in deep devotion, and the 'icing on the cake' of this strange tableau was James Bond, standing just behind him in uniform, with one hand saluting and the other hand holding an umbrella over his head. As he got down from the 'chariot', he and the sadhus broke into a prayer and he walked up to meet Raj Sahab with Bond marching and playing the fanfare!

At RK, Raj Sahab had his own large personal make-up room which, apart from him, only his family would occupy. Me and Jain Sahab accompanied Prem Nath ji to the make-up room which was then already being occupied by Chintu. The first thing he did was pick up Chintu's make-up material and other possessions and threw them out of the make-up room screaming, 'Bond, *humare* room *mein sirf hum aayenge, aur koi* municipality *nahin dikhna chahiye*!'

Bond instantly threw Jain Sahab and me out of the make-up room, '*Bhagwan ke* room *mein koi bhi bina* permission *liye nahi aa sakta*.'

Jain Sahab had a strange look of fear and humour mixed together on his face. I addressed Bond, 'Mr 007, please tell Bhagwan that two mortals have come to narrate the dialogue to him.' Bond sought permission and allowed us in.

Both of us stood there, though Jain Sahab's look was fixed with fear at the bathroom door. Prem Nath ji, sitting on the floor, commanded Jain Sahab to read the scene. The moment the narration finished, he turned to us, '*Abhi kya mere sar par khade rahoge*?' and he yanked me down pretty violently. He took a copy of the scene and rewrote the same on music notation sheet, but not in a line, words kept jumping up and down the lines, like musical notes do in a score, and he kept adding musical instructions, flat, sharp, treble, etc. He started playing the harmonium and reciting the scene over the score being played on the harmonium. Apparently, he was trying to fix the *sur* of the scene and the musical instructions were his cues for punctuation of the tone! A Kafkaesque scenario of prose being recited and played via notations on a music sheet!

While shooting, Raj Sahab was very patient with Prem Nath ji's antics, but there were times when he would get exasperated and tell us, 'I am so irritated that to spite him, I'm going to send Krishna, his sister who happens to be my wife, back to her *maike*.' Krishna Aunty was Prem Nath ji's elder sister and the only living human being that Prem Nath ji was scared of.

Once at a party, he was playing tabla on the bald head of a stalwart producer when somebody announced, 'Raj Sahab and Krishna ji have arrived.' He quickly grabbed his neighbour's plate full of food and started eating it himself. Krishna Aunty, who had already heard of his tabla session said, 'Prem, I heard that you're not behaving yourself.'

'No, no, these are all liars who want to malign me. You see, I am quietly eating my food and I'm leaving immediately.' He put down his plate, respectfully joined his hands and said goodnight to everybody, embraced his 'human tabla' and with a smile whispered, 'Municipality, when we meet again, I will again play the table on your bald head.'

While shooting *Bobby*, Raj Sahab had to pay very close attention to the newcomers as they constituted the driving force of the film. Chintu was easier for him to handle since acting was an inherent part of his genes which made him an unparalleled natural actor. He also understood perfectly what the director expected from his performance. A quality that elated Raj Sahab, who was very proud of his son.

Dimple needed more attention and care. He ran through her performance, coaching her about the nuances in the dialogue, expressions and movements to the extent of instructing her how her hands should be moving while speaking dialogues in a given scene. He had vowed to make her the best.

While shooting *Bobby*, he was very much aware that this was a teenage romance and required all moments that teenagers would actually go through.

He would often take me to town to watch an English film and would follow it with a high tea at Bombelli's on Warden Road. Bombelli's was the only Swiss café in Bombay and was frequented by youngsters. I gradually realized that the purpose of these visits was to observe the behaviour, manner of speaking and gestures of the youngsters of that time. He once told me to write a romantic scene wherein Raja took Bobby out to a café for a sandwich and a Coke. I was not a writer but he wanted me to write this out and even if he did not use the content, my approach to the scene might have inspired him to formulate a romantic scene in the film. This was one of the greatest assets that Raj Sahab deployed – to assimilate pertinent information about the life he wanted to portray in his films and use it to the best advantage in his brand of cinema.

BOBBY: EPISODE 2

WE WERE TO LEAVE for a 15-day shoot in Kashmir. All preparations were being made on a huge scale to fulfil the director's vision. What was surprising to the entire industry was that even though all Raj Sahab's permanent distributors had abandoned him, he was relentlessly going about his work in the same fashion as he always did.

One day, Sardar Vakil Singh ji walked into the studio with a revolver strapped in a holster on his waist. He was a one-time 'theatre representative' of very humble means and had come to acquire the distribution rights of *Bobby* for the territory of East Punjab. To get appointed as a distributor for a Raj Kapoor film was a huge prestigious step in life. Vakil Singh ji had contacted Manoj Kumar Sir and sought his advice on whether Raj Kapoor would entertain him or not.

Manoj Kumar Sir asked, 'Where are you staying in Bombay, Sardar ji?'

'Tip Top Hotel, near Naaz Cinema,' Vakil Singh ji replied.

'If you mention Tip Top Hotel, forget being appointed as a distributor, he will ask the watchmen to physically throw you out of the studio. You have to lie to him that you are staying at the Oberoi Hotel.'

Vakil Singh ji exclaimed, 'That's a very expensive hotel! What if he decides to visit me there?'

'Don't worry Sardar ji, it's very far from his studio and he will not travel that far.'

Vakil Singh ji met Raj Sahab and expressed his intent to be appointed as his distributor. The first thing Raj Sahab asked him was, 'Where are you staying?'

'At the Oberoi, Sir.'

Now came a 'bouncer' to knock Vakil Singh ji out, 'Great, I'm coming to town for a meeting and will drop in to see you at the Oberoi around 7 p.m. and we can discuss the details there.'

Vakil Singh ji, who was yet to get over the 'bouncer', lied again, 'Sir, from the airport, I came straight to the studio and haven't checked in as yet. I'm leaving for there now.'

Vakil Singh ji rushed to the Oberoi, checked into a room and bought a bottle of Black Label whisky for Boss.

The next afternoon, Vakil Singh ji had a meeting with Raj Sahab at four and he arrived with a bag and went into the cottage. Raj Sahab inquired, 'This morning I woke up early and called you as I wanted to readjust the appointment and I was told that you had already checked out last night itself. I was sure that our terms must not be suiting you and you must have left the city late at night. I was a little disappointed because I like you as a person and also judged you to be an honest man.'

Vakil Singh ji replied, 'Raj Sahab, I am not honest and have been lying to you since yesterday, but I think I need to be honest with you now. Actually, when I came to Bombay, I stayed at the Tip Top Hotel near Naaz Cinema, but I had been warned by Manoj Kumar Sir not to mention the truth, in case you asked. So, when you did ask, I had to lie. I rushed to the hotel at 4 p.m., checked into the room at 6.30 p.m., since you were arriving at 7 p.m., and checked out the moment you left at 10 p.m. That way I was charged only 30 per cent for using the room.'

Raj Sahab was not angry, as Vakil Singh ji expected, but had an emotional look on his face. He said, 'This statement of yours speaks volumes about your honesty.' And the first distribution agreement of *Bobby* was concluded.

The unit left Srinagar and Mama ji, Mohan Bali, had taken the responsibility for the travel of the unit. Though he was not there himself, he put us through a harrowing experience – we were chased by sickle bearing villagers, spent a night on a roadside and were almost arrested due to the mismanagement. We really missed our production controller, Om ji, who had passed away recently.

On reaching Srinagar, the tired and exhausted unit was put up in a hotel called the Boulevard, and, Raj Sahab, Chintu, Dimple and Radhu Sahab were staying on the beautiful Dal Lake in a luxurious houseboat. Khan Sahab was busy with some personal work in Bombay and in any case, whatever we shot in the outdoor would need to be dubbed. I had the privilege of staying in the houseboat, sharing Chintu's room, since Boss wanted me around for more effective communication with the unit. I narrated the harrowing journey we had gone through and Raj Sahab was extremely sympathetic and boiling in anger at Mama ji. He called the entire unit over for drinks and dinner and declared that the next day would be a holiday so that we could all relax and start work from the day after.

When we woke up the next day which happened to be an off, Chintu was all ready and said, 'Let's go. We are having lunch with Bunty and Sadiqa [Peerbhoy].'

Bunty Peerbhoy was a childhood buddy of mine and Chintu's and was in Srinagar for his honeymoon, but he had not imagined how his honeymoon would play out because of Chintu. After having lunch, the honeymoon couple said that they wanted to go sightseeing and Chintu was all ready to go with them. So, there was a honeymooning couple accompanied by two idiots, and Chintu spent more time with Bunty than poor Sadiqa. In the evening, we got back to the hotel and I had to discuss the next day's shooting schedule with Boss. He told me, 'Look, the two of you stop behaving like nerds. Bunty is here with his wife on their honeymoon and the couple needs to get to know each other, rather than they getting to know both of you. So, tonight don't disturb them!'

I had to say, 'Sir, Chintu did not come back to the houseboat with me, he went off with Bunty and Sadiqa to their houseboat and asked me to follow when I finished work with you.'

Over dinner, Bunty mentioned that he and Sadiqa would be visiting Gulmarg and Pahalgam. 'Great!' Chintu exclaimed, 'We are also going to these same places for shooting after Srinagar and Rahul will tie up our programme so that the four of us can have a wonderful time together.' I just cannot describe Bunty's and Sadiqa's expressions on hearing this.

Bunty called me at 5 a.m. to inquire when we would be going to Pahalgam as he was supposed to leave in three days' time. I warned him that these were the same dates that we were supposed to go and his immediate reaction was, 'Then we will leave for Gulmarg instead.'

The next day, we started shooting; I think it was at the Nishat Bagh where, lo and behold, we met Bunty and Sadiqa! Raj Sahab realized that things were not fair for the two of them and advised them to go to other locations which were very beautiful and there would not be much of a crowd, and Chintu definitely would not be there!

Anyway, we shot all day and, in the evening, Chintu again said, 'Come on, let's go meet Bunty.'

I said, 'Chintu, stop it! Leave them alone.'

He replied, 'No no, we have to go or Bunty will really be upset with us.'

So, we two, *kebab mein haddis*, landed up at Bunty's houseboat. He was very happy since he was leaving for

Gulmarg the next day and we would be in Pahalgam from the day after. They, our childhood buddy and his new wife, were delighted to finally get rid of us.

The shoot for the next day was erratic since it started raining in Srinagar and we were also informed that the rain was very heavy in Pahalgam, leaving us no alternative but to go to Gulmarg and unleash Chintu on Bunty and Sadiqa.

While driving up to Gulmarg in the freezing cold, we stopped at Tangmarg so that the unit could be fitted with overcoats and gloves to fight the cold. I was standing in a corner and had lit a cigarette. Raj Sahab walked up to me from behind and said, 'I hope the weather is clear in Gulmarg tomorrow.'

My brain had stopped functioning in the cold and with a cigarette dangling from my lips I turned around to him and said, 'I'm sure it will be, Sir.'

He turned away from me and carried on with the conversation. It was his maturity that he understood that I had forgotten about the cigarette and he did not want me to get embarrassed. I, with a frostbitten brain, did not realize that I was smoking in his presence.

We were staying in Gulmarg at the Highland Park Hotel. Bunty and Sadiqa were also staying there and when we reached Gulmarg late at night, Chintu proudly ran to their room, knocked on the door and screamed, 'Surprise! Surprise!'

The next morning at the shoot, Bunty and Sadiqa came to greet Raj Sahab who was very embarrassed with the behaviour of his son and his assistant. He tried finding different excuses to send Bunty and Sadiqa to other spots where they could spend quality time alone but they sat with us at the shoot. I asked Bunty, 'Look, Boss is also trying to get you and Sadiqa away from us. Why don't you just go?'

He turned around furiously and replied, 'You two guys have stuck to me like fucking leeches and screwed up my honeymoon. I don't want to leave you guys and go because knowing both of you, you'll find me. That's why I'm going to spend the entire day with you and go away in the morning, and please don't ask me where we are going because I won't tell you.'

Raj Sahab invited the two of them to have drinks and dinner with the unit in his suite. Raj Sahab, while talking to them, got into his favourite conversation, films. Bunty and Sadiqa were engrossed with this conversation and completely struck by him.

Bunty noted this incident in his diary:

It was September 1972. I had just got married and me and my wife, Sadiqa, were in Kashmir for our honeymoon.

Bobby *was being shot there and my childhood friends, Chintu, the hero of the film, and Rahul, an assistant director to Raj Uncle, were also there.*

Needless to say, we spent almost all our time together, not me and my newly wedded wife but two childhood buddies who unknowingly ruined my honeymoon!

We met Raj Uncle in Gulmarg and he congratulated us and we were promptly invited to dinner in his suite.

On reaching his suite, where Raj Uncle was sitting regally on a sofa, with his entire cast and crew, including both Chintu and Rahul, sitting in a circle around him. As soon as he saw us, he waved us forward and made us sit right in front of him. Very unnerving.

Raj Uncle was extremely warm and welcoming. He insisted that we have a drink. I was hesitant as I had never had a drink or smoked a cigarette in his presence out of respect for him, but he simply insisted and himself poured me a whisky and Sadiqa wine, and thereafter the most incredible and amazing evening gradually unfolded.

That entire evening, going late into the night, he spent just talking to Sadiqa and me as though no one else existed in the room and we were the most important people in his life that evening.

He spoke about his past films and his dream of making a film about a beautiful woman with one part of her face burned, thus disfigured, representing the beauty of the soul versus the body. The inspiration came from his obsession with Lata Mangeshkar's voice. This went on to finally become Satyam Shivam Sundaram.

He also spoke about an idea based around 'Ramcharitmanas' written by the sage Tulsidas, and had also composed a song, 'Sun sahiba sun, pyaar ki dhun'!

It was sheer magic hearing his thoughts about cinema and recitation of two ideas that he had for future films.

Sheer magic. We were completely mesmerized. One of the most amazing experiences of my life.

Shooting in Gulmarg taught me how Raj Sahab translated his thoughts into visuals, no matter how much time, effort or money it cost him. In the song, '*Hum tum ek kamre mein band ho*', there was a 'call' in Bobby's voice post the words, '*hum tum kahin ko ja rahe hon aur rasta bhool jayein*'. This call was recorded much before the shooting of the song, but to justify the words, he had to have the right four-path intersection with a beautiful background. He spent over half a day finding it and finally zeroed in on a perfect location.

In all the shooting that was done in Gulmarg, he made it a point that the natural beauty of the location always stood out.

The interval point of *Bobby* was outside the hut where Raja and Bobby are locked, and they walk out arm in arm, to the music of the song playing in the background. The lovers walking out holding hands, lost to the world, unaware of the opposition which lies ahead. This shot was distinctly one of the most, or I would say, the most powerful visual in the entire film and rightfully deserved the preparation to highlight on-screen the brilliant conception of a scene by Raj Kapoor.

The location that Raj Sahab had picked happened to be the exterior of a room in the Highland Park Hotel, directly overlooking the bedroom window of Boss's room. Raj Sahab started explaining, 'Okay Radhu, there will be a series of shots which will show Chintu and Dimple walking away, and I first require a "master shot" of the camera on a trolley, running parallel with them. I need a 100 feet of trolley track and as the track runs out the camera will pan and we'll see them walking, back to the camera, to give the impression that they are walking towards infinity. The title "Interval" will be superimposed as they are diminishing within the frame. I will use three intercuts to enhance the visual experience.'

The trolley was laid out and Bapu Dada needed time to lay the track and level the same. Radhu Sahab was arranging the reflectors and arc lights for the shot. The moment the arrangements were completed, Raj Sahab gave his instructions to Chintu and Dimple, and after making them run through a couple of rehearsals, he was satisfied that they were holding hands the way he desired and the nuances and movements were up to his satisfaction. As always, he wanted to see a rehearsal, through the lens, so that he himself was satisfied that the coordination between the actors and the movement resonated with the visual that he wanted the audience to see. He kept seeing rehearsals repeatedly and finally said, 'Radhu, there is one thing missing...colours! The shot requires an explosion of colours. The entire ambience should seem like the whole world is smiling down upon the lovers. The visual needs to be more colourful. Let's get some flowers and as the camera is trolleying, we should arrange an array of flowers in the foreground so that we see them engulfed with colours, which symbolizes the bubble of love they are in but when they walk towards infinity, with their backs to the camera, the colours reduce, which in turn symbolizes that they are now heading for turmoil in their love story.'

We set out in search of fresh flowers in Gulmarg, but were told that there is no nursery or bazaar where colourful flowers are sold and at best, we would have to go to Srinagar and source them from the flower market there.

Raj Sahab made up his mind to leave immediately for Srinagar and he himself wanted to source the different colours that he required. This was at about 12 in the afternoon. Srinagar was two hours away and our local driver said, 'Sir, the best time to go to get flowers is 6 a.m. when the flower bazaar opens and the flowers are the freshest.' So, Raj Sahab said, 'Okay. Rahul, you and I are going tomorrow morning. We'll leave here at 4 a.m., reach there at 6 a.m., pick up the flowers and come back by noon and start shooting straight away.'

So, I went with him and he handpicked the flowers himself. We were told that the flowers would stay fresh for two days as long as water is sprinkled on them at regular intervals. We came back to Gulmarg with fresh handpicked flowers.

We got back and Raj Sahab started arranging the flowers. A plank of wood was placed parallel to the long trolley track. Now, Raj Sahab started looking through the camera and placing every flower, individually, keeping their distance between each other, colour-coordinating them and placing them on various levels according to what looked best through the lens of the camera. 'So, this is a red flower, follow this with a carnation, followed by a lily…' He had to make sure that the flowers did not distract viewers' attention from the faces of the actors. He did this till every single flower was placed in its precise position. The process took about three hours and the sun had gone down and thus we had lost shooting light.

Raj Sahab said, 'No problem, we'll shoot it tomorrow morning. Please have the unit ready on location, no later than 10 a.m., and have a setting boy stay up all night and sprinkle water on the flowers so that the fresh look is not lost.'

Radhu Sahab said, 'Raj Sahab, this shot is looking so pretty; the best time to shoot this is between 6.30 a.m. and 7.00 a.m. when the sun is at the correct angle. That's the best time to really get the colour of these flowers.'

Now, we had not shot for two days and that was a huge expense. Of course that didn't bother him and his only reaction was, 'Radhu has finally lost his mind! Shoot at 6.30 a.m.? It's insane but I'll have to do it. Now all of you are aware that we've rehearsed this shot plenty of times. Rahul, everyone should be on location at 6 a.m. Get Chintu and Dimple to rehearse again and when they are absolutely ready, wake me up.'

So, in the morning, at sharp 6 a.m., we rehearsed and were ready to shoot. I went into his room at about 6.30 a.m. and he was sleeping. I went up to his bed and even though I was scared, I woke him up. He stretched out, 'Oh...are we ready?'

I said, 'Yes, rehearsals are done.'

He was still lying down and cribbing, 'Radhu Karmakar has gone mad. *Yeh koi* time *hai* shooting *karne ka*?' He sat up on his bed and opened the window. The location was exactly outside his window. Sitting up on the bed, he looked out and said, '*Chalo,* rehearsal *dikhao*.'

He made small adjustments during the rehearsals and called for a take. He went through a couple of takes and finally being satisfied, he was beaming and said, 'Great shot!

Exactly as I wanted. So, pack up, we've done enough for today', and he went back to sleep! Two days of only arranging a shot and packing up on the third day at 7 a.m. was only possible for a man who had *junoon*, divine madness, for his film.

BOBBY: EPISODE 3

WHEN WE FINISHED OUR schedule in Gulmarg, we came back to Srinagar and had a three-day shoot before we went to Pahalgam. The night before we were to leave for Pahalgam, Raj Sahab called me to his room and he was in a very bad mood, 'You are aware that the unit has to be ready to leave at 6 a.m. and I will not hear any excuses for their not being ready on time as lately I have been seeing that you have no sense of responsibility and my whole schedule is getting delayed because of your incompetence.'

I couldn't understand why he felt like this, but realized that he was angry about something else and taking it out on me. Knowing him, it had to be connected to his actors.

'You are not paying attention to your work and because of you, Chintu and Dimple cannot remember their lines!'

I replied, 'I'm sorry, Sir, I have been doing my best, but I can't force them to remember lines.'

'What do you mean you can't force them?' And he went on to explain how Chintu and Dimple had behaved irresponsibly in the last scene we had shot. I was the scapegoat who bore the brunt of his anger and was expected to make his resentment clear to both Chintu and Dimple. I just stood there, with my eyes downcast, and finally, at 5 a.m., he screamed, 'Now get out of my room! Let me rest!'

I immediately called up the unit at the Boulevard hotel and informed them Boss had just gone to sleep so we would not be leaving at 6 a.m. I came to my room, Chintu had just woken up. I vented my anger on Chintu, 'Because of you and Dimple being irresponsible, he has fired the hell out of me. It's 5.15 a.m., he's thrown me out of the room and just gone to sleep.'

Chintu, not showing any remorse for his irresponsibility or for his 'childhood friend' being grilled all night, responded in a strange way, 'Good, that means we're not leaving at six.' Saying that he got back into his blanket to sleep again.

Even I dozed off and suddenly, Revati ji came bursting into the room, '*Arre*, Rahul Sahab, *aap log so rahe hain*? Raj Sahab Pahalgam *ke liye nikal gaye*.'

I ran out of the room onto the deck and saw him in a shikara proceeding towards Boulevard hotel. Chintu and I were bewildered; we woke up Dimple and rushed out. I was in a huge hurry because I didn't want to give him another chance to be angry at me.

When we reached Boulevard hotel, I saw Raj Sahab in a bus, leaving us and other unit members, including Kala ji, who were not ready.

'The unit members including the actors who are not ready don't deserve to be in an RK film and I am terminating their services right now. I will complete the film without them.' This is what he had said to the manager of the hotel.

My first thought on hearing this was to jump into the Dal Lake and drown myself as I had screwed up very badly by informing the unit that they could relax as Boss would not be ready to leave at 6 a.m.

I knew that he had planned to shoot in the Avantipur ruins, on the way to Pahalgam. I got hold of our taxi driver and begged him to see to it that we reached Avantipur before Boss who already had a 15-minute lead over us. The driver drove at the speed at which people drive in F1 racing competitions, but the fear of the drive was less than the fear of the wrath of

Boss. We overtook the bus just before we reached Avantipur. When Boss got down from the bus, he was shocked to see Chintu, Dimple and me, waiting.

He gave me a dirty look and asked, 'When did you get here?'

'Thirty minutes before you, Sir.'

He kept staring unbelievably and came up with a very feeble excuse, 'I can't shoot without Kala. In fact, I'm going to abandon the film and stop making films since I'm going to throw Kala off the cliff myself!'

As we entered Pahalgam, we saw the most amazing sight. Kala ji was coming out of a barbershop, clean-shaven and with a huge smile on his face. The bus stopped, Raj Sahab came out, stared at Kala ji, then turned towards me, Chintu and Dimple. Without saying a word, he just angrily started walking away towards the hotel. I asked Kala ji, 'How come you reached before the bus?'

Kala ji, reeking with alcohol that he must have consumed the night before, spoke with a triumphant smile, 'Mr Rahul Rawail, S. Kalachandra has superpowers which even Raj Kapoor does not have.'

Anyway, no shooting happened that day and the same format of 'no shooting' followed the day after and the day after that as well. It had been three days and we hadn't shot a single scene. Then on the fourth day, Raj Sahab told me, 'Aren't you ashamed? Three days of no shooting at such a huge expense. I will take about two hours to get ready; there is that small scene in the bus, which you can handle and shoot while I get ready.' I was very excited and happy to be entrusted with this responsibility, and was somewhere hoping that the rest of the schedule would be handled by me and even imagined myself shooting the other scenes. This is a live example of 'counting your chickens before they are hatched'!

After I returned (triumphant, feeling like Alexander must have felt when he conquered the world), we started shooting in the bazaar; I was grounded as I was back to my job as an assistant director. Manmohan Desai Sir was a surprise visitor and came up to Raj Sahab to pay his respects. 'I am here to scout locations for my film, *Roti*. I'm staying at the Pahalgam hotel,' he added.

Raj Sahab replied, 'I, too, am staying there. Can you give me a ride to the hotel, as I need to have my medicines which are lying there?'

He turned to us, 'I'll just go and come back in a jiffy.' He went but didn't return! After about 45 minutes, I wondered what the problem was; nobody seemed to know and I were worried about him. Radhu Sahab and I rushed to the hotel. We found him, sitting in a lounging chair, sipping champagne with Manmohan Desai Sir. He saw my surprised face and said, 'Why are you surprised? I'm celebrating Manmohan coming here. He's my old friend and I acted in his debut film, *Chhalia*. Sipping the champagne, he started singing, the iconic song of *Chhalia*, "*Dum dum digga digga, mausam bhiga bhiga, bin piye main toh gira...*".' By this time, these two iconic pillars of the Indian film industry were high on champagne, furiously dancing, oblivious to a small crowd of hotel guests cheering them; and as they sang the line, '*Bin piye main to gira*', they both actually fell down!

Again, the shooting for the day got cancelled. The next day it suddenly started snowing, which meant 'no shooting' again. But Raj Sahab was in the best of spirits, he said, 'Look, most of the unit members may have only heard of the snow and never seen it. You know, it makes me happy, Rahul, to be instrumental in their witnessing this phenomenon. Wonderful feeling, let's have a party!'

A party was arranged where the entire unit let their hair down and really enjoyed themselves, not that they hadn't similarly enjoyed themselves on other 'no shooting' days as well!

At night, he asked, 'Is it snowing still?'

'Yes,' I replied, 'Can't we shoot a small portion of a song in the snow; we can't afford to waste so much time. How many days have we not shot? It's so expensive.'

He explained, 'Look, Rahul, when I've cancelled shooting, it's because I simply didn't want to shoot. I will only shoot on days I want to. If I don't feel like shooting, I will not shoot. This is the way I make films. Cinema is a creative process and creativity is not ruled by day, date or money. It should be a lesson for every director, if your mind is not working, you will mess up your film.'

We shot in the snow, and once the snow abated, we shot again for two consecutive days. On the third day, when I went to wake Raj Sahab up, he woke up and said, 'Isn't it Dussehra today?'

'Yes, it is,' I confirmed.

He said, '*Tum Dussehre pe mujhse kaam karva rahe ho? Dussehre pe kaam thodi karte hain*! It's an auspicious day, we should be celebrating.' So, we celebrated Dussehra and once again 'no shooting'!

The end result was that we spent 34 days in Kashmir but ended up shooting only for 16 days. We did not shoot for 3 days because of bad weather, and did not shoot for another 15 days but partied. The expenses were way beyond the budget but there was no point in explaining economics to Boss.

At the end of the shooting in Kashmir, I had to stay back for two days to settle all the bills and had the pleasure of getting back to Bombay by flight. After having travelled in third class of Janta Express and a harrowing road journey earlier, this was blissful. Raj Sahab and Krishna Aunty were to go back to Delhi but they wanted to stop over and pay their respects at the Vaishno Devi Temple in Katra.

When he got back to Bombay, after his Katra and Delhi trip, he said, 'This was my first trip to Vaishno Devi and to enter the sanctum sanctorum, one has to crawl under a rock, which left me terrified as the crawl was a very claustrophobic experience. On entering the sanctum sanctorum, I was engulfed with an ethereal feeling and had a tear running down my face as I bowed in reverence. This was an extremely profound experience. I'm not a very religious man but I do go and pay my respects at all religious institutions irrespective of caste or creed. Generally, visits to such blessed institutions have always had a profound effect on me.

'I just had one problem at Vaishno Devi that was the claustrophobic experience that engulfed me and has deferred a lot of other pilgrims, who have returned after seeing the mouth of the cave and the tiny area through which they have to crawl. I have spoken to Mrs Gandhi [she was the prime minister at that time] and requested her to have an entrance via which devotees could walk through comfortably, and as for the devotees who believe the crawling to be an essential part of their pilgrimage, they could use the existing entrance.'

This conversation with Raj Sahab had resulted in the government carving out a comfortable walk-through to the sanctum sanctorum.

This was in tandem with his philosophy, 'Cinema is akin to a religion; it gives you peace and satisfaction and requires the same amount of devotion. However, one should not create hurdles for a human in the way of attaining this blessing. That is exactly why I have always tried to ensure that my cinema also leaves a pleasant taste for the audience and attracts them to revisit the film whenever they need solace.'

After the Kashmir schedule, the borrowed money and insane compounded interest had grown to an unfathomable amount and would grow further as the film was only half complete.

I knew people, I can name them but choose not to as they are creatures who need sympathy, who had rejoiced in the fact that *Mera Naam Joker* did not do well, '*Arre mubarak ho yaar,* Raj Kapoor *ki* film flop *ho gayi.*'

'*Wo zindagi mein* film *nahin bana sakega*!'

The same people, now that Raj Kapoor had already shot half the film and was planning the next schedule, started taking potshots at him with a new tirade. This was the sick tribe that still exist, who have strange sadism in their DNA. They are happier with another's failure than their own success.

'Raj Kapoor is demanding 12 lakh for a territory!'

'He has gone senile!'

'He is a flop filmmaker and will never get that kind of money!'

Much to their dismay, 'he got it'!

His old distributors – who if you ask me were shameless – had made so much money off his films. Once *Mera Naam Joker* didn't do well, they abandoned him, but different people started coming forward to acquire the distribution rights. After Vakil Singh ji, it was Shashi Kapoor, who believed in Raj Kapoor's magic, and bought the Delhi and UP distribution rights of *Bobby*. Other enterprising individuals also made a beeline at RK to get associated as distributors for the balance territories.

Krishna Aunty was ecstatic that all the Indian territories had found distributors and she attributed this miracle to the blessing that her husband received due to his pilgrimage to Vaishno Devi.

Raj Sahab smiled and said, 'This is her faith and the same faith is the foundation of hope for a lot of people. I completely respect the faith that people have in their religion, but for me, the religion that spurns my faith is "cinema".'

BOBBY: EPISODE 4

Our schedule on our return was to shoot the remaining portion of the song, '*Hum tum ek kamre mein band ho*', which was to be shot on a set. For the lines, '*hum tum ek jungle se guzrein aur sher aa jaye*', Boss required a tiger, along with Chintu and Dimple, to justify the lyrics! A tiger was brought from Gemini Circus and was to be released from its cage as soon as the shot was ready. The tiger was accordingly let out of the cage; the song playback blaring through the speaker. A whistle was blown at the end of the shot, a signal for the playback song to be switched off, but suddenly the tiger jumped behind the background screen and disappeared, while the song carried on playing.

We were all frozen in fear. The circus attendants jumped behind the background screen and discovered the tiger sitting calmly in front of the playback machine with a terrified playback operator a stone's throw away from it, who had literally pissed in his pants! The circus attendants got hold of the tiger and said, 'All okay!'

Suddenly, we heard Raj Sahab's distant voice, 'Are you guys sure?'

We looked towards his voice and saw him at the top of the staircase, near the lights, with a revolver in his hand. At that point, we realized that he had walked onto the set with the revolver in his pocket. It reminded me of a day during the shoot of *Mera Naam Joker*, where we were all standing around the lion's cage shooting stray shots of the lions when a young cub scrambled up the cage and jumped out. We just did not know how to react and the cub ran away to the back of the circus and we saw Raj Sahab sitting in the uppermost stand with a revolver in his hand. I guess these were the only two moments when he had 'drawn his gun'!

The introductory scene of Prem Nath ji was to be filmed in a trawler in the open sea. We had organized a trawler that could take us from Versova to Madh Island so that we could shoot the introduction on the trawler and the rest of the day at the Madh Island itself. There was just one hitch; we had to set sail at 6 a.m., as the high tide would set in at 7.30 a.m. making stability difficult on the trawler.

Raj Sahab hated the idea of starting shooting that early and lamented the fact that we had made Prem Nath ji's character a fisherman, we should have rather made him a truck driver!

To save time and eliminate the long drive from Chembur to Versova, he decided, '*Main ek kaam karta hun*, I'll go stay the night at Prem's shack. This way I'll get half an hour more to sleep. Call Revati 10 minutes before you reach the shack and I'll be ready and so will Prem.'

As we were arriving at the shack, I tried calling Revati ji but the line was defective. I got worried that we would be late and miss the slot for shooting, but, 'man proposes, God disposes'.

Standing at the gate was Raj Sahab with a shawl wrapped around his head, and Prem Nath ji sitting and finding the *sur* of the scene on his harmonium! Raj Sahab's face was red and he didn't seem well. I inquired, 'Do you have a cold, Sir?'

His thundering reply was, 'I'm lucky I didn't die. Last night, Prem and I were having a drink in the hall and it started raining. He immediately instructed James Bond, the idiot, to put two chairs at a table in the heavy rain and insisted that we sit in the rain all night. When I pleaded with him to come inside, he said, "Okay then, we go to our rooms and sleep. We will shoot whenever I wake up." I had no alternative but to sit up all night. Have you realized I have been ranting at the top of my voice for the last 10 minutes, and the only effect it has had on Mr Braganza here is that his singing has got louder!'

Luckily, it stopped raining in time for us to board the trawler and the weather stayed dry till we finished the scene. By this time, Raj Sahab was looking really unwell, and it also started raining heavily, so he decided to cancel the rest of the day. He sat in the car with Prem Nath ji, with me sitting in front, and told the driver to drop Prem Nath ji at his shack.

'Stop the car! I need to pee!' Prem Nath ji screamed.

Raj Sahab tried to explain to him, 'Prem it's raining very heavily. If you get down, you will become sick like me. So just hold on, your shack is just 15 minutes away.'

The banter continued with Prem Nath ji insisting that the car should stop so that he could relieve himself and Raj Sahab requesting him to hold on; during this time, the car reached the gate of the shack.

Raj Sahab said, 'Go in quickly and pee your heart out.'

'Too late, I can't wait any longer.'

We had finished the shoot in Kashmir and the edit of the same, and started preparing for the next schedule in Pune. Suddenly, one evening Raj Sahab said, 'I don't like that one scene so tomorrow morning we go back to shoot that scene again.' The next morning, he left with just Chintu, Dimple, Radhu Sahab and a very skeletal unit. They were back after four days and the scene was edited, but now he preferred what he had shot earlier and it finally came back into the film. The second trip to Kashmir turned out to be an 'all expenses paid' holiday for the actors and the skeletal unit.

We left for Pune to shoot the camp scenes where the girls were supposed to be staying. This was the location where the song '*Beshak mandir masjid todo*' was also filmed.

When we left Bombay for Pune, we had no idea where this location that would match Kashmir would be, but Raj Sahab with his elephant's memory drove us straight to a spot in the jungle outside the NDA in Khadakwasla.

On reaching the location, I was amazed how it was wooded, had greenery all around and hills in the background making it a perfect match for Kashmir. I asked him, 'When did you see this, Sir?'

'About four years back,' he replied.

'Wow! So, four years back you had decided on a location that would match Kashmir!'

'No, Rahul. When I had driven past this place, it had appealed to me as a picturesque location and that image was filed in my memory. When I came to a point where I needed to match Kashmir, I mentally went through the catalogue of locations stored in my mind and pulled out the best match.' He looked around and added, 'I have to take care that no overhead electric wires or any other installations are seen. A director is also an illusionist and the illusion that he creates is what the audience sees.'

After the Pune schedule, Raj Sahab was going to Delhi for a couple of days and had left instructions with me to start organizing the dates of the actors for the climax shoot of *Bobby*. I thought I should first confirm the dates with Prem Nath ji and then tie in Pran Sahab's dates accordingly. Prem Nath ji happened to be shooting for Mohan Kumar ji's film, *Amir Garib* at Mehboob Studios.

As I entered the gate of Mehboob Studios, I realized there were four shootings happening there on that day. I saw a huge crowd of unit members, junior artists and actors from all the units, collected on the periphery of the lawn, blocking my view. I met Salim Sahab and Javed Akhtar Sahab, my first meeting with them, who were rolling in splits of laughter as they said, 'Make your way through the crowd, it is a sight that you will never see.'

I managed to push myself to the front and saw Prem Nath ji, relaxing in a lungi and a kurta in the centre of the lawn. It happened to be peak summertime and there were huge buckets of ice water that were being constantly replenished by James Bond. The 'Commander' kept pouring the ice water on his head with a mug and was deeply engrossed in reading the *Illustrated Weekly of India*, a very famous bi-monthly at that time, which happened to be only seven months old! Prem Nath ji even used to read newspapers that were about four days old. I did not have the guts to go up and speak to him lest he makes me hold the mug and pour cold water on myself.

I got back home and was desperate to narrate this incident to Chintu and the unit the next day, but fate had decided a different path.

At 2.30 a.m., I was woken up as Chintu walked in. He was very mellow. I made him a drink and to cheer him up, narrated my encounter with Prem Nath ji. His expression did not change as though he had not heard a word of what I had said, and spoke, '*Bobby* is in trouble, my friend. Dimple is getting married to Rajesh Khanna!'

I was dumbstruck; Chintu added, 'Chunnibhai invited me for dinner to his house, Kaka [Rajesh Khanna] with a couple of his cronies walked in at around 11.30 p.m.; hugs were exchanged all around and one of the cronies addressed Dimple as "bhabhi ji". Rahul, what flashed before my eyes was that my father's film is a teenage love story and the heroine is going to be married. How badly would this affect Dad's film, my debut? Papa does not know about it as yet; he is coming back from Delhi tomorrow afternoon. I have not spoken about this to anybody and won't until you break this news to him when he lands.'

The whole of next day I was in a quandary as to how I would tell Raj Sahab. I was at the airport to receive him. He saw me there and said, 'This is the first time you have come to receive me at the airport so my deduction is that either there is some great news that you want to tell me or the news you have for me is quite disastrous. However, from your trembling lips and pale face, I know that what you have to say is not—'

'Dimple is getting married to Rajesh Khanna,' I blurted.

There was a momentary silence, a smile followed and this was further followed by laughter, 'Raj Kapoor presents "a teenage love story" starring Rishi Kapoor and Dimple Kapadia, the would-be wife of India's biggest star. Hahahaha!'

As we drove into the studio, Rajesh Khanna and Dimple were waiting at the gate of the cottage. Raj Sahab got off and went into the cottage. I don't know what transpired in there. After they came out, he said, 'They came to tell me they're getting married and they want to do it quick. So, I've taken the responsibility of getting them married in the next three days. If they want to do it quick, let me help them do it quicker. I will have all the arrangements made and the wedding will be on 27 March. Rahul, you start making arrangements for shooting the song '*Mujhe kuch kehna hai*' from 29 March in Pune.'

I asked, 'Sir, *shaadi* Tuesday *ko hogi aur hum* Thursday *ko* outdoor *nikal jayenge*?'

He said, '*Haan, ek baar unki shaadi ho gayi to mujhe bhi to apni* film *complete karni hai*.'

So, Rajesh Khanna and Dimple got married on 27 March. Raj Sahab made meticulous and royal arrangements supervising every aspect of the wedding himself, and we left for the outdoor shooting in Pune early morning on the 29th.

The wife of a friend of Rajesh Khanna was Dimple's chaperone and when Dimple came on the set, Raj Sahab called me and said, 'Thank God, they had the good sense of not having the mehndi up to the elbow as most brides do. It is on the palms only and I'll have to manage so that it doesn't show in the song.'

If you see the song, you will not see the mehndi except in one shot, where it is barely visible. Raj Sahab managed to conceal it by shooting cleverly around her. He called up J.P. Singhal, who was designing the posters, and said, 'Replace "Teenage Love Story" with "Love Sublime – Filmed by Raj Kapoor".'

He turned to me and said, 'We now have to finish this film at the earliest!'

BOBBY: EPISODE 5

WE WERE NOW MOVING towards the fag end of *Bobby*'s shooting – the climax. The climax sequence involved Chintu and Dimple eloping and the parents – Pran Sahab chasing them with cops and Prem Nath ji giving chase to the lovers on his own.

Raj Sahab had decided on three locations over which the shooting would be spread – the first chase would start in the Igatpuri Ghats, second at the Shivanasamudra power plant in Karnataka, where the water rushing out of the turbines would be ideal to shoot controlled shots of the actors supposedly being carried away by the fury of a waterfall, and the third at the Hogenakkal Falls in Tamil Nadu. This would all be blended to seem like one area on-screen.

The shoot commenced in Igatpuri and after the first day of shooting, we proceeded to spend the night at Nashik, where he said, 'This location is not exciting, there are much better places in Pune.' So next day, we shifted the whole unit to Pune. He wanted to go via Shirdi so that the entire unit could offer their obeisance at Sai Baba's temple.

We decided to shoot at Katraj Ghats, just outside of Pune, where there was a restaurant at the bottom of the ghats in which Prem Chopra ji's introduction was shot; Raj Sahab himself coined the phrase, 'Prem *naam hai mera*, Prem Chopra!' This phrase turned out to be iconic. We shot extensively there and at a much faster pace, since we couldn't afford any delay as we wanted to complete and release the film as soon as possible.

After finishing the shoot at Katraj Ghats we proceeded towards Bangalore and Mysore, where the 'Bobby' motorcycle – a cute small motorcycle that was manufactured by Escorts especially for the film and was sold commercially after the release of the film – was used in the chase over the rough terrain at the virgin location of Ramnagaram. This later became the location where *Sholay* would be shot. After the release, the 'Bobby' motorcycle, along with Chintu and Dimple, attained 'celebrity status' and was a huge success with the common man.

Then finally we drove to Hogenakkal, an hour and a half away from Bangalore, and camped at the site adjacent to the falls.

Shooting continued but we had started lagging in pace as the heat was intense. There was a shot in the climax, where Chintu and Dimple jump off the cliff into the water. Though the jump was shot with duplicates who jumped off from a great height, we still needed close-ups of Chintu and Dimple off the ledge prior to the jump. Chintu and Dimple had to jump from a rock, only 2½-feet high, and land on sand, thus posing no threat.

I went up to Dimple and explained the instructions Raj Sahab had for her, 'You and Chintu are standing here holding hands, and as Raj Sahab calls "three", you will both jump off. You don't have to worry, it's a very minor height and there is only sand below, so, it's 100 per cent safe.'

Dimple replied, 'Rahul, I won't do this shot.'

I asked, 'You're scared of a 2½-feet jump?'

She said, 'No, I'm not scared but I won't do this shot because I'm pregnant!'

Now, that was the most devastating thing I'd heard. I told her, 'In a unit of 250 people, I'm the only person you found this to tell to?' She did not reply and just went and sat on a chair, next to her chaperone. Now, I did not know what to do in this situation and was completely perplexed how I would break the news to Boss.

I was standing and staring into oblivion when Raj Sahab, who was sitting at a distance, called out, 'Rahul, what happened?' I walked up to him, my heart pounding, and he asked, 'You were saying something to Dimple, she replied and went away and sat on the chair, and since then you are looking like you've seen a ghost. Tell me, what's happened?'

I hesitantly replied, 'Sir, she refused to do this shot because she's pregnant.'

He did not react, just kept looking into space with a wry smile. He suddenly stood up and announced loudly, 'Pack-up!' The unit guys were pretty shocked since it was only around 3 p.m., and the only person who had no reaction to this was Dimple. He turned to the unit and said, 'I'm feeling unwell so I'm going back to the dak bungalow. You guys have a picnic, enjoy yourselves and we'll have drinks together in the evening. I'm just taking Rahul with me to discuss about the shooting.'

Radhu Sahab and the rest of the unit immediately understood that there was some major problem and he wanted to be left alone at the dak bungalow.

As we sat in the car, he sounded hurt, 'This is very irresponsible behaviour. I wish people realized my state. I am shooting a "teenage love story" and have wagered all my material possessions and my family's entire future and reputation on this one film. Everything in my life is at stake.' There was pin-drop silence and tears welled up in my eyes. Looking at me, he said, 'Beta, this is a further lesson and an important one for you to remember. When you will direct a film, you may come across such a situation where you can't afford to scrap the film and feel surrounded by desperation.

Never surrender your arms but prepare yourself to fight this battle and emerge victorious. If your intentions are honourable, the solution will definitely find its way into your heart. Go home, have a drink, and think that your dream and honest hard work is on a funeral pyre which has just been lit; a deluge of rain will not let the fire rise!'

We reached the dak bungalow, he went in for a shower, came out and, though it was slightly early in the day, poured himself a drink. He said, 'You have to organize things. Call Bombay, I need Pran Sahab and Prem within the next four days. We have two cameras, ask the studio to send us two more along with focus pullers for both.' The list of requirements became quite long as he had also planned a second unit shoot to speed up the shooting.

I was dispatched to make arrangements. The telephone closest to the location was at a drive of over an hour and a half away. By the time I got through to Bombay on a lightning call – which proved to be anything but, because by the time I drove back it was two in the morning.

He was still awake, sitting with Radhu Sahab and nursing the first drink he had poured himself a few hours earlier, whilst the rest of the unit had all gone to sleep. As soon as I entered, he asked, 'When will the additional cameras and crew arrive?'

I said, 'They'll be here tomorrow afternoon.'

He replied, 'I don't want this news to spread. Call off the shooting tomorrow, tell the unit we're not shooting because of the heat. We need to plan how the two units will operate.'

After some discussion, he decided that Mansoor Bhai, the fight master, would handle the second unit with duplicates and fighters. The new assistant, Kuku Kohli, who had come on board just before the climax shoot, would assist the second unit, and I would assist Raj Sahab on the first unit shooting portions of Chintu and Dimple before Pran Sahab and Prem Nath ji arrived four days later.

The shooting was now being done at breakneck speed, and even Raj Sahab would be on the set at seven in the morning. It was exhausting but we had finished practically all the work. After four days, Pran Sahab and Prem Nath ji arrived and we had to get both the units together to finish all the work involving the actors.

The morning of the shoot, I saw Prem Nath ji walking towards the location in his full costume, sans the jacket which was an integral part of his costume throughout the entire film. I called for the jacket and it was not ironed. I lost my head at the costume supervisor as to why he did not have the jacket ready, he retorted, 'Kuku *ne bola* climax *mein nahin dene ka hai to maine nahin diya.*'

Kuku Kohli pulled me aside, away from earshot, and said sheepishly, 'I'm sorry, I took it for granted that the jacket would not be required in the action scene.'

I was really angry, 'Are you fucking insane? After shooting the entire action sequence, do you expect us to re-shoot it because you behaved like an imbecile?'

Kuku, very repentant, said, '*Arre yaar galti ho gayi.* Raj Sahab *toh khoon kar denge mera. Mujhe bacha le* Rahul!'

They'd shot the whole climax with Prem Nath ji's duplicate without the jacket!

I was completely at sea and could not understand how we would get over this expensive mistake that Kuku had made. To evade the problem temporarily, I told Kuku, 'Don't talk about this to anybody. Don't even mention it! Let's carry on shooting without the jacket. *Jab* problem *aayegi tab sochenge, lekin* Sahab *se yeh jhooth chhupane ke liye das jhooth aur bolne padenge.*'

We finished the entire climax over the next four days, and the evil side of my brain suddenly woke up to lie further to Raj Sahab. At the end of each schedule, he would always ask me, 'Rahul, *sab kaam khatam ho gaya na*?'

I used to carry a notepad in which I used to note down all the balance shots that needed to be shot. I just opened the notebook and blatantly lied, 'Sir, *ek* shot *baaki hai*.'

He said, '*Kaunsa* shot?'

I said, 'You had said that we needed to take a shot after Prem Nath ji's car stops and there is an insert of Chintu and Dimple being heckled by Prem Chopra ji and the fighters. In the shot that we need, you had said, Prem Nath ji will remove his jacket and run towards the kids.'

He said, '*Maine bola tha*?'

I said, '*ji*.'

He said, 'You are lying! I'm not an idiot to need this kind of stupid shot. Why should he take his jacket off?'

I said, 'Sir, in view of your instructions about this balance shot, we didn't give him the jacket in the climax.'

He said, 'How can it be?!'

I said, 'Sir, you said it.'

He sat down perturbed, talking to himself, 'Raj Kapoor, this tension of completing the film in a hurry has led you to take a ridiculously stupid shot.'

I was extremely worried that he might ask to see the particular page of the notebook where I had noted his instructions, but there was no such page! I quickly diverted his attention and instructed the driver to bring up Prem Nath ji's car and asked Raj Sahab to instruct the shot. We took that one shot; Kuku was relieved and I was pretty disgusted that I had lied to Boss, but also made up my mind that I will go to my grave with this lie.

During the editing, while seeing the rushes, and even at the premiere when that shot showed up, Raj Sahab turned around and asked, 'Did I tell you that I wanted this shot?'

My standard reply was, 'Sir, if you didn't tell me, why would I ask you to shoot it?'

He said, 'How can I be so stupid? It looks so bad.'

He was so sure that I was lying that finally at the end of the post-premiere party, where only a few unit members were around and he was high, he said, '*Chalo beta ab toh* release *ho gayi* film. Did I really tell you about that stupid shot?'

I said, 'Yes, you did!' and then this realization came to me that I was cheating the very man who had put a lot of faith in me. I decided to let the cat out of the bag, 'I have to admit, Sir, that you never asked for that shot and I had to lie to cover a mistake.'

He just looked at me, 'I always wondered why my memory was failing me, which has never happened in my life. Remember one thing, Son, when you lie once, you will lie again to cover it up and this vicious process will never end, and life will never forgive you for the same. Every action takes a full circle and finally comes back to you. So, I am very happy that you finally spoke the truth.'

BOBBY: THE FINALE

BOBBY WAS FINALLY COMPLETED and we were to commence dubbing.

Raj Sahab generally did not attend the dubbing as he had tremendous faith in his sound engineer Khan Sahab. Khan Sahab, of course, would be sitting and monitoring the dub from his recording cabin and it was assistants like me who had to bear the brunt of irrelevant questions that actors would ask, or in the case of *Bobby*, stand in the dubbing room with their heart pounding with the fear of getting beaten to a pulp by a brilliant actor, Prem Nath ji.

Just before our dubbing started, Prem Nath ji had dubbed in the RK theatre for *Shor*. Manoj Kumar Sir's chief assistant, Sikandar Khanna ji, was handling the dubbing. At one dubbing session, he told Prem Nath ji that he needs to improve on his dubbing and Prem Nath ji almost raised his hand against him. I was petrified when I heard this story and called Raj Sahab and told him, 'Sir, Prem Nath ji almost beat up Manoj Kumar Sir's assistant, I hope he does not do the same to me.'

Raj Sahab jokingly said, 'I hope he does. It will be my revenge for all the trouble you have given me during the making of *Bobby*!' and he started laughing.

In preparation for the dubbing, the entire film had to be split into smaller length loops which would then run independently but continuously on the projector, so that, apart from having to repeatedly record a given set of dialogue, a rhythm was also set for the actor to ease them to repeatedly speak the same lines.

Prem Nath ji turned up on the first day of dubbing, sat on the sofa, laid out his harmonium and a bansuri, a new addition to his strange paraphernalia, and said, 'Start!' The loop started and as I was standing just next to him, he again yanked me by my collar, and shouted, 'You bloody municipality, I want to see the reel and not the loop!'

To re-confirm, I asked him, 'Sir, just this reel or the entire film?'

He hit my head with the flute, the sudden shock had musical notes playing in my head, and said, 'The loop you showed me is what I'm going to dub first, the other loops that I need to dub will have to be joined into a reel before I dub those. So, only after seeing a loop, will I express my decision to dub that loop or another.'

This meant that we would need to re-join loops in a reel at random according to his whims and fancies. Finally, he saw the reel, said he was ready and we had to disassemble the reel into loops again. He asked for his entire costume from the scene that was being dubbed and also put on make-up. He started playing the harmonium or flute with the dialogue of the loop playing on the speaker, finding the right *sur* for the dialogue! As soon as the loop started playing, he screamed, 'I told you, I need my costume. The colour of the lungi you have given me is different and there is no topi!' Saying this, he walked out in anger and left the studio. He returned the next morning for the dubbing; I had already laid out all his costumes and accessories since I had understood this eccentric man could want to dub any scene at any time and would require his costume.

The loop started and Prem Nath ji started moving exactly as he had done in the scene. The boom man was aghast as Prem Nath ji had walked away from the mic. He said, 'If you keep walking, how can I adjust the microphone to perfectly capture your sound?'

Prem Nath ji replied, 'No problem, tell Raj Kapoor to reshoot my entire scenes and not give me any movement, then I will not move in the dubbing. If I move, the microphone moves with me.'

Khan Sahab had walked into the studio by then and overheard this conversation. He requested the boom man, 'Dutta, please, you will have to adjust. Just move the mic wherever he is moving and keep moving until he stops.'

So, a strange and hilarious scenario started, though nobody had the audacity to laugh. Prem Nath ji was walking and the boom man was following; Prem Nath ji started swirling and the boom man was swirling with him. Then Prem Nath ji lay down and the boom man was lowering the mic to his face when Prem Nath ji suddenly got up and the microphone hit his face.

I called Raj Sahab up in the cottage, 'Sir, this is what is happening!' And explained everything to him.

He laughed heartily and went, '*Karo karo.* Don't ask me for a solution. The dubbing is for you to manage.'

We came to the climax and I requested Prem Nath ji, 'Sir, when you are in the water, trying to save the kids, I need random calls from you like "Bobby! Raja!" We will place them at various places.'

He said, 'Okay, where's the water?'

I said to Bond, 'Get Commander a glass of water.'

Prem Nath ji said, 'What glass of water? I need water filled in the dubbing theatre. I am supposed to be swimming in the rapids, so without moving in the water, I will not get the correct feeling!'

I said, 'Sir, just give me 10 minutes.'

I ran to the cottage and told Boss, 'Sir, he wants the dubbing theatre flooded! How can I do that? If I say no, he'll hit me!'

Raj Sahab said coolly, 'Don't you dare fill water in my theatre. And if he strikes you, bear it, I have no solution. I have repeatedly said dubbing is your responsibility. Go and handle it.'

I mustered up my courage, holding a handkerchief on my face in anticipation of a slap and told Prem Nath ji, 'I am sorry, Sir, there is no way to fill water in the theatre.'

He replied, 'Take me to a swimming pool, I will dub there.'

I said, 'We can't do that because the atmospheric sound will disturb the dubbed sound.'

He just walked out, fuming with anger, entered the adjacent bathroom, switched on the shower, ran back into the theatre, soaking wet, and screamed, 'I'm now in the character. Start sound!'

He started walking around the theatre, lying down, screaming, 'Bobby! Raja!' At one point he felt he was dry, which he was definitely not, so he ran into the bathroom, stood under the shower once again and ran back to continue his rant of 'Bobby! Raja!'

Finally, on Thursday, 27 September 1973, the film released in Metro Cinema, the most prestigious cinema theatre in Bombay. The advanced booking for the film had created history. On the first day, there were no commercial shows but four 'invitation-only' shows at Metro. The first show was for the staff and unit (wherein I had nicked a number of seats for my friends), the second for the press, the third was a charity show for Campion School and the fourth was a premiere, where the balcony seats were sold for charity to the Cancer Society of India and the stalls accommodated the crème de la crème of socialites and the film industry. I had nicked four seats here too!

While the first show was going on, a strange incident happened. A suited man accompanied by a bailiff of the high court asked for me at the entrance to the theatre.

I went out and was accosted by the suited chap, a solicitor, who informed me, 'The public exhibition of this film has to be immediately stopped as my clients have obtained an injunction from the High Court of Bombay.' The same was handed over to me by the bailiff.

The financiers who had made their money from Raj Kapoor's earlier films wanted the overseas rights of *Bobby* for a pittance. Raj Sahab had refused, as they were not doing him any favour and were in fact charging him a draconian compounded interest that he would have to pay before releasing the film. Thus, he had assigned the overseas rights to a distributor of his choice and got paid a handsome sum of money for the same. Prior to the release, he had cleared the entire account of the financiers and they, to spite him, raised a false claim at the last minute to stop the film from releasing and obtained the injunction. They were truly unscrupulous and did not even consider the fact that Raj Kapoor, via his films, had set them off to become billionaires, nor the fact that they never paid him true profits that were due to him under the agreement which gave their company 'solid legs' to stand on.

There were no mobile phones to contact Raj Sahab who was en route to the theatre and I did not know how to get out of this situation. The assistant manager of Metro, a young chap, came up with a temporary solution to keep the show running.

He told the solicitor, 'The injunction says that no public exhibition of the film is allowed. Today, all of our shows are "invitation-only" shows and do not constitute public exhibition. Hence the injunction does not stand good today.'

The solicitor had no answer and left the theatre. When Raj Sahab came, along with Dabboo Sahab, he was apprised of the situation and he immediately rushed to court with his solicitor and cleared the injunction.

The press show was a great success. They loved the film except for one idiot who told me, 'This film will be a flop because the climax is in the water. No film with a watery climax is successful.' I wanted to slap him or rather drown him at that moment.

At the Campion School charity show, the principal was talking about how proud the school was that an alumnus of the school, Rishi Kapoor, was starring in a Raj Kapoor film; he also praised Chintu for his achievements in academics. Raj Sahab standing behind whispered, 'I don't think this idiot knows that Chintu had failed in his ninth standard, I had to donate a trophy to the school for them to promote him and then he had again failed in the eleventh standard.'

At the post-premiere party, the industry couldn't stop gushing over the film. A proud Raj Sahab came up to the members of the unit, poured us all drinks and said, 'I need to thank you guys for this achievement, which would not have been possible for me alone.'

The next day, Friday, when the film released in all the theatres, I witnessed nothing short of hysteria in each and every screening that I attended to gauge the reaction of the audience.

By the end of the day, as per the reports, the film had received a tremendous response from all over the country except Delhi and UP where the film could not be released due to the unscrupulous financiers using a false ploy to delay the same. Vakil Singh ji made a lot of money due to the delay in release in Delhi and UP. He was running extra shows in Faridabad since that was in Punjab and there was no restriction on the release there. The hysteria was such that there were special 'Bobby Buses' that transported people from Delhi to Faridabad and back just to see the film!

After six weeks, the objection to the release was cleared and the film released in Delhi and UP. We attended the premiere in Delhi and were witness to unprecedented crowds and appreciation for the film, even though most people had repeatedly seen the film in Faridabad.

Vakil Singh ji insisted that we come to Punjab. So, we went to Amritsar, and while driving from the airport we saw 'Bobby Laundry', 'Bobby Tailor', 'Bobby Barber', 'Bobby this', 'Bobby that' and also 'Bobby Butcher'! *Bobby* had turned into a true cult classic.

We drove to the cinema hall, where *Bobby* was now running in the seventh week, but the crowd was more than what one expected on the first day of an eagerly awaited film. The booking board showed 'House Full'.

We walked in and I saw the booking window open, though the board had showed the house was full, and two women were selling tickets. I asked Vakil Singh ji, 'Who are these two women?'

He said, 'One is the theatre owner's wife and the other is his daughter-in-law.'

I said, 'How can they sell tickets for a show that is already full?'

He said, 'Black market!'

As we entered, it was claustrophobic inside the theatre because of the sheer number of people.

I said, 'The crowd is overflowing, what is the capacity of the theatre?'

He said, '*Ji,* capacity *kya hoti hai. Jitne log aa jaye, utni* capacity.'

I said, '*Seeton ka koi* number *toh hoga*?'

He replied, '*Arey* Rahul Sahab, *kaun puchta hai* number *kya hai?*'

It was a 3 p.m. show and it was already 3.15, but the film had not started. The seats were full, extra chairs were put up in the aisles, some people were standing crushed in the aisles, others sitting on the floors, but in this entire madness, there was one row in the centre of the theatre, with backrests placed on the seats, which was empty.

I asked, 'Why is this row empty and why is the film not starting?'

He said, '*Jo* theatre *ka maalik hain, uske bacchon ka* school *ka* masterji *aur unka khandaan abhi tak nahi aaya. Unke liye yeh* row *khali rakha hua hai. Unke aane tak* film *shuru nahi ho sakti.*' Welcome to Punjabi culture!

Then we went to Kolkata for the premiere. In Bengal, I saw a strange practice, which I've seen in their weddings also. In the film, the moment they saw something exciting, they wouldn't clap or whistle, but would take out expensive perfume bottles and start spraying perfume in the air. This practice led to the cinemas, screening *Bobby*, smell like a strange mix of different fragrances!

So, this somewhat sums up the whirlwind that was *Bobby*. The lessons I learnt during its making, the inception, the casting, the handling of actors, the wedding and pregnancy of the leading lady, were all great inspiration for me. I learnt about the nuances in a director's work, his zeal to adapt to every situation and overcome them while staying dedicated to his craft.

GOING FORWARD

Bobby turned out to be one of the most successful films in the country! Rishi Kapoor, my childhood friend, turned into a megastar. I decided to launch my own film as producer and director with Chintu in the lead. I spoke to Raj Sahab about my plan and he was extremely supportive of my endeavour advised me to take every step carefully, but like a fool, I did not. My launch film took eight years to make, drove me penniless and happened to be my fourth film to release! Through my various debacles and victories over those seven years, Raj Sahab's lesson of resilience was the force that kept me going.

Picking out 'geniuses' was a natural trait of Raj Sahab. From my years spent at RK, there were hordes of incidents that translated into lessons. I learnt not only from Raj Sahab but also the people he worked with. One such person was Prem Nath ji.

Prem Nath ji was right in insisting that the choreography for a fisherman's song, '*ghe ghe ghe ghe ghe ghe re*', could only be conceived by him. He had gone so far as to 'bop' the senior choreographer, Sohanlal ji, repeatedly on the head with a trumpet because he didn't agree to his dance movements.

Even though eccentric – so much so that people laughed at his antics – his true sense of humanity ran like an undercurrent in all his endeavours, which would emotionally move people when they recounted encounters with him.

At one time he was planning to produce and direct a film starring Dabboo Sahab, and Prem Nath ji was ecstatic and proud of the title he had finalized for the same – 'Havaldar Dharti Dhakel Singh'!

Dabboo Sahab, controlling his laughter, asked, 'Which other actors will be performing in this film?'

He replied, 'I've got the best actors ever to work together for the first time. Ruby Myers, Mubarak Sahab, Nana Palsikar and the "heartthrob", Poppy Jairaj. They have not acted in a long time and "Havaldar Dharti Dhakel Singh" will be their reincarnation.' From his list of actors, the youngest was eighty years old!

Dabboo Sahab, with his strange sense of humour, said, 'Uncle, I asked you the star cast of a film, you are reciting the roll call of an old age home!' Though we all had laughed about it, in hindsight I realize, living in a world where even current actors are 'out of sight, out of mind', the level of his compassion was unprecedented as he yearned to have long forgotten actors face a camera again. Benevolence was one of those unseen and unnoticed facets that made him unforgettable. Yesterday, I happened to see *Bobby* once again after a long time. I saw one of the greatest performances by Prem Nath ji, and I don't think any other actor will be able to replicate it.

Dabboo Sahab was the only other director I assisted in *Kal Aaj Aur Kal* and partly in *Dharam Karam*.

Kal Aaj Aur Kal starred Prithviraj Kapoor Sir, Raj Sahab and Dabboo Sahab, who was also directing the film. A huge task undertaken by a director for his debut!

Dabboo Sahab, a chip off the old block, steered the film in the true desired fashion. I learnt from him a very smart technique when he was picturizing the song, '*Aap yahan aaye kisliye*'. The setting for the song was that of a beach and two sets had been erected to achieve an extended depth in the location. Half the set was erected on the largest stage of RK, and after concluding that shoot, the other half of the set was erected on the same stage.

This required meticulous planning as at times, two different shots from both the halves were to be joined in the editing, a panorama that seemed like continuous shots on a long location. A masterful stroke of technique creating a grand visual.

On the first day when Prithviraj Kapoor Sir, Raj Sahab and Dabboo Sahab were shooting together, Dabboo Sahab was slightly hesitant about giving instructions to his grandfather. He asked Raj Sahab, 'I need to tell Papa ji [Prithviraj Kapoor] that the tone he is using is not correct for me.'

Raj Sahab replied, 'Go and tell him! On this set, you are not his grandson, you are the director. I am sure he will appreciate it like I appreciate you, the director, correcting me when I am wrong.'

Then, Raj Sahab narrated a very funny incident from *Awaara*. The film had Prithviraj Kapoor Sir playing Raj Sahab's father and in the courtroom scene, Lala Basheshwarnath Nath (Bade Papa ji), Raj Sahab's grandfather, was playing the judge. Raj Sahab said, 'He used to sit on the judge's chair all day, reading issues of *Mastram*!' *Mastram* was a Hindi pornographic magazine.

'He would not pay attention to what I was saying, and would invariably forget his lines as his concentration was on *Mastram*. I lost my head one day and screamed at him, "*Aapko* dialogue *kyun nahi yaad rehte hain*?" And his *jooti* flew out of nowhere at me and he screamed at Papa ji, 'Prithvi, *main aaj ke baad kaam kya*, Raj *ki shakal nahi dekhunga. Aisa badtameez ho gaya hai tumhara beta*!'

Raj Sahab carried on and said, 'Papa ji will listen to you as he is a very competent actor; Bade Papa ji was not an actor.'

There was an incident that happened on the sets of *Kal Aaj Aur Kal*. While shooting a party scene, Papa ji came on the sets and noticed one junior artist. He went up to him, embraced him and burst out crying like a child! The junior artist said, 'Prithvi *tu roh kyun raha hai*?' We were taken aback that he addressed Papa ji with his first name, 'Prithvi!'

Papa ji turned to Raj Sahab and said, 'Raj, *tumne pehchana inko*?'

Raj Sahab touched the feet of the gentleman (I can't remember his name; it was a Parsi name) and turned to us, with moist eyes, 'This man was a very big star in Wadia Movietone. I have stood in line for 2–3 hours to buy a ticket for his movie in which he was the leading man, and today he's working here as a junior artist. This is something that really hurts, and tells of the uncertainties of this industry.'

By this time, tears had welled up in his eyes, but he continued saying, 'My respect for him has really grown today as he has faced the ups and downs of life bravely and is still working. This should be a lesson for all human beings, "never give up"!'

Once, on the set, I was asked by Dabboo Sahab to go to Papa ji and to tell him the correct pronunciation of a word. For me, this was one of the proudest moments of my life. Me, a mere mortal, was going to correct the pronunciation of Emperor Akbar! Having read about the emperor in history classes in school and seeing the film *Mughal-e-Azam* as a child, I was, and still am convinced that Prithviraj Kapoor was actually Emperor Akbar in disguise!

The crowning glory for me was the day Raj Sahab asked me to direct a film for RK, to be produced by him.

A story he had heard that he wanted me to direct was a comedy titled, *Biwi-O-Biwi*. I have extremely fond memories of the film. I got an opportunity to direct Dabboo Sahab and also veterans like Shashikala ji, Dina Pathak ji and Rajendra Nath Sir. To top this, I got to direct the unparalleled actor Sanjeev Kumar Sir and observe his way of approaching his performance very closely, which helped me in my career.

I wanted Chintu to do a cameo in one scene. The moment I asked him, he immediately said yes and this added another feather in my cap – directing Rishi Kapoor!

Raj Sahab, the producer, was a director's dream. He gave his director a free hand and would never come to the shooting. Whilst shooting, he did not see a single scene from the film and saw the film only after it was complete. He came back with some suggestions and said, 'These are only suggestions. To retain them or reject them is your prerogative. Always remember, the director reigns "supreme".'

The Master had influenced me to a great extent. Lessons I had learnt working under him and observing him closely had embedded a lot of knowledge in me. During the climax shooting of *Bobby*, I had seen how he overcame the hurdle which Dimple's pregnancy had created, and his way of overcoming a hurdle came in handy when I was directing *Aur Pyaar Ho Gaya*.

I was working with a very well-known actor, I don't want to name him, who decided, on the last day of the shoot, that he would not turn up for the shooting. I was on my way to the shooting, 'blew a fuse' and wanted to crucify the actor. I realized 'blowing a fuse' was not the solution and this hurdle had to be tackled like my boss would have done!

I called the actor and said, 'I thought I should tell you that I don't need you anymore as your work is complete.'

He asked, 'What about the one day I had today?'

I replied, 'You said you will not come for shooting, so I imagined that I had just returned from your funeral at the Santacruz crematorium, after consigning you to the flames, and while driving back, I was trying to find a solution to the problem your fucking dying created for me. Viola! The solution came to me and I don't need you anymore for the film.'

I reached the shoot and was having a cup of tea in the vanity van when after 10 minutes, my assistant came and informed me, 'Sir... [the actor] has arrived.'

This was just one stray incident about the influence of Raj Sahab on my work. His influences were unending; I would like to take you through four films that I directed which impacted the audience and were heavily influenced by Raj Kapoor.

LOVE STORY

LOVE STORY IS THE only film in the world which does not carry the name of a director! All the people, including the film industry, the actors in the film and me, are convinced that I actually directed the film, but an order from the High Court of Bombay barred the film from carrying the name of the director in all publicity material and titles of the film. The root cause of this high court order was a petition filed by Mr Rahul Rawail, that is me. Sounds strange, but there were concrete reasons for me to take this step. Let me take you through the influences that governed my creativity in the visual narration of *Love Story* and finally led to my filing a petition in court, which further led to me not being credited for my creativity.

When I had started my first film, *Gunahgaar,* along with Chintu, I had cast Rajendra Kumar Sir to play Chintu's father in the film. The film had been in the making since 1974, but there had been no progress in my career. In 1978, Raj Sahab asked me to direct *Biwi-O-Biwi* and within two months of that announcement, Rajendra Sir asked me to direct his film which would also launch his son, Kumar Gaurav.

Though Rajendra Sir had always acknowledged my work as a director, in *Gunahgaar*, it was after Raj Sahab decided that I should direct a film that he will produce, Rajendra Sir decided to entrust me with directing *Love Story*. I presume that my being Raj Kapoor's film's director influenced him in his decision.

I was on top of the world since, from having no work at all, I had suddenly two of the most prestigious films to direct. I went to meet Raj Sahab with a box of mithai and told him about my acceptance to direct *Love Story*.

He was very happy and said, 'You have my eternal blessings and am more excited than you about your achievement. I just want to add, I presume you have taken on Pajendra's [that's what he called Rajendra Kumar] film after giving it a lot of thought. In any decision that you take, always weigh the pros and cons.' At that point, it never struck me that this was a veiled warning, spoken by the one man, my guru, whose wisdom I should have embraced and trodden this path carefully, without getting carried away.

The story narrated to me by the Mirza Brothers was a straight lift from the 1958 Hollywood film, *The Defiant Ones*, that starred Sidney Poitier and Tony Curtis, both nominated for the Oscars for the same. As a matter of fact, the film won two Oscars and had seven nominations. The film's concept was based around racism since the protagonists belonged to two different races, black and white, who are handcuffed together. Mirza Brothers had cleverly tweaked the story to include two youngsters, a male and a female, who hate each other's guts. Fate throws the two into a situation where they are handcuffed together and what follows is hatred blossoming into love.

I found this premise interesting and exciting for a love story. The challenge of two fresh faces making their debut, and me being at the helm of it all, presented me with a great opportunity to put into practice whatever I had learnt from Raj Sahab during the making of *Bobby*, probably the greatest teenage love story made till date.

Rajendra Sir said, 'It would be a great idea if we assigned Radhu Karmakar ji to be the cinematographer on the film. What do you think?' I was the happiest man in the world!

The screenplay given to me by the Mirza Brothers was handwritten on three double-sided A4 sheets. This was shocking to me and it drew me back to the cottage to seek Boss's advice.

Raj Sahab's instant reaction was, 'Wow! I would love to meet the so-called writers. They have come to you with a plagiarized story and a three-page screenplay. I hope they will write the dialogue for the film or will they just say that they have thought of giving a new dimension to this film – silent, no dialogue!'

I just burst out laughing and replied, 'Sir, I had a talk about the dialogue with Rajendra Sir and he assured me not to worry about the same as he would write the dialogue himself.'

Raj Sahab reacted, 'I have worked with Pajendra on two films and his flair for writing dialogue is quite commendable. You will be in good hands, as long as his prowess stays only to writing dialogues and does not interfere with your responsibilities as the director. Now, regarding your concern about the screenplay having no detailed descripted scenes, you should be happy since the entire treatment and narration of the film is going to be in your hands alone. You were an integral part of *Bobby*, and if you have learnt any lessons from the making of that film, and I am certain you have, then consider yourself fortunate that so early in your career, you have an opportunity to artistically and technically display your own individual creativity.'

I was overwhelmed with the faith Raj Sahab had in me, and I excitedly went on to tell him that Radhu Sahab would be the cinematographer on the film.

Instead of sounding pleased, a strange smile played out on his face, 'Pajendra is taking Radhu as a cinematographer? I must say he is ambitious. Knowing how meticulously Radhu works and the time it takes for him to light up a shot, one needs to have large pockets and a large heart to put their hand into that pocket. I fear that a false overambitious attitude could turn a man into a greedy and selfish narcissist.' This was the second time that I was cautioned with a veiled warning, which again, like a fool, I did not decipher!

The shooting of *Love Story* commenced and I was always looking at it with what I imagined to be Raj Kapoor's method of thought and technique of execution. When I suggested the casting of Amjad Khan Sir, the dreaded dacoit of the iconic *Sholay*, as the funny, sweet and humane Haryanvi cop, there was an expected opposition from most of the unit, 'How can you imagine a villain to play a comedian?' I feel sorry for people who typecast actors and have somewhere forgotten that characters in a film have to be humane as well and a good actor will always be a good actor irrespective of the shade of his character.

What made my belief extremely steadfast was that Raj Kapoor had got Pran Sahab, who was also a dreaded villain to sing a song in *Jis Desh Mein Ganga Behti Hai* that showed his emotional and human side. When nobody was getting convinced, I finally lied and told Rajendra Sir that it was Raj Sahab who made the suggestion and on hearing that he immediately agreed.

Situations from Raj Sahab's films that were embedded in my psyche and I was waiting for an opportunity to reincarnate those situations in *Love Story*. The song '*Kya gazab karte ho ji*' provided me with a situation to reincarnate, '*Main ka karun Ram, mujhe buddha mil gaya*'. Just like the original song had been shot in a hotel room, my song was shot in a small room of a lodge. The area was really small and had three characters with plenty of movement. In fact, one character, Aruna Irani, was oblivious of Vijayta Pandit's presence. While shooting this song, I honestly had this feeling that Raj Sahab's blessings were guiding me. In fact, I have always felt that Raj Sahab has been omnipresent and has guided me throughout my career.

Rajiv Kapoor or Chimpu, the youngest of Raj Sahab's sons, was working with me as an assistant director. Raj Sahab landed up in Pahalgam with the excuse, 'I was in Delhi so I thought Pajendra *ki* shooting *chalke dekhte hain.*' I am certain that he was missing his son, and like every father, he too wanted to meet him.

I was very happy seeing Raj Sahab there, but he was happier meeting Chimpu! We were sitting with him and telling him about our experiences while shooting in the exotic locations in Kashmir, but Chimpu had a problem, 'Papa, there is one big problem that the air here really stinks. Being in such a beautiful exotic area and having to smell the stinking air is horrible.'

Raj Sahab replied, 'Son, the problem is not with Kashmir's air quality, the problem is being born and brought up in Bombay. You only know the smell of pollution and trash, which is the reason why the unadulterated and fresh air of Kashmir stinks.'

Whenever Raj Sahab used to visit the location, I used to be very nervous in his presence. Once when he came to the shoot, it became very cloudy early in the afternoon and it seemed that no further shooting would take place that day. Chimpu immediately called out, 'Setting, *ek kursi leke aao.* Spot boy, *ek* glass *pani jaldi lekar aao*!' Holding Rajendra Sir's hand he said, 'Sir please sit down, don't take tension, have this Calmpose.'

Raj Sahab was very intrigued by Chimpu's action and asked me, 'What's happening?'

I replied, 'The problem is that it gets cloudy here in the valley at any unpredictable time and then the shooting gets delayed or cancelled. This creates a lot of stress for Rajendra

Sir. You must have seen his face has gone white, his lips are quivering, all because he is completely paranoid about the loss of money. This act of Chimpu is repeated every time it becomes cloudy.'

Raj Sahab looked at me with a sarcastic smile. I also narrated other similar incidents which had happened over the shoot. He laughed and said, 'I thought he was a very ambitious producer? If you love your money, don't make a film. And you, Mr Director, be careful!' My dumb brain could still not fathom the repeated warnings which this time was more direct.

Being an actor himself, Rajendra Sir would try and impose his own 'sense of performance' into his son Kumar Gaurav's performance. However, he seemed to be caught in a 'time warp', unable to exit from the 1960s and upgrade his performance to the 1980s. This was irritating and interfering with my vision. I thought to myself, 'I might as well drop his son from the film since he will be performing like his father and would become a laughing stock in the industry.'

One day when Raj Sahab was on location, I decided to 'give it back' to Rajendra Sir for interfering in my concept and performance. There was a shot where Kumar Gaurav had to rush down a slope whilst singing. The slope was extremely slippery and lined by rocks on both sides. I explained the shot to Kumar Gaurav, who was apprehensive that he might slip since the path was covered with wet soil. I turned to Rajendra Sir, who was sitting with Raj Sahab, and called out to him, 'Sir, I want Kumar Gaurav to come down this slope, singing the song with some style, but he is scared that he will slip and fall. I'm requesting you, Sir, with your experience, you'll be able to guide him as to how he should move in this shot and how safe it will be for him to come down the slope.'

Rajendra Sir was very thrilled that I said this in front of Raj Sahab and with a contemptuous smile he turned to Raj Sahab and said, 'These kids including the director should be happy to have me around so that I can guide them the right way. You know children need confidence to be instilled in them and that can only be done by an experienced person.'

Rajendra Sir proudly took Kumar Gaurav's position. When the playback was switched on, he started enacting the song in his own style; however, as he started moving down the slope, he slipped and fell! He was bruised, but when all of us jumped up and tried to help him, he, though in pain, put on a huge act of bravado saying that for actors the injury means nothing, it's only their performance that should bother them.

Raj Sahab went up to him and saw that the bruise was superficial and Rajendra Sir was not injured in any way. Raj Sahab turned to me and whispered, 'Come to my room in the evening, I need to talk to you.'

In the evening, Chimpu and I went to his room, he sternly said, 'You are doing this on purpose.'

I innocently said, 'Doing what?'

'Putting poor Pajendra's life at risk!' Saying that he burst out laughing, 'I don't understand why people should poke their nose into other people's craft.'

There is one scene in *Love Story* where Rajendra Sir lands up in a dak bungalow and by chance, is brought face to face with Danny Sir and Vidya Sinha ji. From the time I read the situation which said Ram Dogra, Danny Denzongpa, Vijay Mehra, Rajendra Kumar, Suman Dogra and Vidya Sinha meet face to face, I had formed a series of mental images for its visual presentation. It would be akin to the iconic climax scene that Raj Sahab had executed in *Sangam*. Ever since I started directing, I was always looking to shoot a scene that would be my homage to my guru, and this particular scene from *Love Story* was my attempt at doing the same.

As mentioned earlier, in *Sangam*, the three actors maintained a triangular position throughout one particular scene. The visual impact of the triangular position hits the bulls' eye vis-à-vis the message of the scene and Raj Sahab's mastery has to be admired. In *Love Story*, the scene starts between Vijay and Suman and then Ram enters the room. I managed to bring Danny Sir into a position where a distinct triangle is visually formed between him, Rajendra Sir and Vidya ji. From here on, through the scene and movement within the characters, I had to maintain the 'visual triangle' until it rose to a crescendo with Danny Sir's dialogue, '*Iss waqt aap mere aur meri biwi ke beech ek deewar banke khade ho*!'

I had achieved the desired tableau. Danny Sir said, 'Very nice, Rahul', which was followed by a round of applause from the unit, and even though I was gloating at the appreciation, my mind wanted me to tell all these people, 'Go to the cottage at RK and repeat the appreciation and applause for Raj Kapoor, the unseen force that guided me here.'

Raj Sahab's veiled warning started becoming clearer at yet another instance. One evening, I finished shooting a scene from *Biwi-O-Biwi* at about 8.30 p.m. and was given a message that Raj Sahab wanted to see me at the cottage.

He offered me a drink and I respectfully told him, 'I'm sorry, Sir, I have some editing left to do for *Love Story*.'

He said, 'Why are you jumping between two different films in one day?'

Though I never wanted to tell him about my problems with Rajendra Sir, but having reached a breaking point, I blurted out, 'Rajendra Sir is getting unnecessarily edgy and rude! He keeps saying that I am only obsessed with *Biwi-O-Biwi* and not bothered about *Love Story*. He keeps cribbing that his work is suffering because of me.'

He looked me straight in the eye and said, 'I asked you to have a drink because I wanted to tell you something. Vakil Singh saw a preview of *Love Story* today and came to see me with Rajendra Kumar.'

I was taken aback slightly because this was the first time that he referred to Rajendra Sir as Rajendra Kumar and not Pajendra.

Raj Sahab carried on, 'Vakil Singh was extremely thrilled with what he had seen and paid me a great compliment when he said that Rahul Rawail is your true disciple. But Rajendra Kumar was upset and angry. He told me that he is feeling very cheated because people who have seen a preview of *Love Story* talk in superlative terms about the director and nobody praises him for the tremendous job he has done as a producer. Therefore, I am calling off the shooting of *Biwi-O-Biwi* until you get him out of your system!'

I was extremely upset after hearing this and did not go home but went to a bar at Bandra Station and got drunk. When I got home at 1 a.m., Rajendra Sir called up and started screaming, 'You did not go for my editing! You know how much money I lost because of you? I had to pay for everybody's dinner though no work was done!'

I was boiling mad but I apologized and told him, 'From tomorrow, Raj Sahab has decided to hold back his shooting till the time I finish all my work on *Love Story*.'

From that day onwards, there was a definite strained relationship between Rajendra Sir and me, and it was evident to the entire unit. I immersed myself in finishing the shooting, editing and the final edit with an unrelenting focus. A final preview was screened for all the people involved in the film, including Rajendra Sir, R.D. Burman and Mangesh Desai ji, the re-recording engineer at Rajkamal Studios. The final version was much appreciated by everyone who saw it, and thereafter, I even had detailed discussions with R.D. Burman about the background music that was to be recorded.

Ten days before the background music was to be recorded, Rajendra Sir told me, 'I have decided to put a romantic song between me and Vidya Sinha at the beginning of the film.'

I flew off the handle and said, 'You have decided? I am the director of the film and my conviction says that a song of you and Vidya ji is the most hilarious and obnoxious suggestion I have ever heard!'

A screaming match started and he shouted at the top of his voice, 'I am Rajendra Kumar! People call me "Jubilee Kumar" and you find a song with me to be obnoxious?'

My reply, one octave higher, was 'The audience want to see Rajendra Kumar's son, not Rajendra Kumar himself! That is why I have reduced, to the bare minimum, the prologue between you, Vidya ji and Danny Sir.'

The reply came in the highest octave possible, 'You are destroying my career! I have the highest number of fans in the country. It is my money, my film and I will decide what is best for it.'

In the meanwhile, the photosets of *Love Story* had been printed and I was completely shocked when I saw them! The legend on the photoset said – 'Rajendra Kumar's *Love Story*. Music: R.D. Burman. Lyrics: Anand Bakshi.' There was no mention of the director!

'Why isn't my name mentioned here?' I asked angrily.

He said, 'There is no place to fit your name.'

I replied, 'There is space for the names of the producer, music director and lyrics writer, and no space for the director's name?'

He had a rude reply, 'R.D. Burman, Anand Bakshi and Rajendra Kumar are names that "sell" and are essential for publicity.'

I could not believe what I had just heard! I called up Raj Sahab and told him the situation I was in and he said, 'I don't believe you.'

I said, 'Why would I lie to you about this, Sir? I am telling you the truth.'

He consoled me saying, 'If truth be told, I suspected this might happen since Pajendra is over ambitious and wants people to give credit only to him for making the film. I hinted to you at various times but I guess you did not see the storm brewing, and frankly, I did not expect the problem to reach this far. So, what is the next step you are contemplating?'

'Sir, I am planning to file a complaint against the producer with the Indian Film Directors' Association.'

Raj Sahab said, 'Yes, you can try it but I don't think any good will come out of it. The governing committee of the director's association is full of sycophants, who would rather suck up to Rajendra Kumar and bend over backwards to please him.'

Exactly what Raj Sahab had said, happened.

The governing council passed an order that said, 'The producer has every right to supervise the creative content of a film and the director's right is only limited to his remuneration.'

I walked out in a huff and went straight to RK to meet Boss. He patiently heard me out and remarked, 'This is an order passed by the Indian Film Directors' Association?' He laughed heartily and said, 'This is what is expected of sycophants!'

I, hurt and angry, said to him, 'Sir, I feel like informing the association that my name should be removed as director of *Love Story*.'

Boss hugged me and stood up with a salute saying, 'I salute a very brave man! This action of yours has convinced me that there are still directors around who believe in their conviction. Remember, one day, like a *besharam*, he will come back to you and ask you to direct a film for him. The other thing I want you to do is take precautions that no other name appears as the director, since he will want to put his own name as the director.'

The next day, I called for an emergency meeting of the association and Rajendra Sir, and informed them of my decision to withdraw my name as the director of the film.

Rajendra Sir jumped up happily and said, 'Wonderful!'

I added, 'I would also like to inform the committee that the producer had verbally committed a remuneration of ₹1,50,000, and I have only been paid ₹25,000.'

The committee said, 'Verbal commitments don't mean anything. In the absence of an agreement, he has to pay you a minimum amount of ₹50,000, and since you have admitted receiving half the amount, he is only bound to pay you the balance, that is ₹25,000.'

Apparently, all these decisions were made by the association to protect my interest!

I turned around and said, 'I will donate the balance due to me to the Spastic Society of India.'

Rajendra Sir intervened and screamed, 'It is my money; what right does he have to donate it to charity?'

I laughed out loud and said, 'Mr Rajendra Kumar, the money due is mine, I can give it to whomever I want. I would also like to warn this "mentally deranged committee" that no other person's name can appear as the director of *Love Story*.'

The sycophants spoke in unison, 'That is Rajendra Kumar's prerogative. He can decide any name that he would like to give, including his own. If you have an objection to this, obtain a court order that bars him from using any other person's name.'

This was the only time the association gave me advice that I cherished. I filed a suit in court, got a favourable order from the judge and personally went and threw the order in the face of the committee.

The news spread like wildfire; most people in the industry took pleasure in hearing that my name would not appear as the director, but a handful of people were sympathetic towards me as they were very well aware that directing a film was an art and producers at that time didn't know the *ABC* of that art!

Mangesh ji called me to Rajkamal Studios and asked me the reason behind this ugly problem. I explained to him in detail; he was shocked to know about the song and scenes, featuring himself, Rajendra Sir wanted to add. He told me he would convince Rajendra Sir not to do this stupidity and reinstate my name as the director. I thanked him for this gesture and added that I would not like my name back in the film, as I could not forget his elation when I withdrew my name. However, I would be forever indebted if the film releases in the same version that I had completed.

Rajendra Sir agreed immediately with Mangesh ji. I presume he was revelling in the fact that my name would not be there. He got just one scene added to satisfy his ego which was straight from the 1960s – a stupid family get together at the wedding reception of Pinky and Bunty. He had Saawan Kumar Tak shoot that scene, but Amjad Khan Sir refused to take any instructions and said, 'The director of the film is Rahul Rawail. Either he comes and instructs me or I do whatever I think is right.' God bless his noble soul!

The premiere of the film, the version that I had finalized barring the stupid family get together scene, was held at Metro and I was not invited.

Late at night, after the premiere, Raj Sahab came to my house and was extremely delighted about my effort as a director.

While leaving, he just asked me, 'Why didn't you come for the premiere?'

I replied, 'I was not invited.'

He simply shook his head in disbelief, left in his car and was immediately followed by Dabboo Sahab and R.D. Burman, who had also come to congratulate me. I had tears in my eyes and was thankful that my effort had paid off. Dabboo Sahab insisted that I have a 'success' party the next evening. I agreed, called all my friends and even met Rajendra Sir to invite him to the party. Neither he nor his son Kumar Gaurav came.

Love Story turned out to be an unprecedented success, Kumar Gaurav turned into a cult star and the director was sitting at home unemployed.

BETAAB

POST THE MEGA SUCCESS of *Love Story*, the days ahead got very difficult for me to cope with, since I had withdrawn my name from the film. I was surrounded by despair. My mind was warped and I couldn't think straight.

In this period, I met Raj Sahab one day and he asked me what I was doing.

I replied, 'I have joined the ranks of the educated-unemployed.'

He said, 'You have only yourself to blame for becoming part of the educated-unemployed. The failure of *Biwi-O-Biwi* does not bother me and I will always be happy to employ your services whenever you are willing.'

When he had spoken these words to me, I should have been over the moon with joy, but given my mental state, it did not register. There is a very famous idiom in Hindi that described my situation – *Vinash kale vipreet buddhi*! (When doom approaches, your intelligence fails you!)

As more time went by, I was at the point of a nervous breakdown. I even seriously contemplated the most cowardly of all actions, the final solution! But God had other plans.

Dharam ji's brother, Ajit Sahab, came to my house with a message, 'Dharam ji is planning to launch a film with his son, Sunny, and would like to meet you at his house tomorrow.'

My heart was pounding and I said, 'Why tomorrow? I'll come right now.'

I met Dharam ji and he said, 'I saw your film, *Love Story*, and want you to launch my son. Would you be keen?'

I thought this was insane! Asking me if I would be keen? 'Yes, Sir,' I said this and left his house immediately not giving him time to change his mind!

The first person I shared this news with was Raj Sahab, who responded, 'I told you, talent can never be suppressed.'

What excited me was the fact that a man of Dharam ji's stature had asked me to direct his son's debut film, which gave me an opportunity to further demonstrate the lessons I had learned working with Raj Sahab. I had made up my mind that the film would be a love story, and this is something I believe in till today. When Raj Sahab decided to make *Bobby* with a new pair of young actors, he had said, 'Essentially, this story of teenage romance requires only new talent for the lead, as they do not have any "image" that has been formed in the minds of the audience and therefore makes it more believable.'

When I met Dharam ji the next day, he asked me if I had a story for the proposed film. In my school days, William Shakespeare's *The Taming of the Shrew* was a part of my literature syllabus, and I was convinced that with a modern background and debutant young actors, a film based on the same would draw a favourable reaction from the audience.

I narrated *The Taming of the Shrew* without revealing the source to Dharam ji and was expecting to earn brownie points for having thought of such a remarkable story.

The moment I finished narrating to him, he said, 'This idea of yours to remake *Aan* is wonderful.'

My dream of receiving accolades for my 'story', came shattering down. *Aan* was a film made by one of the masters,

Mehboob Sahab, and had gone on to become a runaway success. As a matter of fact, this gem from William Shakespeare has been adapted for cinema 28 times in various languages, with different backgrounds and unique visual forms. I would like to add that *The Taming of the Shrew* has been made over eight times in different Indian languages, which include four in Hindi itself!

Javed Sahab was brought in by Dharam ji to write the film. Javed Sahab gave the script a totally fresh outlook starting with the character of Sunny, a trainer of wild horses, which had never been seen before. All the characters had to be approached with a unique flavour; old wine in a new bottle.

Sunny's farm, where most of the film took place, also needed an exotic location. I had traversed the road from Pahalgam, which went up north towards Chandanwadi, earlier during the shooting of *Love Story*. There was one piece of vacant land, with a stream running through it, that had captured my imagination. I needed to see the vista from the ground level before making my decision. I remembered Raj Sahab saying, 'Locations or visuals that a director imagines may or may not be the same until you actually reach that location. You have to make a significant effort to actually scout the place that you might have seen from a distance, irrespective of the path leading up to there. Only when you actually visit the location will you be able to make a decision whether the location fits the parameters that you have imagined for the film. If you forego this exercise, because of your laziness, you will, through your life, regret that you may have missed an idyllic setting.'

Armed with this conviction, I along with the cinematographer, Manmohan Singh, and local production assistant drove down to the nearest point where the stream was on level ground, waded through the stream to the opposite bank and started an arduous walk, heading north estimating that we were on the right path.

After walking through the forest with stretches of slush along the way, the path opened up and revealed 'heaven'! At that moment, all I could think was that had it not been for Raj Sahab's insights, I, being as lazy as I am, might have missed out on this spellbinding visual that affirmed the fact that 'seeing is believing'. Thank you, Boss!

The shooting of *Betaab* was a very creatively satisfying process. Having debutants who immersed themselves into the characters, veterans like Shammi Kapoor Sahab, Nirupa Roy ji and Prem Chopra ji, an extremely talented cinematographer and a brilliant writer, all contributed to the successful making.

We shot a major part in Kashmir but the location we picked for Shammi Sahab's estate was in Bangalore, the geographic backdrops of both locations being on the opposite ends of the slate.

A scene at the stud farm that I had shot with Shammi Sahab and Prem Chopra ji, alternated between focusing on the big close-ups of both the characters and then cutting away to a combined mid-shot. I knew that the cut was jerky but couldn't understand why. Raj Sahab offered me extremely valuable advice, 'Your opening of the scene with the focus being shifted has a great impact but since the background is all out of focus, I do not understand what is the location of this scene. You should put a distant sound of a galloping horse, thus alerting my mind that the location is the stud farm and overlap the sound of a neighing horse over the cut to smoothen out the visual jerk.' That repair work on the soundtrack made a huge difference.

Raj Sahab always maintained, 'Whatever you show the audience, they will believe, provided the narrative is interesting and captures their imagination. If you are shooting a film on two or three vastly contrasting locations and the narrative is arresting, the audience will start believing that these contrasting locations are actually neighbouring areas. Remember, if you go around trying to justify the geographical discrepancies, you are surely in trouble because you are moving the attention of the audience from the narrative to the description of the location. Similarly, in the narrative of a film, never commit the time and date on which an event will take place but leave it ambiguous unless the time and date are extremely crucial to the impending event in the narrative.'

Keeping this in mind, I strove to make the narrative as interesting as possible and the transition from Kashmir to Bangalore was never commented on by any viewer. I am convinced that filmmakers are all liars. The make-believe world of cinema just fooled the audience into believing that Kashmir was in the backyard of Bangalore!

While editing a sequence, I came across a shot of Sunny entering Amrita's house, walking through the corridor, the camera trolleying back with him, and at one point the camera turns with Sunny into the bedroom where Amrita is waiting, and he goes in and embraces her. It was all in one shot to depict his urgency and fearless zeal in entering the bedroom of the girl he was in love with.

There were three complete okay takes and they created a dilemma for me. I had to select any one take when each of the three takes had their own irreplaceable portions. When I used one of the takes, a portion of the other take was so strong that I would replace the selected take but then miss the nuances in a portion of the earlier take. This was followed by a perfect movement in the third take sending my mind into a tizzy. After much deliberation, I decided to do a 'Raj Kapoor' in this shot. I found the best matching frames between the three takes that enabled me to jump from the first to the second and on to the third take in the same continuous shot. My assistants rejected this experiment saying that even though the jerks were minimal, they were definitely noticeable and unforgivable. I got hold of a background score, synchronized the musical bangs at the visual jerks and played the edited shot back and nobody noticed the jerks anymore. When the final background score was recorded, I asked R.D. Burman to replicate musical bangs as I had done in the rush print.

When the film was completed, I went to ask Boss when he would like to see the film. He was very busy with the editing of *Prem Rog* and expressed his inability to watch the film at that time but wanted me to show it to Krishna Aunty and her friends. A preview was arranged for them at RK. Raj Sahab was in the editing room, adjacent to the theatre, and as soon as the preview started, he came and stood at the entrance door to the theatre and watched the entire film. This gesture made me very happy but I was apprehensive about the comments that he may have about the film.

'It was wonderful!' he remarked, 'But there are a couple of things that I felt should be brought to your notice. Staying with the same or rectifying them is your decision…'

He mentioned the sequence where Sunny comes to train the wild horse at Amrita's place. According to him, Sunny riding his own stallion while entering the stud farm would have been far more effective had it been dramatized with him riding and jumping the fences on horseback. He was absolutely right, but unfortunately, it was too late to reshoot the sequences.

He mentioned another scene in which Amrita runs away from her home and comes to meet Sunny. She meets his mother in the compound since he is not home and says to the mother, 'I've run away from home to be forever with Sunny because my father will not let us get married.' The scene goes on to become a highly emotional moment between Nirupa ji and Amrita. This particular scene did not move Raj Sahab at all, in fact, he expressed apprehension that a portion of the audience may even snigger at moments.

I agreed with him and told him that when we edited the scene, we had identical feelings, and though we could not go back to Kashmir, we reshot the scene in the garden area of Chandivali Studios and the outcome was the same. Nobody was getting emotional and we could not understand the problem. The scene was just not working!

Raj Sahab gave me the reason for it not working and the solution also, 'It is shot at the same location in which the love story blossoms. By the time you reach this scene, the location has become a beautiful, integral association of the romance and in the same location, an emotional scene between the lovers would work, but your scene is not between the lovers. The attachment that the audience has with the lovers and this location, shatters their conviction in this momen and therefore they are rejecting the scene. Shoot this scene again by erecting an L-shaped piece of the set, and trust me the result will surprise even you.' Going by his conviction, we reshot the scene as guided by him and I have to admit, the scene moved people to such an extent that handkerchiefs appeared in the hands of some viewers. It was the experience and wisdom of Raj Sahab that taught me how every element, major or minor, plays an indelible part in a motion picture. A location had upset the applecart and a change of location propped it up.

Betaab finally released on 5 August 1983 and I was a nervous wreck with the ghost of *Love Story* riding on my back. I went to meet Raj Sahab a day earlier and he was very confident that the due credit for the success of *Love Story* would be rightfully attributed to me. Vakil Singh ji, who was also present at my meeting with Raj Sahab, had the distribution rights for *Betaab* for both Punjab and Bombay territories. Raj Sahab laughed reminiscing about the fact, 'Vakil Singh had bought the rights of *Love Story* for Punjab because he saw you shooting in Kashmir and taking 30 takes for one close-up. I'm sure he saw you in Kashmir again taking 60 takes of one close-up in *Betaab* and bought two territories!'

Vakil Singh ji was very confident that *Betaab* would create history on its release the next morning.

The first show in Punjab was at 6 a.m. I did not sleep that night in anticipation of what the response to the film would be. We had no mobile phones in those days and I kept trying to call Vakil Singh ji, who was in Bombay on that day, for feedback on the response. There was no reply from his room at Tip-Top Hotel.

At around 9.30 a.m., I heard someone yell at the door of my house, 'Oh Rahul Sahab, *mubarak ho*!'

Vakil Singh ji walked in with an entourage of six to seven people doing the bhangra, '*Mubarak ho ji! Kamal ho gaya!* Rahul Sahab, *ek toh mar gaya. Chaar* hospital *mein pahunch gaye, balle balle*!'

I was watching him in disbelief, rejoicing in the fact that a man was killed and four others were hospitalized when one of his cronies, who was on the phone screamed, '*Mubarak ho ji, dooja vi chala gaya*!'

Vakil Singh ji was overjoyed, '*Oh ji, dooja vi chala gaya! Yeh toh kamal hai, shaam tak paunch, chhah aur chale jayenge*!'

I asked, '*Kya hua*?!'

He said, '*Itni bheed thi, itni bheed thi ki* police *ne goliyan chala di* crowd *ko* disperse *karne ke liye*!'

I was unsure whether I should react with pleasure that my film was accepted in a big way or repent this macabre incident happening on the release of my film.

Raj Sahab had a big laugh when he heard about this, 'Rahul, Vakil Singh is lying! He is making up this weird incident so that you would be happy and would narrate the same thing to Dharam who, according to him, would have been happier.'

Betaab turned out to be a bigger success than *Love Story*. God had been kind to me. The same people who bitched about me when *Love Story* had released were now passing comments like, 'I always knew that Rajendra Kumar was not capable of making a film like *Love Story*.'

'He is basically a fool!'

'I'm so glad that you have vindicated my faith in you by directing the blockbuster *Betaab*.'

In life, failure leads to even your near and dear ones abandoning you and success breeds a new 'father' every minute!

Dilip Kankaria, a film financier, along with Bhaiji (Shri Bhairuratan Pachisia), whose valuable fatherly advice has helped me through my career for which I am indebted to him, came to meet me with an offer to direct a film. Dilip asked, 'Tell me, Rahul, would you direct a film for Rajendra Kumar?'

I started laughing, 'Are you serious?'

He said, 'Very serious. I was talking to him this morning, and he said, "Listen, I don't have a *jhagda* with Rahul, he is like my son. I didn't throw him out of *Love Story*, he was childish and walked out after making a wonderful film."'

Bhaiji said, 'Don't do it! After what has happened, there will be problems starting with your remuneration, which will be far more than what he paid you for *Love Story*.'

I told Dilip, 'I'm sorry I can't go against Bhaiji's advice. However, I admire Rajendra Sir's honesty, after all, he never threw me out of the film, I was the chutiya who walked out himself!' Me at my sarcastic best.

Post *Betaab*, being credited for the success of *Love Story* coupled with Rajendra Sir offering me his film to direct solidified my faith that there was a new 'soothsayer' in my life – Baba Raj Kapoor!

ARJUN

THE FRIENDSHIP, THE RISE and the enmity between the D Company (Shabir Ibrahim Kaskar and his brother Dawood Ibrahim Kaskar) and the Pathan Gang (Amirzada Nawab Khan and his brother Alamzeb Jangrez Khan), their manipulation by politicians leading them to become criminals, coupled with the then pandemic of the educated-unemployed prompted Javed Sahab to pen a film script and set a record of some kind.

Let me give you a short background prior to Javed Sahab finalizing the script of *Arjun*.

While *Betaab* was being shot in its last schedule, Sunny's childhood friends, Karim Morani, his brother Aly Morani and Bunty Soorma joined hands to produce a film which would star Sunny, of course, written by Javed Sahab and directed by me.

Javed Sahab narrated a story idea that I liked but required two heroes. We first thought we'd take Kumar Gaurav and Sunny Deol together in the film as it would create a huge publicity blitz, but when we approached Kumar Gaurav, he expressed his inability to feature in this film.

Then we signed Rishi Kapoor to star in the film along with Sunny Deol. We started working on the script, and while discussing the story with R.D. Burman, he was inspired and sang a traditional Portuguese song, '*Mamaiya ya kero kero kero mama*'. This song swayed us off our feet and we decided that even though the script was still being written, we would make a situation for both the heroes to sing this particular song. We even went ahead, recorded the song and it became an instant rage with the unit. Unfortunately, as the script reached the climax, we realized that it was not working and we would have to drop it and find a new script. This was a very embarrassing situation for me and sheepishly, I informed my dear childhood friend, Chintu, about the unfortunate turn the script had taken. I was extremely apologetic, but Chintu, being Raj Kapoor's son, said, 'Rahul, the script is the cornerstone of a film. When you find a crack in the same, you abandon construction and start erecting a fresh cornerstone all over again. Believe me, I'm happy with your decision and will always be there to support you; however, I have one request, or rather a condition – whatever script you finalize, incorporate the song "*Mamaiya ya kero kero kero mama*", don't lose a winner.'

The producers were also insistent that the song had to feature in the film. So, now we did not have a script but we had a song! We struggled for months to find a script that would fit the song at an essential junction, but the song kept becoming a hurdle. One eventful Sunday, in Khandala over breakfast, we were having a general talk about the educated-unemployed pandemic and how it was psychologically affecting the youth and incidentally, on the same day, we read an article in the *Sunday Times* on the rise of the Dongri Gang and Pathan Gang. This general conversation steered by Javed Sahab, an extremely knowledgeable and keen observer of life, carried on till about ten at night. We retired for the night into our respective rooms. Suddenly, I was woken up by Javed Sahab at around three in the morning and he narrated a detailed script based on the conversation we had had during the day. Javed Sahab set a record wherein a simple conversation led to a detailed script within 20 hours and had an ideal situation for the coveted song.

This script fascinated me! A script breaking all conventions, not narrating a story in the true sense, but narrating the life of an 'educated-unemployed' character, manipulated by a politician, gave me the opportunity of divulging into a realm which I had never attempted before. The thought of wading through uncharted waters gave me an adrenaline rush!

I went to Raj Sahab seeking his advice on this step that I wanted to take. He said, 'When you narrated the gist of the script, I could see and hear an excitement within you, and this will lead you to make this film with great conviction. Just remember one thing, make this film "free-willed"; throw all filmmaking conventions to the wind, don't be bound by any rules and let your conviction drive the narrative that you envisage. Filming an unconventional script without any fear or boundaries will be your strength. So, break convention, but break it with conviction and you'll be successful!'

New confidence instilled into me and I didn't look back after that. I had the Master's blessing!

The fabric of *Arjun*'s script, in my vision, dictated boundaries that had to be maintained. I knew the film had to be based in Bombay city, and more so in and around the Parel area since it represented the milieu of the middle class. Another conscious decision taken was that the film would not move out of Bombay city at any point. Even romantic songs, which are generally shot in picturesque outdoor locations, were filmed at the Hanging Gardens.

Generally, in our films, the male lead had a name but never a surname. To establish the ethnicity of the character, Arjun had to have a surname and he had to essentially be a Maharashtrian. Thus, was born, Arjun Mavlankar! Most of the other characters were also assigned surnames, of mixed ethnicities, to establish the diversity of the metropolitan city of Bombay.

Arjun needed unique faces, and good performers, even for the minutest roles to give more authenticity to the film. Casting directors did not exist at that time and we underwent a Herculean task to find the right faces for the characters. It was in this process that we discovered an extremely talented and versatile actor, Paresh Rawal. The character of Shiv Kumar Chowgule, the principal antagonist, had to be performed by an actor who had not been seen as the 'villain', which led us to watch a preview of the wonderful Mahesh Bhatt film, *Saaransh*, and resulted in our casting another brilliant actor, Anupam Kher.

Even though we had decided on the Lalbaug area for most of the filming, shooting for long periods in the crowded area of Lalbaug was unfeasible and would lead to creative compromises. So, we decided to erect a set of streets, by-lanes, houses, etc., in the outdoor area of Rajkamal Studios. The studio provided a huge comfort zone for the shooting and was situated in the Parel-Lalbaug area. The set combined with the surrounding areas would complete the 'Lalbaug feel' that we were looking for.

The outlay of the set was heavily inspired by the street set erected in *Shree 420* where the song '*Pyaar hua ikraar hua*' was picturized. Lanes and by-lanes were laid out in a similar manner as the *Shree 420* set. I insisted that a bridge was required and it turned out to be an exact replica of the *Shree 420* bridge. I guess that image must have been imprinted in my mind and was therefore recreated when the other set demanded the same.

The construction of the set was a mammoth task. My art director, Madhukar Shinde, was pushing the envelope to make the set so realistic that the audience would believe that they had been transported into a living locality in Bombay and not on a set. As the set neared completion, owners of a barbershop, a dhaba, a mithai shop, a paan shop, a tea stall, all came up with a request that they would set up these essential facilities at their own cost. The only rider they specified was that, since the set would require a large number of junior artists, they should not be prevented from using these facilities. They were smart and shrewd vendors who found this as an opportunity to earn a quick buck. Other vendors were also contacted to set up retail shops with their signage and brand cut-outs, for no payment, which they readily agreed to. Parle set up a soft drink shop where an unlimited quantity of Thums Up was distributed free of cost for the unit and junior artists. Kwality ice cream was also keen on the same arrangement but we had a condition that there would be an unlimited supply of various flavours of ice cream including the most coveted cassata. The junior artists and the unit were told that their families were welcome on the set and would be treated to free ice creams and soft drinks. It became a win-win situation, the families who visited on the weekends were ecstatic and we had a larger 'free' crowd on the set. I have to add, the clever vendors who set up consumer shops saw a huge rise in their sales!

Three or four days before shooting started, I was surprised to see Raj Sahab walking towards the set. Apparently, he had come to meet Anna Sahab and had heard about the street set, so he wanted a guided tour of the same. 'I love the authenticity and details that have gone into the set. I am sure you will have a BEST bus also running on the set.' I had not thought about this and admitted the same to Boss. He said, 'A BEST bus is a signature archetype of Bombay and will strengthen the belief that the film has been shot on an actual location. Also make it a point to shoot some scenes in the dhaba, barbershop and other such consumer shops. Exploit this magnificent set to the best of your ability and make sure that this unconventional film that you are making shows the city of Bombay in a never-seen-before light.

The city of Bombay has to be treated as a character who would play an integral and essential part in the narration.'

Armed with Raj Sahab's suggestions, the producers made arrangements with the BEST depot, which happened to be adjacent to Rajkamal Studios, that we would have a bus available as and when required on an hour's notice. I informed the producers that we would require two or three taxis to be available to us as and when required.

When I went on the set on the first day, I saw the production guy had got three autos instead of taxis. I said, 'Look, the film is based in Lalbaug and autos don't run beyond Bandra Masjid.'

The producers said, 'It is cheaper to hire three autos as they are giving us a great deal. We will save at least 25,000 bucks in this schedule.' The financier, Dilip Kankaria, said, 'In any case, we should save money since you have burned my money by putting up this horrible set. It looks so real that nobody will realize the amount of money that has been spent. Terrible! You have no economic sense.'

I started laughing hysterically and they added, 'What is the need to identify the area?'

I replied, 'By identifying the area, we show the strata of society that exists in the industrial areas of Bombay and where the inherent violence springs up from. The demographic brings to light the economically underprivileged. Even the underworld has its roots in a similar area – Dongri. Our film is based around an educated-unemployed underprivileged boy being exploited by politicians.'

In keeping with the concept of identifying the area around the set, I went up to the rooftop of Rajkamal Studios. Seeing the city and its congestion laid out below prompted me to have the roofs of all the structures on the set strengthened as I would definitely want to share this unique visual as a facet of the character that was Bombay. A scene filmed on a rooftop, between Arjun and his sister, wherein he talks about his frustration of being unemployed in this vast city added to the intensity and emotion which he was undergoing.

The very first scene that depicted his frustration was the 'carrom scene'. The scene required to visually carry the impact and state of mind of Arjun. This scene had no guideline in the script that I could adhere to and still I had to visually convey, without dialogue, the turmoil of the character. I started imagining how Raj Sahab would have tackled such a situation. Taking a cue from his command of the craft, I planned that portraying the confusion of the character would be best told when done through a confusion of shots with brief moments of no activity and suddenly resuming the visual confusion. Raj Sahab's creative use of sound, and lessons learned about the same, opened up a path for me to milk the scene and create a resounding impact. Sunny playing carrom and a close-up of the carrom board, each was shot from 24 different angles and magnifications. The scene would be played in complete silence, with no background music and the only sound that would be heard was the effect of the striker hitting the wall of the carrom table and the sound of the striker rebounding off all four walls. Before the shots were assembled in the editing room, it was necessary to lay the sound effects track to act as a guide for the shots to follow each other. Every time the striker rebounded off the walls of the carrom table, all 24 different shots with different magnifications interspaced with the shots of the carrom table were spliced together in random order synchronized to the sound. The brief moments of 'no activity' were created in shots where Sunny places the striker back on the starting point of the board after it has rebounded.

The outcome of this strange audio-visual narrative clarified the dilemma of the character and set a tone for the entire film.

Arjun Mavlankar was a complex character who challenged Sunny to deliver a performance keeping the nuances at the forefront. What was more difficult was to perform the sequences where 'no performance' was required. Sunny was required to remain stoic; a difficult demeanour to portray. With the inherent vulnerability that is inbuilt into Sunny's persona, he was at his best in this film. The complexity of the character gave a great opportunity to 'revel in emotionless silence', landing an extremely hard-hitting punch in the guts of the audience.

According to Raj Sahab, a close-up is 'the ultimate tool in the hands of a director to accentuate the emotions and, in turn, overpower the audience. We used close-ups extensively with extreme magnification, the chin and forehead being cut off within the frame. The use of such close-ups did help in the visual narration, especially where silence played a major hand, but required long shots to be juxtaposed to further enhance the visual experience. Throwing all the so-called 'rules' to the wind, I decided on a format to jump from an extremely magnified close-up to an extreme long shot. Jumping in this manner was considered blasphemy, as the order of the day was following a protocol of extreme long shot to normal long shot to mid-shot and finally to a close-up or vice versa. This was not the only area where *Arjun* defied the convention and followed a path that was dictated by the heart. A lot of colleagues who saw the film at previews were sceptical about this new normal that I experimented with. I quoted Raj Sahab to them, 'As long as you are convinced and excited, you will set new rules for filmmaking.' I was definitely excited and convinced!

The greed for making this film as visually exciting as possible was creeping up more and more on me. But I did not want to go into an area where I would disengage from the audience. Their interest should never waver.

The 'umbrella sequence' threw up its own challenges. The sequence involved Arjun's friend who is chased through the streets and is brutally killed. In the scene preceding this sequence, it is foreshadowed in the dialogue that some form of doom awaits Arjun or his friends, and therefore the 'umbrella sequence' had to have the audience prepared for the 'doom' that was to follow. The only tool to create this atmosphere was to recreate a scene that I had seen on many occasions during my tenure as an assistant director, and also a personal experience that I underwent just a week before the shoot.

Raj Sahab used the Deccan Queen whenever he travelled to Pune. I used to normally reach VT Station an hour before the departure so that I could eat a snack at the Pancham Puri House, a very well know eatery, situated a lane away from the station. Around 4.45 p.m., the office crowds moving towards the station would descend en masse onto the street and in the monsoons, one was subjected to a sea of black umbrellas on the entire street. A visual that enamoured me forever. This visual would perfectly set the tone of 'doom'. To make the sequence memorable, the sea of umbrellas would be coupled with a gory scene that had happened before my eyes. I was returning from a wedding at about four in the morning when I spotted seven to eight guys with swords drawn, chasing a chap on Linking Road. The screaming man was trying to open the doors of cars that were parked overnight to save himself but unfortunately, he slipped and fell and was engulfed by the assassins. At that point, I hurriedly drove away but it was apparent that the victim could not outrun his destiny.

I discussed the sequence with Baba Azmi, the DOP, and described to him that the whole street would seem like a sea of black, and just the umbrellas would show since we would be shooting mainly from a top angle. Through the black, we would only see the swords shimmering in silver, above the black umbrella tops, thus creating a more eerie atmosphere. To add to the eeriness, Baba wanted an overcast sky so that the rain would look more natural. We called for a crowd of 1,000 junior artists and each one would be holding two umbrellas, one in each hand, thus multiplying the visual splendour the scene would create. Finally, we achieved the right ambience as the hunted, Mohan, was the only human being who was seen as he weaved his way through the umbrellas and finally met his gory death.

The ultimate contribution in making this sequence memorable came from the background score composed by R.D. Burman. Initially, the background score recorded by R.D. Burman did not live up to his own expectation, 'The background score is making this brilliant sequence seem poor, whereas it should be lifting the visual experience.' There was a pause of about two hours and a disturbed R.D. Burman kept walking around the recording studio looking as worried as a man would normally be when his wife was delivering a baby. Suddenly he asked for the recorded score to be played back and sang a couple of abstract musical sounds over the track! Till today people remember this revolutionary background music score.

Audiences then, and even to this date, consider Arjun to be an 'action' film. They are wrong! The film had minimal action; drama was the backbone of the narrative. Drama that emanated from suppressed violence due to the circumstances Arjun lived in, swayed the audiences to believe that they had watched an action film. As Raj Sahab, on seeing the film, had remarked, 'The characterization, belief in the pathbreaking visual narration is the takeaway of this film.'

The song '*Mamaiya ya kero kero kero mama*', though recorded for another script had to be dubbed to suit the milieu of Arjun. I was hellbent on the song being given an unusual visual narration, staying within the parameters of the script. The natural progression of the script demanded an action scene but I wanted to incorporate action into the song. My inspiration for the execution of the song came from the Robert Wise directed and Jerome Robbins choreographed/co-directed masterpiece *West Side Story*. The song started with a small action sequence filmed at the Cooperage Football Stadium and moved onto a park at Chembur, a BEST depot and Linking Road at Bandra with the actual crowd on the street. Shooting this song was an exhilarating experience.

Flora Fountain, in the heart of Bombay, was the location I finalized to shoot the sequence in which Arjun chases Mohan's killer. At lunchtime, the crowd in this area is phenomenal and truly represents, the diversity of the people of Bombay. I made a conscious decision to shoot then, as it was most crowded and traffic would also be crawling due to the lunchtime crowd rushing around. The sequence seemed like a logistical nightmare as we could not use junior artists nor orchestrated traffic, which was essential to capture the right ambience, and to top it all, the police would never give us permission to hold back the crowd and traffic at that given time.

I called the producers and the unit together and said, 'This is going to be a "guerrilla" shoot. We shoot at one in the afternoon with concealed cameras and nobody should realize that they are witnessing a make-believe chase at the end of which a guy gets beaten up. The natural reactions of passers-by will range from fear to awe to excitement and also sadistic pleasure. For some strange reason, crowds love to watch anybody being beaten up as long as it is not them! The authenticity of their reactions and movements would be unparalleled. But let's not forget, we are leading the people of Bombay to believe in something which is unreal and it will take them a maximum time of a minute and a half to realize that this is actually a shooting, after which all reactions would change.'

We unanimously decided to take up this challenge. On the day of the shoot, we got seven cameras with seven cameramen. The producers had spoken to six different offices, located at six different places around the area, and they were kind enough to allow us to shoot from their premises. They also allowed us access to their offices at 4 a.m. to set up and rehearse the shots. One camera was concealed in a van and parked at a vantage point from where we could obtain closer shots of the action.

The cameramen were told that there would be no communication between any of us, so at 1 p.m., they would see Sunny and the antagonist get off a blue and white striped fiat car, and that was the cue for all the cameras to start rolling. 'You guys have to capture as much footage as you can. You can zoom in, zoom out, pick up the camera, move it to the right, to the left, it's all for you guys to decide. The moment you see that people have realized this is a shooting, four junior artists, dressed as cops, will immediately exit the van, catch Sunny and the antagonist and lead them away.' We set up and rehearsed from 4 a.m. to 5 a.m. and left to eat a delicious breakfast. We reassembled at about 12.30 p.m. and all the cameramen went up to their respective positions. I sat on the mezzanine floor of the iconic Pyrkes restaurant from where I had a bird's eye view of the happenings but was blind to how it was being captured in the various cameras.

The shooting finished and all the cameramen came to Pyrkes. They were excitedly describing how they had captured the action and I was silently praying that I would have enough variety of useable material to piece the sequence together.

We were watching the final cut of *Arjun* and a brainwave struck me, but the reaction it had on everybody else was that due to the stress of shooting this film, I had lost my marbles! I seriously said, 'Dimple has no constructive contribution in the narrative of the film and the film can do very well without the two songs she features in. So, I am removing her track from the film and *Arjun* will be a rare film without a heroine.'

Pandemonium erupted in the preview theatre.

The reactions ranged from, 'Rahul has gone insane!' to 'How can a film not have a heroine?!'

'The film will become 18 minutes shorter, which means there will be two reels less. When the audience sees the censor certificate showing a lesser number of reels, they will create a ruckus that we are cheating them by showing them less than what they have paid for!'

I finally had to unwillingly accede to the demands of the producers though I still maintain that showing more material in a film than what is required is 'hazardous to its health'.

I firmly believe that such a step would have not made an iota of a difference in terms of monetary profits.

When *Arjun* was completed and the final print was ready, I took it to RK to show the film to Raj Sahab. At the interval, Dabboo Sahab said, 'The sequence you shot at Flora Fountain is breathtaking, how did you manage to shoot it with all the crowd?'

I told him about how we placed the cameras and rehearsed early in the morning. He asked, 'How many cameras did you use?'

'Seven,' I replied.

Raj Sahab immediately retorted, 'If you used seven cameras why were there only six angles and not seven? Where was the seventh angle?'

His sentence struck me like a thunderbolt. After editing, the sequence had 127 cuts. Different angles, zoom in, zoom out, moving the camera left and right, and this man turned around and asked, 'Where was the seventh angle?' How had this genius deciphered that there were only six angles and not seven? The camera which was placed inside the van had failed and there was no footage to use. So, he was the only man who had rightly spotted the fact that only six cameras were used! When Javed Sahab heard about this, he had only one reaction, 'I don't believe this!'

Till today, I cannot get over this incident and wish my understanding of cinema would be close to matching his.

Post interval, when it is revealed that Arjun was just a pawn in a game of chess being played by Shiv Kumar Chowgule, Raj Sahab stood up and clapped and exuberantly said, 'Just stop the film! This is a twist in the tale that I could not even imagine. It is one of the biggest surprises I have seen in cinema. Let's finish seeing the film and then I would like to see it again, right away.'

After finishing the second screening, he reacted, 'I love the way you have set the tone for the audience that they will be viewing an unconventional film by having no sound while the titles are playing. This silence during the titles creates the biggest noise this film can make from the word go!'

I went on to tell Raj Sahab about my only regret being that I could not remove Dimple's track from the film as her track had no contribution, but the producers were up in arms. He said, 'They probably think your endeavour to make a revolutionary film has twisted and turned your mind. I wish their minds had twisted and turned instead!'

The film released and garnered great appreciation from the audience and the press. The film critic of the *Times of India* wrote in his review that the amount of attention paid by the director to create the right ambience was remarkable. He wrote about a shot in the climax where Arjun is trapped against a wall that has a huge election poster of Shiv Kumar Chowgule; he has been cornered by the politician's thugs and has no means to escape. The critic went on to say that at that very moment, we see a rat scurrying across the frame giving *Arjun* the impetus to break through the cordon of thugs. To the critic, this was a defining moment created by the director. I was the director and I had never seen that rat which the critic saw. I went back to the cinema hall to see the climax and my attention was only on the moment when that rat would cross the frame. When that rat appeared, I was seeing it for the first time! Under normal circumstances, had I seen the rat while shooting, I may have taken the shot again as it would disturb the audience, but here I was in a situation where I was being praised for creating a cinematic moment that I had not even thought about. Raj Sahab used to say, 'While making a film, there are unplanned moments that elevate the visual narration. Remember one thing, that even though this had nothing to do with your creativity, always take credit for the amount of thought and effort you had to put in for achieving that particular cinematic moment which you had supposedly put in.' Which I did!

DACAIT

DURING THE MAKING OF *Arjun*, I had committed to doing another film, *Samündar*. The film was being shot in the beautiful and picturesque location of Maldives islands, a somewhat unseen location for Indians. One day, through a long shooting spell, I heard the producer speak to the production manager on the phone, 'What is cheaper today in Male, fish or chicken? For lunch, bring the cheapest of the two and also the cheapest vegetable available.' Overhearing this conversation upset me and the stinginess of the producers kept showing up on various occasions. They were not bothered about the quality of the film, they were only interested in making money. The moment we came back to Bombay, I was in a good mind to withdraw my services as the director but I was being paid a huge remuneration for the film and so decided to just complete it and get all the money that was owed to me. In hindsight, I realize that this was a cardinal error from my end; money had prevailed over creativity!

I spoke to Raj Sahab about the mental conflict that I was fighting and he explained to me, 'Rahul, you had earlier removed your name from *Love Story* and now you want to take a similar step. You will become a laughing stock among people. You have also confessed to me that you had been shooting half-heartedly, I hate you for this and can never excuse you for doing injustice to your work because of money. I was very proud but am now ashamed to say that you are my one-time assistant. Remember that you got all the credit for the success of *Love Story* and the entire discredit for *Samundar* will also fall on your shoulders, and if you disassociate yourself from the creative credibility, it would be the most dishonourable thing to do.'

I was completely shaken up by what he had to say and there was more, 'The only remedy is to start shooting another film with a story that excites you and put all your heart into it. I wish that what you churn out is considered to be a remarkable piece of Indian cinema. Make me proud that my assistant director has demonstrated his worth.'

Armed with this pep-talk, I went and met Javed Sahab and said to him, 'Sir, I need a story that washes off all the sins that I have committed in *Samundar* and resurrects me.'

Javed Sahab narrated the story of *Dacait* to me and it bowled me over completely. A lot of dacoit films had been made, but here Javed Sahab wanted to portray the human aspect of a dacoit. He said that his dacoit would not be portrayed as dacoits were generally shown in our films. The dacoit would not wear a pagdi nor a dhoti kurta, there would be no prominent long red *tikka* on his forehead and he would not have a perpetual scowl to make him look menacing. He would be dressed like any other person in jeans and a shirt. There would be no mandatory sequence of the dacoit with his gang, going to a *devi ma ke mandir* on a festival day where the cops would have laid a trap for him, but he would manage to get away!

I went to Chembur to take Raj Sahab's advice and after hearing the story, he said, 'I have to admit that the passion I saw in your eyes when you were narrating it to me, ignited a *junoon* within you. This *junoon*, I am sure, will translate into the "memorable film" that I expect from you. Let me give you one piece of advice. Since you have decided that your dacoit has to be looked at as a human, it is essential that the habitat that he lives in is also real. We all know that dacoits fester in the ravines along the Chambal River, between the triangular borders of Madhya Pradesh, Uttar Pradesh and Rajasthan. You should actually visit the area and I am certain that seeing the terrain will make your and Javed's mind more fertile and help in the script. In fact, go to Gwalior jail and meet Phoolan Devi for first-hand advice on the lifestyle of dacoits.'

Javed Sahab was excited about conducting a recce in the Chambal area and meeting the legendary female dacoit, Phoolan Devi. I knew Vitthalbhai Patel Sir very well since he was the lyricist of *Jhooth Bole Kauwa Kaate* and was also a minister of state in the Madhya Pradesh assembly. Even though I knew him myself, I wanted to use the good offices of Raj Sahab, who at my behest asked Vitthalbhai Sir to extend and facilitate my recce and the shooting thereafter. On Raj Sahab's recommendation, Vitthalbhai Sir himself accompanied us to the Chambal area, and that opened up all locks for us.

We had an eventful two-day meet in Gwalior Central Jail with Phoolan Devi, the only living female dacoit, and even spent an evening having dinner with 83 dreaded surrendered dacoits! All the 83 dacoits were housed in an open jail, only Phoolan Devi had an individual cell away from the others and she had filed a writ petition demanding that she should not be discriminated against and be housed in the open jail with her own community. The authorities that segregated her believed that staying in an all-male open jail could lead to serious issues like violence, molestation and possibly rape. She had expressed, to the jailor, that since she had lived a life full of violence, she would be happier living within the shadow of violence rather than an umbrella of security.

Phoolan Devi was a rather short and frail-looking woman, contrary to the image that I had of her. During all our conversations, she would oscillate from her cruel hard-hitting persona to an emotional side, with occasional tears welling up in her eyes, and mine too as I listened to her.

She provided pertinent insights into her life, pre and post her becoming a dacoit. She knew the ravines like the back of her hand and on a map of the ravines, in and around Bhind-Morena (the epicentre of the dacoit clusters), she marked out the exact locations that the script required with the logistics to access such locations.

The lady used the foulest of language in every sentence and spoke unabashedly even though a minister and the highest-ranking members of the Madhya Pradesh Police were all present during our meeting. Replying to one of the questions that I asked her about how the dacoits obtained stocks of ammunition, she turned around to the inspector general of police and asked, '*Behenchod, bataun kya inko*?' There was laughter all around, except a sense of shock for Javed Sahab and me. The minister replied, '*Jo batana hai, sach sach batao, koi bhi yahan tum par action nahi lega*.'

She turned sharply to the deputy superintendent of police and gave a stinging reply, '*Yeh madarchod Dipti SP bechta tha*!'

After the enriching meeting with Phoolan Devi we went on to Bhind-Morena to actually see the ravines and gather as much information as we could. We met the local superintendent of police who was undergoing a photo session with his family in the town centre surrounded by a crowd, while holding the heads of two dacoits who he claimed were killed by him in a fierce encounter. We were told by one of his own inspectors that the two people shot dead by him were not dacoits but poor villagers. They were labelled 'dacoits' and a photo session was arranged so that the visiting film director and writer could witness his heroics. We also met a school teacher who was the contact point with the dacoits and carried messages between them and corrupt policemen.

During the five days that we spent in Bhind-Morena, and as more information seeped in, Javed Sahab wove in the grotesque and absurd facts into the script. I estimated that we would be shooting in Bhind-Morena for about sixty days and the logistics would have been practically impossible without the support of Vitthalbhai Sir. He arranged for the security of the actors and technicians, accommodation for a unit of 150 persons, organized 2,000 policemen to feature in one sequence for three days, and helped us arrange for guns, ammunition, explosives and horses.

Shooting in the ravines was indeed a challenge. The Chambal River keeps changing course and the ravines change positions automatically. The ravines are a web formed between hillocks of loose mud which also, at times, alter the topography of a particular area overnight. We needed to create visual markings of the path that led us from the location to the base where the vehicles were parked.

The dacoits used to move only on foot as riding horses would make them an easy target for the forces which were hunting them on practically a daily basis. We used horses in only one sequence, where Chawli is snatched away by the dacoits from the hands of the police. This sequence looked more dramatic because of the pursuit of the police jeep by dacoits on horses. Barring this, most of the sequences did not use horses. The deputy inspector general of police told us that there were days when in pursuit of the dacoits, they would be walking in the ravines and the adversaries would be walking on the same path and direction separated only by the hillocks.

After about six days of shooting, I realized that something was missing, a thought which had been nagging me from the second day of shooting. The realization of the problem dawned on me when I had lost my way and climbed up a hillock to look for the unit. Standing atop the hillock, without anyone in sight, I realized that the sheer intrigue of the labyrinth formed by the ravines was missing in my execution of the visual narration. Raj Sahab always said, 'If a location plays an integral part in the story, treat that location as a principal character of your film and never let the audience start missing an important character as that will create a disconnect from the film.'

I scrapped the six days of shooting, arranged for the police security force to be increased from a 100 to 400 so that the crowd could be kept much further away, thus giving me an undisturbed gigantic landscape of the ravines. The lenses used, the camera movement and the positions of the actors always kept the audience embraced by the ravines, a principal factor in the life of a dacoit.

After about 40 days of shooting, we had to leave the Bhind-Morena area as the temperatures started shooting up above 45 degrees, making work impossible. We returned to Bombay and immediately started erecting sets for the village, police station and the haveli. To keep them realistic, we avoided using wood to build the set but erected the same, in the outdoors, using bricks and mortar.

The time I had in hand whilst the sets were being erected, was utilized by me to finish *Samundar*. (By the time it was released, the shooting of *Dacait* had created a lot of hype and *Samundar* 'coming and going' was overshadowed, but I cannot shirk away from my responsibility for the outcome of the film.)

The defining moment in *Dacait* was the sequence in which the Thakur and his henchmen attack Sunny's village while festivities to celebrate his sister's marriage are underway. The attack turns into a massacre and 30 to 35 people are brutally killed. Sunny and his elder brother are tied to a tree. Thakur has Sunny's mother brought out and decides to humiliate her in the presence of her children and village bystanders. He holds up her *choti,* with the intention of shearing her hair and devastating her humility. The three elements which were essential to the shot were Thakur's sadistic pleasure, the *choti* and the mother's shock at the humiliation she was undergoing. This moment gave me an opportunity of using Raj Sahab's technique of employing a pan-focus shot since that would best convey the essence of the drama.

A lens having a focal length of 75mm, generally but not necessarily, used in shooting close-ups was here being used as a three shot and required all three elements to be in sharp focus. This was a night sequence and the shot entailed increasing the exposure from f4 to f16, causing a five-time increase in the lights. The lighting took about five hours and when they were switched on the heat emitted became unbearable, but to the credit of the actors, Rakhee and Raza Murad, they withstood the burning heat straight on their faces as the impact of the shot was of utmost importance to them. This dramatic shot led to the mother with the sheared hair dancing to the beat of a drum.

This heart-wrenching moment brought not only tears, also but had audience sobbing uncontrollably. While watching the preview, Kamal Haasan couldn't stop crying his heart out, and a lady even passed out. At the end of the film, there were two different reactions. Either the film received a standing ovation or people were exiting the preview still crying uncontrollably.

On seeing the film, Anand Bakshi ji told me, 'Rahul *yaar,* Raza Murad *ke marne ka tarika accha nahin tha.* Sunny *ko usko haveli se nikal ke, uske baal mundne chahiye the, usse* dance *karana chahiye tha aur phir bolna tha,* "Dance *karo! Naccho haramzade jaise meri maa ko nachaya tha." Aur phir usko goliyon se chhalni kar deta! Aise mujhe bahut* satisfaction *milta, jo abhi mujhe nahin mil raha hai.'*

My immediate reaction to this statement was, 'Bakshi ji has lost his mind and has made this obnoxious suggestion. Here I am proud of having made a film with the impact that had the audience gasping for breath and praising it endlessly, and there he wants me to end the film with a typical "filmy" climax!'

Raj Sahab saw the film, and at the interval, he said, 'This sequence of Rakhee's hair being cut is leaving a huge impact on me, I am breathing heavily and my heart is pounding. I need a small break to compose myself and then we'll continue watching the second half.'

When the film finished, he said, 'Very good, very well shot, brilliantly depicted ambience and execution of the scenes. I only wish the end was more impactful and not tame as it is now. I would have liked to see the zamindar being ruthlessly massacred. This particular film will be considered a milestone of Indian cinema, my only fear is that the commercial outcome may not be satisfactory.'

I remembered Bakshi ji giving me similar advice that I had shunned while Raj Sahab saying it triggered a mental conflict. However, my perverse sense of 'overconfidence' fogged my mind; having directed three super successful films, my false ego prevailed. How could any person tell me that I was wrong?!

But, I was wrong and for the first time, I did not pay heed to my guru's suggestion.

I still consider *Dacait* to be the crowning glory of my career, but it being a non-starter at the box office affected me then and even does now. Given a choice between glory or materialistic gains, I guess I made the right choice but also hate myself for not discussing Raj Sahab's reaction further with him, which I am sure would have guided me to an unblemished 'middle path'.

Let me be candid and honest, pride overshadowed a lesson that was readily available to me and I will forever regret that I did not take advantage of it.

IMMORTALITY

On 2 May 1988, Raj Kapoor was to be honoured with the most prestigious award for his cinematic achievements in Indian cinema – the Dadasaheb Phalke Award.

The presentation ceremony was held at Vigyan Bhavan and presided by the Honourable President of India, Shri R. Venkataraman. It was attended by many celebrities of Indian cinema.

Raj Sahab, who had been ailing with severe asthma, entered the auditorium along with his wife, Krishna Aunty, to a standing ovation. As reported by the press, he seemed visually disoriented even though there were no signs of his being unwell.

The President came onto the dais and delivered his customary address and the award presentation ceremony was underway. While various awards were being presented, Raj Sahab was struck by an asthmatic attack. There was a state of slight panic and in a quick flurry of movement, the President's physician was summoned. He administered oxygen to Raj Sahab who seemed stable for the time being. The ceremony continued and when Raj Sahab's name was announced, to come up to the dais and receive his award, the oxygen mask was removed from his face. He struggled to stand and just plopped back into his seat, unable to withstand the stress.

The Honourable President showed an unprecedented gesture. He walked down towards Raj Sahab. The audience gave a full-throttle standing ovation and Krishna Aunty helped Raj Sahab to stand. The President handed him the citation and put the medal around his neck and at that precise moment, he joined his hands in acknowledgement and slipped into a coma. An extremely dramatic moment for the man whose life was cinema.

He was quickly wheeled away on a stretcher into the President's ambulance and rushed to the All India Institute of Medical Sciences, where a top-notch medical team wheeled the stretcher into the intensive care unit. At that point in time, nobody realized that this was the beginning of the end.

By the second day, his entire family including his children and brothers had arrived in Delhi to be by his side. Chintu, who was shooting in Kathmandu, flew down immediately. I flew down to Delhi as well, with a prayer in my heart that he would recover from this catastrophe.

People from all over the country and other parts of the world were very concerned about his health, but he was not progressing towards recovery. Daily news about his health became a national concern and updates were issued regularly. The then prime minister, Shri Rajiv Gandhi, and other cabinet ministers visited the hospital regularly and so did members of the diplomatic missions of various countries.

Some members of the film fraternity also made trips to meet the family and express their solidarity. Dilip Sahab, an old friend of Raj Sahab's, visited him and was the only person, apart from the immediate family, who was allowed into the ICU. Chintu had accompanied him and witnessed, according to him, an intense and emotional 'conversation' between the friends. Raj Sahab was in a coma and Dilip Sahab was speaking to him, in Punjabi, about the start of their friendship and how it had grown over the years. Eventualy, Dilip Sahab had tears running down his face and his language graduated into Pashtu, the language of the Pathans which Raj Sahab also used to speak. Even without understanding the language, Chintu was overwhelmed by the emotion he saw on Dilip Sahab's face and tone of speaking, which varied between laughter and sadness. This was Dilip Sahab's desperate effort; he thought that on hearing his voice, his friend may come out of the coma. Unfortunately, that was not the case.

Practically every second or third day, Raj Sahab would develop different health problems and the situation was getting more and more perilous. One evening, All India Radio made an announcement that Raj Kapoor was no more. This news spread like wildfire but apparently, it was an error since he was still alive. The announcement led to the prime minister driving his own car into the hospital without any security. Apparently, he was having dinner at the residence of the Chinese ambassador where he received this news and just jumped into his car and drove off. There were no protocol officers to receive him as nobody had news of this sudden visit. He rushed to the ICU and met Krishna Aunty who told him about the fake news. By this time, the hospital corridor was swarming with his security and aides and a very annoyed prime minister summoned the I&B minister, Shri H.K.L Bhagat, and was vociferous in expressing his displeasure in everyone's presence.

I had made five trips to Delhi to meet the family and would not stay for over a day on each trip, as I thought it was essential not to disturb the family during the hour of crisis. It was 2 June when I was at a dinner in Bombay when the breaking news was announced on Doordarshan that Raj Kapoor had succumbed to his prolonged illness. I was in a state of shock, I had lost the one man who had taught me whatever I knew and was always there for me whenever I needed him.

I drove back home and called Chintu. I was told by him that the prime minister had just visited the hospital to offer his condolences to the family and requested Krishna Aunty, 'Ma'am, I would like him to be placed in-state at Delhi itself for a day so that the common man can pay his last respect to the Master.'

Krishna Aunty apologized because she just wanted to take him back home with her as soon as possible. The prime minister respected her wish and instructed his personal secretary to have an aircraft waiting at Palam Airport to fly the family and the mortal remains back to Bombay at whatever time they decided.

I telephonically informed Shri Rakesh Maria, ex-police commissioner of Bombay, who was then the DCP, Zone IV, Bombay, and his jurisdiction comprised of Trombay, RCF and Chembur police stations, the area where Raj Sahab lived. He had already received the news and the police had been alerted. He only made one request that the flight with the mortal remains should land in Bombay by 6 a.m. so that before the news spread and crowd starts collecting, the family could be driven back home.

In Delhi, they decided to take off at 3.45 a.m. Chintu told me that when they reached the VIP departure complex at Palam Airport, they were all shocked to see the prime minister with his entire cabinet in attendance to pay their final respects. He also instructed Shri H.K.L. Bhagat to accompany the mourners as the official representative of the Government of India.

When the flight landed in Bombay at 5.45 a.m., the family started disembarking. Rajesh Khanna, who had gone to Delhi to see Raj Sahab was also on the flight. The DCP who was there at the airport was taken aback on seeing Shri H.K.L. Bhagat disembarking as he was a 'Z-security' designated VIP and suitable arrangements had not been made. The efficient DCP set the wheels rolling and before the cavalcade was ready to depart, all security arrangements had been made.

Raj Sahab entered his house for the last time before his mortal remains were to be consigned to flames. News had started spreading and crowd gathering. People from the film industry were pouring in and there was an overall atmosphere of grief. His associates and friends flew into Bombay to pay their last respects. Amitabh Bachchan and Manmohan Desai Sir flew in all the way from Srinagar to express their grief. Later, from the house, his mortal remains were placed on an open truck and driven to RK where, for two hours, people were allowed to file past him and pay their last respects.

The security and traffic were handled brilliantly by the Bombay Police. Chembur was swelling with people and honour was paid to him not only by the Indian film sector, which shut down the industry and closed all cinemas for the day, but also by Pakistan by shutting their industry and cinemas. The video pirates also shut down their illegal business for a day in reverence to the passing away of Raj Kapoor!

The funeral procession left RK and walked the 2-kilometre distance to the crematorium. The mortal remains were carried to the pyre by the family. Most of the mourners, whose eyes were moist, could not come to terms with the death of Raj Kapoor.

I stood alone, in a state of shock, and could not fathom that my guru, philosopher and guide had left me orphaned. I was wondering how this would affect my life in the journey ahead. Whom would I turn to for advice and who would be the harshest critique of my creative journey? Would I creatively progress or stagnate? I have to admit that his going away had affected me deeply.

After the rituals were complete, the funeral pyre was consigned to flames by the three sons. The flames engulfed the mortal remains of the Master and as the fire rose, it heralded the birth of the immortal Raj Kapoor.

ACKNOWLEDGEMENTS

This book is a product of a lot of hard work by various people whom I would like acknowledge:

Apurva Asrani, for planting the seed in my mind for writing this book.

Sachin Chatte, for his valuable inputs.

Mama ji, Vishwa Mehra, the oldest living, closest associate of Raj Sahab, who, even at the age of 94, shared all his wonderful experiences that were invaluable while I was writing the book.

Bunty and Sadiqa Peerbhoy, who have always supported me in all my endeavours.

Shri Chaitanya Prasad, Director of the Directorate of Film Festivals, for his unending support.

Shivali Kalra, for her encouragement.

Asha and Sumant Batra, for their valuable insights.

Cinemaazi, the website dedicated to Indian cinema.

Rajeev Masand, for his valuable contribution.

Sanjeev Goenka of Filmistan Studio, for his support.

P.K. Bajaj of Mayapuri Publications, for contributing photographs.

Zarine Jandesova, from Russia, for contributing photographs.

Rajan Bedke, for helping me source photographs.

Kalash Pandiya, for transcribing my narration.

I also pay my respects to all the wonderful artistes and technicians who are no more with us and who gave R.K. Films and Studios their unending support.